外国语言学及应用语言学研究丛书

U0608245

An Ecological Critical Discourse Study
of Shen Shixi's Animal Narratives

沈石溪动物叙事的
生态批评话语研究

林 晶 著

ZHEJIANG UNIVERSITY PRESS
浙江大学出版社
·杭州·

图书在版编目（CIP）数据

沈石溪动物叙事的生态批评话语研究 ＝ An
Ecological Critical Discourse Study of Shen
Shixi's Animal Narratives：英文 / 林晶著. — 杭
州：浙江大学出版社，2022.12
　　ISBN 978-7-308-23075-9

　　Ⅰ．①沈… Ⅱ．①林… Ⅲ．①批评—话语语言学—研
究—英文 Ⅳ．①H0

中国版本图书馆CIP数据核字(2022)第175240号

沈石溪动物叙事的生态批评话语研究

An Ecological Critical Discourse Study of Shen Shixi's Animal Narratives

林　晶　著

策划编辑	董　唯
责任编辑	董　唯
文字编辑	黄　墨
责任校对	黄静芬
封面设计	项梦怡
出版发行	浙江大学出版社
	（杭州市天目山路148号　　邮政编码310007）
	（网址：http://www. zjupress.com）
排　　版	杭州林智广告有限公司
印　　刷	广东虎彩云印刷有限公司绍兴分公司
开　　本	710mm×1000mm　1/16
印　　张	14.00
字　　数	300千
版 印 次	2022年12月第1版　2022年12月第1次印刷
书　　号	ISBN 978-7-308-23075-9
定　　价	58.00元

Preface

Representation of animals has been the site where the relationship between humans and animals is constructed. Anthropomorphism in animal narratives functions to construct animals as both rhetorical symbols and sentient beings, serving the dual purposes of rendering back the visibility of animals as the subject of a lifeworld and evoking a reflection on human selves and society. Previous studies on anthropomorphic animal representation fail to capture the dynamic nature of anthropomorphism in animal narratives as the continuum between the human domain and the animal domain. In addition, the nature of anthropomorphic animal representation as being ideologically manipulative has been overlooked. A linguistic approach to studying animal representation in animal narratives, which aims to justify anthropomorphic animal representation as an effective resource to facilitate meaning construction and construal, is thus necessary. In the field of ecolinguistics, no satisfying attempts so far have been made to offer systematic and cohesive interpretation for the existing framework of ecolinguistics from the perspective of critical-cognitive discourse analysis. Considering these factors, the present study attempts to construct an ecological critical-cognitive discourse analysis framework of animal representation. Against this background, the study endeavors to explore anthropomorphic representation of animal images in Shen Shixi's animal narratives. It attempts to answer how language resources and discursive strategies help to construct anthropomorphic representation of animals. It delves into investigating how anthropomorphic representation of animals can be legitimized. And it seeks to explore how anthropomorphic representation of animals is conceptualized. Furthermore, it puts the topic in the broad social and cultural context in an attempt to reveal the three-dimensional interaction between human beings, discourse and animals.

Among the major findings are: 1) Referential and predication strategies work to construct the constituted reality about animals in Shen Shixi's animal narratives. Referential strategies involve individualization and assimilation. Individualization is the referential strategy of names and naming, aimed at individualizing animals as subjective beings. Assimilation involves the referential strategy of the pronoun use of "you", which blurs the boundaries between humans and animals. Predication strategies in Shen Shixi's narratives are realized by using action verbs and mental predication. The use of action verbs constructs animal behaviors as meaningful and authored; the use of mental predication acts to shape animals as sentient beings. 2) Legitimization strategies are used to endorse anthropomorphic representation of animals in Shen Shixi's animal narratives. They are manifested through grammatical cohesion, evidentiality and epistemic modality. 3) Metaphor as the way of conceptualizing animals in animal narratives is inherently ideological. "Humans are animals" and "animals are more or less the same as humans" work to construct interrelationships between animal and human domains. The impositive metaphor "humans are animals" tags value judgment sanctioned by human society on anthropomorphic representation of animals in narratives. The approximative metaphor "animals are more or less the same as humans" appraises animals from the lens of humans on the basis of emotional similarity. 4) Human perspective and animal perspective negotiate with one another in anthropomorphic representation of animals. By writing out a pleasant blending of human and animal horizons, anthropomorphic animal representation in Shen Shixi's animal narratives offers prospects for eradicating dualist conceptuality on the relationship between humans and animals. In resonance with Chinese harmosophy, it can be deemed as ecologically harmonious.

It is concluded that anthropomorphic representation of animals in Shen Shixi's animal narratives is effective in manipulatively shaping people's construal of animals and providing meaningful discoursal resource for promoting a harmonious relationship between humans and animals. The study contributes an insightful observation of animal representation in Shen Shixi's animal narratives, offers a possible and plausible perspective to anthropomorphic animal representation research and adds an extension to current literature on ecolinguistic study. It is helpful in facilitating an intercultural dialogue between the Eastern and Western eco-discursive paradigms, thereby making a joint effort in improving ecological consciousness worldwide.

CONTENTS

Chapter 1　Introduction

Chapter 2　Literature Review

Chapter 3   Theoretical Foundation

Chapter 4   Representation Strategies in Anthropomorphic Representation of Animal Images

Chapter 5   Legitimization of Anthropomorphic Representation of Animal Images

Chapter 6   Metaphorical Conceptualization of Anthropomorphic Representation of Animal Images

Chapter 7   Ecological Attribute of Anthropomorphic Representation of Animal Images in Shen Shixi's Animal Narratives

Chapter 8   Conclusion

Chapter 1   Introduction

1.1   The "erasure" and "reminding" of animals

On the planet where all the components are supposedly interconnected, humans and animals constitute a strong symbiotic alliance. The intimate yet complicated bond with animal counterparts has consistently been at the core of human life. Seen from the biological point of view, human beings are animals by essence—humans, like animals, are multicellular, eukaryotic creatures; on the societal level, animals are indispensably constitutive of human life—humans are surrounded by animals and dependent on animals for food, clothing and companion. It is safe to say that human society is largely shaped through interactions with animals in that "animals of all kinds have figured prominently in the material foundations and the ideological underpinnings of human societies" (DeMello, 2012: 4). More to the point, human society is based to a great degree on its exploitation of animals to fulfill human needs (DeMello, 2012; Stibbe, 2012; Cook, 2015).

However, the lifeworld of animals as sentient beings has long been overlooked. Because of this, animals are alienated and distanced from human beings, becoming "the very embodiment of 'otherness'" (Beardsworth & Bryman, 2001: 85). Thus boundaries between humans and animals are no longer fluid as they should be. The fundamental reason should go back to the long-held belief in the categorical and qualitative difference between humans and animals—the so-called "human exceptionalism" or "human centralism". Deeply rooted in traditional Western thought (e.g. classical philosophy and Judaeo-Christian theology), human exceptionalism asserts human dominion over other species, which has become the default view in contemporary human society. Under its influence, along with the impact of ever-expanding urbanization, intensified farming and commercial incentives, animals are increasingly marginalized and objectified. In consequence, animals, although constantly connected to human life, are vanishing or disappearing from not merely the physical world but also people's consciousness. Animals are, as Stibbe (2012) states, "erased".

Another crucial factor contributing to the erasure of animals resides in the dramatic change in the nature of humans' encounters with animals. To be precise, people's experiences with animals are more and more mediated through symbolic representations in fictions and documentaries. It is through representations that animals are "socially-constructed" (DeMello, 2012: 285). More specifically, in the current anthropological context, animals do not represent themselves, but feature social and cultural meanings in various ways through representations made by humans. Compared to their physical identity, the symbolic identification of animals is more emphasized. "Animals exist as mirrors for human thought; they allow us to think about, talk about, and classify ourselves and others." (DeMello, 2012: 14) Through the process of making representations, humans are not aiming at a greater knowledge of animals but attempt to understand themselves better as humans. In this way, animals do not emerge and exist as subjective and sentient beings; instead, they become cultural symbols and linguistic metaphors. The very stage of mediation between humans and animals in the real world is extremely significant given the fact that "representation increasingly will become the site where the future of many species of animals is determined" (Jacobs & Stibbe, 2006: 2).

The increasing importance of representation is ascribed to the fact that "language use is neither a neutral tool nor simply ancillary to the worldly phenomena depicted" (Crist, 1999: 83), and divergent linguistic representations of animals will give rise to the discrepancies in people's construal and conceptualization of animal life, which will greatly impact their attitudes towards animals. Just as what DeMello has put forward, "Human-Animal Studies is about getting to the core of our representation of animals and understanding what it means when we invest animals with meanings" (2012: 11), it is critically important to probe into how representation is linguistically processed and how it is manipulated by social force. Nevertheless, it is not until recently that academia has shown interest on the topic. So far, there have been some inspiring studies on linguistic representation of animals (Dunayer, 2001; Cook, 2015; Glenn, 2004; Stibbe, 2001, 2012), directed at uncovering the workings of the symbolic world in representing animals. Among these the most impressive study is conducted by Stibbe (2012), who, focusing specifically on the invisibility of animals in linguistic representation, endeavors to disclose the mechanism of discursive erasure and insulation. He distinguished three forms of discursive erasure, namely, the "void", the "mask" and the "trace" (Stibbe, 2015: 149). Of prominent relevance in the context of animal representation is the "mask", referring particularly to the kind of representation by which "the image masks and denatures a profound reality" (Stibbe, 2012: 3).

An evident indicator of the "mask" is the anthropomorphic depiction of animals. Anthropomorphic language is ubiquitous in the representation of animals. Conventionally, anthropomorphic interpretation of animal behaviors is deemed as notoriously harmful for the coordination among species, because in anthropomorphic representation, animals are masked and denatured as "mirrors for human identity" (DeMello, 2012: 296). In other words, anthropomorphism allows human beings to project their own thoughts and feelings onto animals to demonstrate their power and superiority in the universe. By this token, anthropomorphism can be regarded as something allied to anthropocentrism. The situation gets complicated when some scholars make their efforts to rehabilitate anthropomorphism. They assert that there is no neutral language available to construct absolutely objective representation of the world as it really is, so animals have the opportunities to "take on a life of their own" in anthropomorphic representation; in rendering behaviors meaningful and authored, the anthropomorphic portrayal opens the door to appreciating the "marvelous world of animals" (Crist, 1999: 222). Such being the case, anthropomorphism and anthropocentrism can "tug in opposite directions" (Daston & Mitman, 2005: 4). Anthropomorphism is conducive to bringing back animals to our mind as the subject of a lifeworld, which can be regarded as a means of "reminding" (Stibbe, 2015: 161). The proposal of "reminding" is a response to the erasure, or "sequestration of experience" (Giddens, 1991), of animals in a time when there is a growing demand for the harmonious co-existence with animals.

"Erasure" and "reminding" are a pair of complementary antonyms within the ecological and symbolic realm. Whether anthropomorphism is a self-referential symbolic system that leads to the "erasure" of animals or a way of "reminding" that animals should be viewed as privileged and performative agents remains contestable. The study aims to explore this paradox by concentrating on the mechanism of anthropomorphic language in representing animals. To this end, an elaboration of the notion "anthropomorphism" will be necessary and helpful.

1.2   Anthropomorphism in animal representation

Anthropomorphism, noted for centuries, still remains inexplicable throughout human thought. With a long history of scrutiny, anthropomorphism in animal study has had both proponents and opponents, with the latter being the majority by far. For those who warn against it, anthropomorphism is a mistake and should be rooted out. The most compelling indictment is that anthropomorphism is merely an extension of humans' worldview and represents a kind of "universal tendency" among humans to conceive everything as being humanlike.

However, whether anthropomorphism is necessarily an error or not "hinges largely on the writer's definition and explanation" (Guthrie, 1997: 52). Definitions of anthropomorphism vary widely in light of the employment or the recognition of the failure in human mind's powers of "pattern-discovery" (Guthrie, 1997: 52). Accordingly, they can be categorized into three overlapping types, namely global, inaccurate and subjective anthropomorphism respectively (Mitchell, 1997b: 407). Global anthropomorphism is an inclusive term, referring to "an expectation (perceptual or theoretical) that things in the world are like human beings or are caused by human beings or humanlike entities" (Mitchell, 1997b: 407); under the rubric of global anthropomorphism, people regard anthropomorphism as either a fundamental element of human cognition (Guthrie, 1997), i.e. the innate tendency to approach animals with expectations of humanness, or a methodological attitude towards animals (Knoll, 1997). They stress the similarities between humans and animals by clinging to the evolutionary linkages. For them, there should exist a continuum of species, and thus anthropomorphic attribution is justified.

In contrast, the other two types, inaccurate and subjective anthropomorphism, emphasize the dichotomy between humans and nature, admitting humans' intellectual failure in discovering the "pattern". In consequence of the "disparity between the infinite complexity of the world and the limited powers of the mind" (Guthrie, 1997: 53), people under these two categories are apt to view anthropomorphism as the misattribution of human mental traits to animals, hence a categorical mistake. To be specific, inaccurate anthropomorphism indicates the mistake in describing animals as "having (uniquely) human characteristics (usually psychological)" (Mitchell, 1997b: 407); subjective anthropomorphism stresses the psychological characterization of animal behaviors. Although subjective anthropomorphism could be accurate or not by itself, it is notable that the rise of behaviorism challenges any mental attribution of animals. Therefore, "anthropomorphic subjectivism" turns out to be a self-evident error in the realm of animal behavior study.

Seemingly, at the core of all the puzzles concerning anthropomorphism lies the unsettling question of whether the mind is unique to human beings or whether animals have minds. Grounded in evolutionary continuity, Darwin's anthropomorphic portrayal of animals signifies that animals have rich mental life. His representation of animals tends to suspend the overwhelming criticism of anthropomorphism as distorted and erroneous representation of animals in reality, and bring back to the public's attention the "unbroken continuum between humans and animals in all respects, including behavioral patterns and mental faculties" (Crist, 1999: 18).

Following the tradition of Darwinian anthropomorphism, the anthropomorphism of the naturalists shows the effect of depicting animals' world as a lifeworld—in their writings, the abundant language of a meaningful world saturated with actions enables animals to emerge as the subject, which endows the ascription of mental life to animals with credibility and forcefulness. Just like Darwin's anthropomorphic language in describing animals, the naturalists' anthropomorphic portrayal yield a close correspondence among species by creating a conceptual environment in which the existence of animal mind is natural, scenic and indispensable. Together, Darwin and the naturalists' anthropomorphic depictions give an alternative understanding of animal life, and help to achieve an alignment between the human and animal world. In this sense, anthropomorphism has its merits and should be rehabilitated. However, given the historical consistency of its pejorative label, especially among the ethologists, misgivings about animals as the subject with mentalities are aired loudly. Viewing anthropomorphism as an irrational and should-be-rejected likening among species, they maintain a mechanistic conception of animal behaviors and prefer the mechanomorphic approach to representing animals. The most salient characteristic of mechanomorphic portrayal is that animals are likened to machines and depicted as mindless puppets with the employment of a technical-causal language. One inevitable consequence of deploying technical language is, as Crist points out, "the epistemological objectification of animals" (1999: 84); in other words, the subjectivity of animals is drastically destructed, and even erased. In denying animal mind, mechanomorphic representation of animals leads to the insulation between human and animal realms.

Within behavioral science, the development of sociobiology witnesses the emergence of so-called "new anthropomorphism" (Kennedy, 1992). Influenced by a number of interacting factors, the decline of behaviorism and the rise of cognitive ethology in particular, sociobiology strives to study both human and animal social behaviors in a single yet encompassing biological-evolutionary framework. That is not to say, sociobiology favors the idea that animals have the mind. Conversely, sociobiologists are similarly skeptical towards animal mind as behaviorists. For example, they prefer to displace agency to genes rather than ascribe the language of intentionality directly to individual animals. Even so, the sociobiological use of social-category concepts, concepts of "social action, structure, relations, or attitude" (Crist, 1999: 136), unavoidably erodes their skeptical stance on the issue of animal mind. To put it in another way, the application of the social-categorical terms accessible to both realms of humans and animals, terms such as adultery, altruism, caste, cheating, class, contest, and cooperation, functions as a mirror between them, which overcomes the dividing line between the two realms, and hence creates an alliance among diverse species.

As mentioned above, controversies about anthropomorphism in animal study continue to grow. Yet an investigation into different approaches to studying anthropomorphism could contribute to some telling insights on the topic: 1) anthropomorphism involves imbuing animals with humanlike characteristics; 2) anthropomorphic depiction of animals is not merely about attributing mental experiences, and "the direct attribution of ostensibly human mental experiences is not a defining or even necessary feature of anthropomorphism" (Crist, 1999: 80), as is exemplified by the naturalists' approach; 3) anthropo-morphism itself is an ambiguous and electrified concept; global argument against anthropomorphism cannot secure its place any longer; "the ascription of concepts whose natural home is in describing human features and behaviors may very well apply to nonhumans" (Mitchell, 2005: 105) because of biological relatedness; thus whether anthropomorphism is justified or merely a mistake depends on the researchers' interest and explanations; 4) anthropomorphism is mainly employed in the service of heuristic purposes and anthropomorphic language acts as a technique for describing and interpreting animal behaviors; 5) anthropomorphic depiction of animals plays a formative role in readers' understanding of animal world and anthropomorphism in portraying animals is not restricted to be "a logical or empirical problem" but regarded as strategic and ideological manipulation.

To conclude, anthropomorphism is really something of a paradox. It is a perpetual conflict of praise and blame: opponents regard it as a form of self-centered narcissism, and even an ally of anthropocentrism, while proponents see it as a powerful transformative force and persuasive rhetoric contributing to the continuity between humans and animals. The present study, instead of highlighting its binary oppositions, prefers to viewing anthropomorphism as a continuum. The key to tilting the balance dwells on how anthropomorphic language is strategically deployed. Therefore, compared to the accuracy of anthropomorphism, the study is more interested in the validity of anthropomorphic description of animal world. On this view, the study will focus on discussing what discursive strategies are employed in anthropomorphic representation of animals, as well as what cognitive effects anthropomorphism produces upon the readers. Not surprisingly, to examine anthropomorphic portrayal of animal world, it is crucial to have a close look at narratives of animal life given that "the presentation of animal behavior within a story is the factor which most saliently propels us to a humanlike (and potentially accurate) psychological interpretation" (Mitchell, 1997a: 151). Animal narratives, when combined with anthropomorphism, can "create a method of interpretation" (Mitchell, 1997a: 151). To better reveal the intertwined relationship between anthropomorphism and animal narratives, the next section is dedicated to an illustration of what animal narratives are about.

1.3   Understanding animal narratives

In modern society, dwindling wilderness, deteriorating environment and diminishing biodiversity are pressing for a re-evaluation of the relationship between humans and animals. People are tempered with a commitment to improve and reconstruct their connections with animals. Symbolic representation seems to be the perfect medium for a greater engagement with animals that are increasingly erased from the human world. Among diversified ways of representing animals, animal narratives emerge as an obvious choice since they seek to make animals visible again. In contrast to the dominating discourse that attempts to "standardize, de-individualize and automatize the behavior of animals" (Krebber & Roscher, 2018: 1), in animal narratives, the captivating life of individual animals, both real and fantastic, has kept people hooked for a long time, through which readers not only develop renewed understandings of animals, but also build up a strong and positive link with them. It appears that animal narratives are "a response to the urgent call for a return of human nature and a solution to the ecological degradation" (Tang, 2010: 13). Nevertheless, it can never be easy to understand what an animal narrative entails, as it is elastic and comprises encyclopedia accounts. To make explicit what the term implies, teasing out its relevance with animal folk tales and children's animal literature will be of vital importance.

On the one hand, animal folk tales, consisting of both literary fables and oral legends, serve to entertain. On the other hand, they can be educational; for example, most fables are created for imparting moral lessons. In these fables, animals that are cast as the leading roles are usually characterized, such as sly foxes, loyal dogs and brave lions. In so doing, they are regarded as "stand-ins for humans" (DeMello, 2012: 23) and made to "ventriloquize human morals and social norms" (Langdon, 2017: 1). Through reading these folk tales, readers can gain "a glimpse into the worldview of the people who created them" (DeMello, 2012: 307). Seen from this perspective, animal folk tales like these should not be considered as a literal representation of animals; on the contrary, "the literal animal is absent, replaced by the metaphorical or symbolic animal" (Hobgood-Oster, 2008: 15). This is evident particularly when animal folk tales attempt to create the human-animal hybrid, in which animals can be transformed into humans, and vice versa. In addition, "talking animals" are popular among animal fables. In *Collection of Aesop's Fables* or *Grimm's Fairy Stories*, they can be seen everywhere. Even nowadays, "talking animals" can be found in many children's stories.

Children's animal literature derives from animal folk tales, as most of the animal tales, heavily-animal-featured children's stories are composed for the purpose of educating and entertaining children. Children can get into the make-believe world created by these stories, with a sense of substitution evoked through the encounter with the fantasy creatures and talking animals. Thus children are able to understand the strong affinity with animals, and get access to lessons on morality, friendship, perseverance or valuable social skills. Animals in children's animal literature are mainly represented in two ways, either as human models, dressing, behaving and speaking as humans do, or as real and sentient animals that are imbued with integral qualities such as love, hatred, fear and loyalty, and have the ability to communicate their emotions.

Different from animal folk tales and children's animal literature, the point of departure of animal narratives is not to teach lessons, at least not in an explicit way. Definitions of "animal narrative" differ greatly among scholars (e.g. Sun, 2010; Tang, 2010), yet it is agreed upon that animal narratives highlight the ontological value of individual animal life, and prefer the realistic portrayal of animal world from an ecological perspective. As such, most animal narratives are committed to making visible animal subjects by ascribing individual traits to them and reconstructing the intimate interlacing between humans and animals. To capture the individuality of animals, episodic description serves as a powerful heuristic vehicle. "An episode is an actual and specific sequence of observed behaviors of notable though varying durations." (Crist, 1999: 69) Accordingly, the episodic portrayal of animal life choose to document concrete and actually-witnessed animal events. That is, they tend to record singular instances of specific animals rather than their generic behaviors. Concentration on narrating striking and extraordinary events brings out conspicuously the uniqueness of individual animals, representing vividly "a complete, self-contained" (Crist, 1999: 69) animal image. Moreover, narrating an episode with fine-grained details creates a world of mundane life, and thus advocates a tacit standpoint of being realistic, which is considered to be another prominent feature of animal narratives. Being "realistic" means that the depiction of animal behaviors in animal narratives adheres carefully to the biological characteristics and genetic features of animals in the real world. This is further favored by moderate participant observation. The role setting of human observers in the animal narratives as professional biologists or zoologists, who record animal behaviors after long observation in natural surroundings, lends credibility to the realistic representation of animals.

To sum up, what the notion of "animal narrative" connotes is mostly captured in Shen Shixi's words: the representation of animal images in animal narratives is in strict and full compliance with the biological features, physiological characteristics and behavioral patterns of real animals; animal narratives place prominent position in psychoanalysis of animals with an aspiration to conveying reliable knowledge to readers; animal behaviors in animal narratives are depicted as individualized instances through the format of typification; and animal narratives should not be degraded as an analogy or the symbol of human life—instead, they involve the distillation of animal world and the artistic reflection of human life. Notably, the very dualism of animal narratives is mainly realized through the anthropomorphic representation of animal images. As the common feature of most animal stories, anthropomorphic language is deployed extensively in animal narratives. Animals in fables and children's animal literature are fully anthropomorphized to impart moral lessons, while anthropomorphism in animal narratives serves the dual purposes of rendering back the visibility of animals as the subject of a lifeworld and evoking a reflection on human selves and society.

It is by means of anthropomorphic language that humans are brought to be in alignment with animals. In view of this, the anthropomorphic perspective in animal narratives "deserves serious attention" (Crist, 1999: 10). This study, with anthropomorphism at its core, investigates the discursive strategies for anthropomorphic representation of animals in animal narratives. In addition, it delves into how anthropomorphic depiction of animals is cognitively operated.

1.4   Research questions

Studies on animal representation is a multifaceted undertaking. The way in which animals are represented has direct consequences, either positive or negative, upon human-animal relationship. It thus becomes clear that inquiries into animal representation is interdisciplinary, and should be considered as a matter of "pressing environmental, social, economic and philosophical concern" (Cook, 2015: 587). Concerns on animal representation can be effortlessly found across the social and natural sciences, e.g. anthropology, literature, history, philosophy, behavioral science, and animal psychology, to mention a few. Within the realm of human science, the interdisciplinary tendency has in particular drawn attention from scholars working at Human-Animal Studies (DeMello, 2012; Taylor, 2013) and Animal Studies (Gross & Vallely, 2012). Following the trend, a linguistic approach to studying animal representation will undoubtedly add a valuable extension to the literature.

Language plays a powerful role in the portrayal of animals. On the account of the "ideological dimension" of language (Fairclough, 1989, 1992, 1995; Fowler & Kress, 1979; van Dijk, 1998), linguistic and discursive representation of animals can never be neutral. Divergent linguistic mediums tend to yield discrepancies in understanding animals, which will in turn affect how people view and treat animals in the real world. The intersections between linguistic representations of animals and human-animal relationship in reality can be best elaborated by the theoretical accounts argued by academic scholarships within the field of Critical Discourse Studies (CDS). CDS is "an interdisciplinary approach to language in use, which aims to advance our understanding of how discourse figures in social processes, social structures and social change" (Flowerdew & Richardson, 2018: 1). As is seen, on the top priority of CDS' agenda, "a specific is not 'a specific discipline, paradigm, school or discourse theory'" but "pressing social issues" (van Dijk, 1993: 252). Animal representation concerning human-animal relationship should be regarded as one of these issues. Thus, CDS can be deployed as a vigorous tool to explore discursive representation of animals in this study. Meanwhile, studies on animal representation is an ecological enterprise by nature. Therefore, it is advisable to approach the subject under a broader framework of ecolinguistics, which has contributed a great body of literature to issues concerning animals (e.g. Dunayer, 2001; Goatly, 2006; Sealey & Charles, 2013; Sealey & Oakley, 2013, 2014; Stibbe, 2001, 2012).

To make it clear, the present study adopts a three-level approach to examine animal representation in animal narratives, namely macro-, meso- and micro-level perspectives. On the macro-level of ecolinguistics, the special genre of animal narratives makes it a kind of "ambivalent discourse", which is neither "destructive" nor "beneficial" and could be either "destructive" or "beneficial" according to the principle of ecosophy (Stibbe, 2015). On the meso-level, the study will resort to two main angles from CDS—the dialectical perspective and the perspective of social-cognition—to explain how animal world, linguistic (discursive) representation and human society interact, as well as how the interaction is mediated through social cognition. Specific discursive strategies in representing literary animals are discussed on the micro-level. Meanwhile, the conceptualization of animal representation is also studied.

With approaching literary representation of animals at the heart, the present study chooses Shen Shixi's animal narratives as materials for analysis. Shen Shixi, one of the most prolific and influential animal novelists in contemporary China, has been honored as "the king of Chinese animal narratives". He has given full play to his literary imagining in creating animal novels and initiated a creative form of writing in telling animal stories. In the stories, animals are depicted vividly as the subject of their own lifeworld, providing possibilities of diversified construal of animals and attracting a wide readership (mostly young ones) in China. His writings are categorized, more often than not, into the scope of children's literature (Chen, 2018). This is arguable, however, because what the stories convey is far more than imparting lessons to children. Therefore, this study tilts towards placing his writings under the genre of "animal narratives".

In line with his interpretation of what animal writings should be, animals under his pen are ascribed with unique individuality and colorful inner world by ways of anthropomorphic description. Although the anthropomorphic tendency of his animal narratives is generally acknowledged (Chen, 2018; Sun, 2010; Tang, 2010; Zhu, 2005), few studies so far have dug into how anthropomorphic representation of animals is realized by linguistic means in his novels.

The purpose of the present study is to uncover the profound role language plays in anthropomorphic representation of animal images in Shen Shixi's animal narratives. What is at stake is how the anthropomorphic portrayal of animals can be realized through techniques of linguistic expressions and how they are conceptualized and legitimized. Moreover, the ecological attribute of Shen Shixi's animal narratives can be identified on this basis. Taking the above into account, the research will revolve around the following questions:

(1) What discursive strategies are applied to achieving anthropomorphic representation of animal images in Shen Shixi's animal narratives?

(2) How is anthropomorphic representation of animal images in Shen Shixi's animal narratives legitimized?

(3) What is the cognitive mechanism of anthropomorphic depictions? More precisely, how can anthropomorphic representation of animal images be metaphorically conceptualized?

(4) What is the ecological attribute of anthropomorphic representation of animal images in Shen Shixi's animal narratives in terms of Chinese ecosophy?

1.5　Methodological layouts

To save space and tedious work, research on linguistic representation of animals in Shen Shixi's animal narratives, with anthropomorphism as the core issue, will be conducted on five of his novels, i.e. *Dream of the Wolf King* (《狼王梦》), *Gorge Leaping Gorals* (《斑羚飞渡》), *The Seventh Hound* (《第七条猎

狗》), *The Last War Elephant* (《最后一头战象》), and *The Old Hark* (《老鹿王哈克》). There are several considerations for this choice. The first is accessibility: all five are available both online and in paper. The second is the diversity of animal species involved: animals in the selected writings vary widely, ranging from domestic to wild ones, and they are extensively depicted. The third is their representativeness: those novels differ from each other in length, some being full length and others being medium length or short pieces; they represent distinctive perspectives of telling animal stories (some of them are narrated in the third perspective, some told in the second perspective and others created in a mix of the first and third perspectives); they all enjoy wide popularity and high reputation in society. The last is systematicity: Shen's animal novels are intertextual by nature and composed in a homogeneous way especially when some of them are aimed at conveying similar themes (Zhu, 2005); the novels under investigation in the study cover most of the thematic metaphors he tries to express in his writings, e.g. metaphors of competition, success, economy, sacrifice and altruism. An overview of the collected materials is presented in Table 1.1.

Taking clarity into account, summary of each novel can be presented as follows.

Dream of the Wolf King mainly tells the story of a female wolf Zilan. In order to fulfill its husband's last wish to be the wolf king, it was determined to train its own son to be the "super wolf" at any price. Its plan was in tatters when, unexpectedly and tragically, its four wolf cubs lost their lives in succession. Even so, it didn't give up and placed all its hopes on its grandchildren. At the end of the story, in order to make its grandchildren no longer threatened, it died together with the golden eagle in a fierce fight.

Gorge Leaping Gorals tells the story about a group of gorals who were forced to a steep cliff in the hunter's pursuit. The only way for gorals to escape from the hunting was to jump across the cliff which was barely possible at that time because the narrowest distance between the two mountains was too far for these "jumping champions" to jump to the opposite side. For the sake of the survival of the whole goral population, the older gorals volunteered to sacrifice themselves, serving as

Table 1.1   An overview of the collected materials

Book title	Year of publication	Chinese characters	Leading character	Perspective	Metaphorical theme	Social impact / Honor / Others
Dream of the Wolf King 《狼王梦》	1990	100,000 (full length)	Wolf	Third-person	Competitiveness / Success	• The Fourth Yang Huan Award for Children's Literature; • The First Prize of the Second National Excellent Books for Children; • Among 100 Excellent Books Recommended to Young People by National Copyright Administration in 2008
Gorge Leaping Gorals 《斑羚飞渡》	2006	4,257 (short piece)	Goral	Third-person	Altruism / Sacrifice	• The People's Literature Publishing House's First Selection of Chinese Literature Award; • On the List of Chinese Textbooks of Junior High School Published by People's Education Press
The Seventh Hound 《第七条猎狗》	1985	8,680 (short piece)	Hound	Third-person	Altruism / Sacrifice	• Shen's Signature Work; • The First National Outstanding Children's Literature Prize of the China Writers Association; • Among 10 Best Children's Books selected by China Times in 1994
The Last War Elephant 《最后一只战象》	2008	4,684 (short piece)	Elephant	Third-person	Altruism / Sacrifice	• On the List of Chinese Textbooks of Elementary School Published by People's Education Press; • The adapted play was put on stage at the National Opera House in 2019
The Old Hark 《老鹿王哈克》	1994	17,091 (medium length)	Deer	Second-person	Altruism / Sacrifice / Success	

Note: There are a total of 134,712 Chinese characters of the five books.

the "stepping stone". In this way, the younger gorals are able to survive and thrive.

The Seventh Hound unfolds a story between a hound called Chili and its owner Zhao Panba. At the beginning of the story, Zhao Panba treated Chili as the most treasured possession for the reason that Chili was as ferocious as a tiger in hunting as a descendant of army dogs. Nevertheless, one day, Zhao Panba attempted to beat Chili to death with a stick because he never expected that Chili would behave cowardly when he was attacked by a boar, which turned out to be a mistake. With the help of Zhao Panba's grandchild, Chili escaped and ran into the woods. Several years later, at the critical moment when Zhao Panba and his grandchild were attacked by a group of jackals, Chili turned up and sacrificed its life to help them get out of the danger.

In the War of Resistance Against Japanese Aggression, the last war elephant Gasuo survived, who was the animal protagonist of *The Last War Elephant*. With a sense of foreboding that its life was going to come to an end, Gasuo once again put on the elephant saddle, and came to the banks of the Dalo River to remember the past. After that, it buried itself in a pit next to the elephant mound where its companions were interred.

The Old Hark presents the readers with a story of a deer king Hark. Foreseeing the arrival of death, Hark decided to do something extraordinary for the population of deer. When the deer population was desperately threatened by a wolf, Hark was determined to fight against the wolf alone to save the deer herd from danger. To this end, it gave up its throne. Even though a fierce struggle arose inside its heart, Hark overcame it and finally perished together with the wolf.

In order to address these issues, the present study tends to adopt a qualitatively-oriented approach. There are several reasons. Firstly, the analytic commitment of (ecological) CDS is to study discourse as social practice, and to disclose the hidden power of language and its effects, rather than examining linguistically-coded discourse as an abstract entity, i.e. a set of grammatical rules or lexical patterns. Therefore, with an aim to uncover the functioning of language in anthropomorphic animal representation and its possible impacts upon people's outlook towards animals in particular, intuition and retrospection probably weigh more than statistics and quantification in this study. Secondly, animal narrative, as a form of literature, has established itself as a register which is expected to represent its own discoursal context. "Interpretation" of animal narratives, therefore, involves the "contextualization process in which texts are indexically 'made to fit' a particular context" (Blommaert, 2005: 43). This is especially true when anthropomorphic representation of animals is mostly realized in episodic depiction in animal narratives. Each episode creates its own discoursal context, any aspect of which "is responsible for the interpretation of an utterance in its particular locus of occurrence" (Auer, 1992: 4). In this regard, qualitative analysis, which is agreeably supposed to provide greater richness and precision, conforms to the needs of studies on context-sensitive animal narratives, which are basically explanatory instead of descriptive. Thirdly, there are good reasons not to quantify, as Wood and Kroger (2000) argue. The fundamental issue is that quantification risks reducing analysis to "counting the countable" (Ding, 2018: 31). Functional importance of language could probably be mistakenly equated with frequency of occurrence in quantitative analysis (Phillips, 1985).

For the sake of credibility and reliability, examples cited in the current study are extracted from the above-mentioned five novels and are selected painstakingly and justifiably based upon the following reasons. First and foremost, the examples are selected in terms of their relevance to the research questions of the project. In the second place, representativeness is always a major concern. Equally important is the thematic relatedness on the account that animal narrative as a literary work invested with rich episodic description is a form of highly contextual-restricted discourse. In addition, to avoid biased selectivity and interpretation, cross-examining and reflexivity are necessary.

1.6   The organization of the book

The book consists of eight chapters. Following this introductory chapter, Chapter 2 is devoted to reviewing relevant literature. A close scrutiny of the literature suggests that literary and linguistic approaches to studying animal representation are highly complementary. In addition, studies on Shen Shixi's animal narratives are presented analytically to pave the way for further explorations.

Chapter 3 is intended to lay a solid theoretical foundation for the study. It starts with an elucidation of the dialectical relationship between animal world, discursive representation and human society. It goes on to pinpoint the mediated function social cognition performs in the interface. Further, it discusses at length how the model of ecological critical-cognitive discourse study will be helpful in doing the present study. Under this theoretical framework, the subsequent four chapters are dedicated to providing detailed analysis of anthropomorphic representation of animal images in Shen Shixi's animal narratives, each with a specific focus.

Chapter 4 centers on disclosing the discursive strategies deployed in anthropomorphic representation of animal images, revolving round referential and predication strategies. Chapter 5 proceeds to study how anthropomorphic animal representation can be legitimized. Strategies of legitimization, including grammatical cohesion, epistemic modality, and evidentiality are investigated. Chapter 6 looks at the cognitive mechanism of anthropomorphic language in representing animal images. It delves into the process of metaphorical conceptualization of anthropomorphic animal representation in the materials. Metaphors like "humans are animals" and "animals are more or less the same as humans" take the central stage of the study. Chapter 7 shows an attempt to identify the ecological attribute of anthropomorphic representation of animal images in Shen Shixi's animal narratives. It discusses the way in which animal perspective and human perspective are negotiated in anthropomorphic animal representation. It also introduces traditional Chinese philosophical thoughts as Chinese ecosophy, based upon which identifying the ecological attribute of anthropomorphic animal representation in Shen Shixi's animal narratives is made possible.

Chapter 8 is the closing chapter. In this chapter, the major findings of the study as well as its theoretical and empirical implications are revealed. Moreover, limitations of the current study are acknowledged and promising avenues of future research are provided.

Chapter 2　Literature Review

2.1　Introduction

In this chapter, a survey of literature on animal representation studies will be conducted. The review of previous studies takes different dimensions into consideration, including animal representation in literature, linguistic representation of animals, and animal representation in Shen Shixi's animal narratives, with an aim to offer a panoramic view of what is going on in the field of animal representation studies. The literature review can serve as the background against which a novel and interdisciplinary perspective into studying animal representation in Shen Shixi's animal narratives is introduced.

2.2　Studies on animal representation in literature

2.2.1　Crude anthropomorphism in animal-related literature

Since the Romantic Movement of the nineteenth century, critics have shifted their attention to the ecological evaluation of balances in living systems. Alongside the emerging eco-criticism, literary scholars are attracted by ecological concerns, reflecting on human's position in nature through literary works. The continuous interplay between eco-criticism and literary study not only contributes to a genuine understanding of how people are situated in the world, but also gives rise to an increasingly critical interest in literary animals. Literary animal studies as a field has become a constellation of many concerns, covering ethology, sociobiology, neurophysiology, animal rights, literature, evolution and linguistics, and hence represents the convergence between scientific and literary explorations. The complementarity between science and literature provides an innovative and crucial perspective to explore ecological issues, stated as follows:

> Writers imagine situations that help readers experience the ethical problems of certain kinds of science and technology, to live vicariously in potential worlds our science might bring to pass by its manipulations, to make "visible" through fictional situations the "invisible" environmental dangers that their readers could not have imagined. (Garrard, 2012: 75)

In the late twentieth and early twenty-first centuries, animal scholars started their advance in critical and theoretical work on the creatures of literature. Ever since, there has been a rapid growth of literature on literary animal studies, most of which endeavors to raise readers' awareness of "how language itself is contaminated by our human inheritance of human exceptionalism" (Wesling, 2019: xii). Specifically, scholars are more attentive to how animals are represented in animal-related literature as well as the dynamics between animal representations in literature and the underlying ideologies.

A leading role in promoting the development of critical study of animal representations in literature is Cary Wolfe, who is considered to be one of the most thoughtful voices in critical arguments on human-animal relationship. He proposes a special focus on literary animal studies within the broader domain of Animal Studies. His interdisciplinary background makes possible the birth of new-type critical theory and practice, which takes its root in the posthumanist thought of "human" as the outcome of the liberal philosophical tradition. His posthumanist framing sheds new lights on understanding animals:

> … the animal has always been especially, frightfully nearby, always lying in wait at the very heart of the constructive disavowals and self-constructing

narratives enacted by that fantasy figure called "the human". (Wolfe, 2003: 6)

Deeply influenced by him, Parry (2017) has conducted an extensive examination of animal representations in twenty-first-century novels. Her research suggests that animals, seemingly pervasive in texts, are not readily noticeable for the reason that "[a]ny study of a text on the non-human always becomes a study of humanity in some sense" (Clark, 2011: 187), even though the supposedly clear and uncrossable boundaries between humans and animals are obscured in "a structure made of symbols, significations, and discourses of mastery" (Parry, 2017: 2). Among the fictions she selects to interpret, *Animal's People*, with its title foregrounding the categorical discrepancies between animal and people, is a story of a human animal and his resistance against categorical prejudices that model him as "worthless less-than-human" (Parry, 2017: 16). As a literary entity, its hero is, as Parry posits, "folded into a complex of political, cultural, and philosophical encounters with the idea of the animal" (Parry, 2017: 16). The representation is imbued with the discourses of animality, characterized by bestial traits such as irrationality or lower intelligence, and hence locates both other species and othered people in an inferior position. In this way, *Animal's People* implicitly discloses the capacity of zoomorphism (the counterpart of "anthropomorphism") in creating reductive associations, which serves the aim of provoking forceful questions concerning how humans imagine themselves. In this regard, animals become unseen.

Another overt example can be found in her exploration of the metaphorical representations of ants in twenty-first-century fictions. Although the texts examined are of various genres, they share some common features: one is that ant representations bear imprints of biologically real ants, like their perceived thrift and organized social life; the other is that representations of ants in these novels are exploited metaphorically to figure and analogize human's reflection of themselves, i.e. to explicate human political and social organizations. That is to say, the ant in literary works has largely acted as "a vehicle for describing forms of human sociality, and retains its analogical power as a method for critiquing humanistic individualism" (Parry, 2017: 67). Despite the contribution ants make to humans as a method of comprehending the true meaning of being human, the figurative representations of ants by means of the so-called "crude anthropomorphism" (Parry, 2017: 42) may to a great extent distort the actual ants. These two examples, among the others, reveal the truth that in animal-related literary works, animals are reducibly yet unavoidably transformed into figural and cultural representations which elicit both humans' self-imagining and their reactions to animals. In this sense, "animal representations tend, therefore, to be characters whose furred or feathered exteriors clothe the concerns, beliefs, and interests of humans" (Parry, 2017: 42), and animal narratives will turn to be anthropocentric by nature. Parry expresses her concern about this fraught condition of literary animal representation, and advocates a vital recognition that people should concern more about animals (either real or fictional) per se than just their engagement in the story of humans.

Parry's study is fruitful and insightful in the following aspects: Firstly, it attempts to respond to the categorical distinctions drawn between humans and animals in the twenty-first century; secondly, it uncovers how the concept of anthropocentrism is evolving in fictional animal representation; thirdly, it probes into the possible effects the textual politics of depicting fictional animals will have upon the future trajectory of human-animal relationship; fourthly, it poses questions about anthropomorphism and analogy in animal-related stories, contending that crude anthropomorphism—completely overlooking animals' subjectivity and imposing human thoughts upon animal life—will "produce only humans wearing a superficial coat of animal fur or a chitinous shell" (Parry, 2017: 66). In the meanwhile, she favors a critical form of anthropomorphism which shows respect to animals' subjective life and uses the language and concepts of human behavior to depict animal world in non-anthropocentric and careful ways, arguing that it is helpful in emancipating people's minds from the restriction of exceptionalism.

2.2.2 Critical form of anthropomorphism in animal biography

The critical form of anthropomorphism has found its widespread use in the genre of animal biography. Animal biography, under the umbrella of literary animal study, is a vital form of literary narration concerning animals. It acts as an approach to trace the individuality of animals, and hence makes animals noticeable as individuals. In animal biographies, the agency of individual creatures is foregrounded with the presentation of their own personal traits and idiosyncrasies. The prominence of subjective experience of animals, together with their dynamic intersection with the (natural and human) surroundings, fulfills the individual's making of his or her biography. The tendency of individualization in animal biographies deconstructs the collective identity animals hold as being principally the same, reframing them as subjects of (at least) their own lives. In addition, as a genre specialized in narrating and recording animals' lifeworld, animal biography is created as a blend of fact and fiction. The co-existence of scientific objectivism and vivid depictions of animal anecdotes in animal biographies contributes to transgressing the borderline between science and art, allowing a space for differentiation and deviance.

Recent literature pertaining to animal biography centers on four main dimensions, consisting of "explorations, reflections, constructions and experiments" (Krebber & Roscher, 2018). Explorations of animal biography are made by focusing on the interlinkages between animals and human participants. Kean (2018) traces animal appearance back in archival materials and suggests that the relational and emotional connections between humans and animals are at the heart of a biographical account, indicating the symbiotic relationship between different species. Also disapproving of the species-specific readings of animal biographies, Middelhoff (2018) challenges the reliability of the encounter between a real animal and the text's author, which is considered to be the very source of creating fictional animals. Upon a closer examination of literary autozoographies, she argues that the overt relationships between the narrator and the author should be told apart to consolidate the empirical foundations in exploring the animals' autobiographical selves. Far from merely presenting the individual animal's life story, animal biographies also serve as an access to perceiving the contextual constraints.

Reflections on animal biographies are directed towards a deeper dialogue between fictional animals and the socio-political as well as cultural contexts. Skabelund (2018) digs into the challenges and possibilities of writing animal biographies, exemplifying the high adaptability of animal representation to nationalistic idealization. A reflection on methodology is of interest for Shah (2018). By examining the practice of primatologists, she asserts that their fieldwork is characterized with participant observation and recognition of individual animals. The animal biographies—byproduct of primatological fieldwork, she continues to point out, enable the ascription of agency and subjectivity to individual animals, and the individualization of animals in biographical discourses can be perceived by referring to a socio-political concept, that is, intersubjective recognition. The reflections on the biographical representation of animals, with their individual lives as the focal point, break the biological confinement of animals and entail profound significance.

The third dimension, constructions, investigates into how biographical discourses regarding animals are constructed. Driven by the passion of understanding whether individuality is the premise for framing the historical subjects, McHugh (2018) conducts her study on the interrelationship between taxidermy and literary representation. Her research suggests a disentanglement of constructing culture from nature (biology). A similar claim is available in Wolf's (2018) dissection of biographical representation of animals in films. Drawing on the concept of "becoming animals", he demonstrates the evolutionary process of constructing either human or non-human identities, at the core of which lies the question of anthropomorphism. His detailed elucidation of anthropomorphism, combined with the analysis of biographical narration of the protagonists, exposes the underlying "humanist framework" behind anthropomorphism, which elicits a call for disentanglement of categories of similarity and identity construction.

Experiments exhibit some insightful and inspiring perspectives in potential pattern, narration and embodied structure of animal biographies. Obsessed with the concerns for animal rights, scholars have pioneeringly studied creative forms of animal biographies on an experimental basis. Subramaniam (2018), by using textual fragmentation rather than narrating biographical stories in a linear fashion, addresses the importance of human participation in the presentation of animal biographies. Stallwood (2018), for the sake of animal well-being, advocates studying animal biographies in a broader framework than just highlighting animals' behaviors. Most importantly, he stresses that creating animal biographies is a useful help in reminding people of what some of the autonomy animals possess which otherwise is routinely denied in a human-centered world. DeMello (2008) inquires into the biographical representation of animals on social media. She posits that biographical construction of online animals function no less than their fictional counterparts in written materials to evoke readers' compassion and empathy for animals. In addition, she shows confidence in the anthropomorphic nature of online animals, asserting that it will provoke innovative thinking and understanding of animal's identity as subject.

2.2.3 Discussion

Animals, whether fictional or real, are irreducibly complex syntheses of imagined and real characteristics. Therefore, human's responses to and engagements with animals largely depend on their understandings of this composition. However, in an era when animals are diminishing rapidly, literary representations of animals appear to be the optimal choice for humans to approach them. An overview of the literature on literary animal studies is ready to shine some enlightening lights on comprehending animal representations in literature.

To begin with, fictional representations of animals in literature initiates a challenge to the scientific account of animals as being mindless and objectified "others". Taking individual animals at the central stage, animal narratives (biographies) attempt to reconstruct animals' identity as the subject of their own lives which has been obscured for a long time. Acknowledging animals' agency will, in turn, have a positive impact on people's attitudes and treatment of animals in reality. Seen from this perspective, literary representations of animals have "material consequences" (Parry, 2017: 230) for themselves, which account for the claim that "the granting of rights to animals should thus include the right to a biographical narration that accepts the claim that animals are subjects, at the very least, of their lives" (Krebber & Roscher, 2018: 14).

Nevertheless, reshaping animal images through a biographical lens doesn't necessarily lead to the expected emancipation of animal agents via individualized representations. In animal narratives, the perspectives of the narrated and the author are inextricably interwoven, and the portraits of the protagonists, their lives and distinctive characteristics included, count on how the author makes the story through organizing the fragmentary materials and his or her language. It seems that fictional representations of animals might surpass their biological individuals. They could be mirrors or symbols of human society and culture. In effect, narrations of animals are "incapable of stepping outside its preoccupations with human concerns" (Parry, 2017: 66). On this account, it is not surprising to find that animal narratives are always imbued with authentic and metaphorical depictions. This dualism of animal representation in literature is best manifested in the paradox of anthropomorphism which is widely used in portraying animals. The employment of anthropomorphic depiction of literary animals is justified for one reason that there exists no single semiotics amenable and accessible to read and tell animals' minds; for another, anthropomorphic representation of animals lends voice to the agency and visibility of individual animals. Extensive use of anthropomorphism in animal representation might negatively strengthen the walls erected between humans and animals. Important though it is, so far, there is still a shortage in studying how fictional animals are represented via anthropomorphic language. A linguistic approach to studying animal representation in literature will be of great necessity.

2.3   Studies on the linguistic dimension of animal representation

2.3.1 "Ecolinguistic turn" of animal studies

Linguistic approaches to animal study have arisen from an emerging discipline called "ecolinguistics". Propelled by the paradigm of "the ecology of language" (Haugen, 1972), ecolinguists were initially interested in exploring the interrelations among languages in multilingual communities as well as in human cognition. Accompanied by a growing awareness of environmental degradation, the ecological dimension of linguistic study is increasingly concerned with how language can impact the ecosystems that life on the earth depends upon.

Among scholars on this vital topic, M. A. K. Halliday is an early exponent in critiquing the potential destructive effects that language contributes to the environment. In his remarkable article "New ways of meaning: The challenge to applied linguistics" (Halliday, 1991), he points out how the topics of growthism, sexism, classism and "speciesism" are implied in our languages both lexically and syntactically, which, according to his "linguistic constructionism", will make a difference in people's construal of the world and impose detrimental influence upon the ecological environment. Following the line, Goatly (2005) reveals the fragmentation of the world caused by grammatical divisions of languages, advocating a more "consonant" grammar which is good for developing a view of wholeness towards the universe and advancing inseparable connection between human and nature. The critical tendency of ecolinguistic study can also be found in Trampe's work. Centered on the language system of agriculture, Trampe (2005) criticizes anthropocentrism and commercialism of language, bringing to light the fact that living organisms are ideologically objectified to meet the commercial needs of the human world.

Apart from system-focused criticism shown above, another strand of critical ecolinguistic study resorts to discourse analysis to uncover how the product of social environment, language in particular, could undermine the physical surroundings (Fill & Mühlhäusler, 2001). Inextricably intertwined with the advent of CDS, discourse-oriented critical ecolinguists have a growing awareness that "all discourse about natural phenomena is highly selective" (Fill & Mühlhäusler, 2001: 5), and thus are dedicated to analyzing how linguistic choices and discursive strategies contribute to creating solidarity or separation between human and the environment (e.g. Alexander, 2009, 2018; Berman, 2005; Hansen, 2018; Howlett & Raglon, 1992).

Discourses under their investigations cover a wide range, varying from advertising to economics, from environmentalism to energy, from natural resources to animals, and so on. Diverse as these studies are, they share some common features, which can be summarized as: 1) they are all motivated by a deep concern for ecological issues; 2) they all stress the significant role language plays in ecological destruction or protection; 3) they attempt to reveal the impact of language on ecology by examining clusters of linguistic features through discourse analysis; 4) by means of critiquing ecologically-destructive language practice, their ultimate goal is to raise people's ecological awareness and promote alternative forms of language use that are potentially helpful for the environment. Ecolinguistics, in this sense, can be defined thus:

> Ecolinguistics, then, is about critiquing forms of language that contribute to ecological destruction, and aiding in the search for new forms of language that inspire people to protect the natural world. Ecolinguistics can explore the more general patterns of language that influence how people both think about, and treat, the world. It can investigate the stories we live by—mental models that influence behaviour and lie at the heart of the ecological challenges we are facing. (Stibbe, 2015: 1)

Along with the rise of ecolinguistics, the development of Animal Studies has gone through an "ecolinguistic turn". The reality that animals are vanishing from both the physical and the mental worlds of human beings calls for a serious attention to the question—how animals are erased and how they can be reminded of. Considering that most animals nowadays emerge as "linguistic signs" (Abram, 1996; Stibbe, 2001, 2012), more researches on linguistic representation of animals are required. So far, linguistic approaches to studying animal representation have mostly underlined the fact that animals are socially constructed for human's exploitation and oppression (e.g. Abram, 1996; Berger, 1980; Dunayer, 2001; Glenn, 2004; Freeman, 2009; Stibbe, 2001, 2012), that is, viewing from the perspective of linguistic representation, animals are "typically objectified and regarded as inconsequential" (Tønnessen, 2013: 257) in various kinds of discourses.

Notably, critical ecolinguistics of animal representation, corresponding to the divergent directions of critical ecolinguistics, follows different pathways too. There is the prescriptive approach and the discourse-oriented approach. Prescriptive approach aims at providing linguistic norms that prescribe how animals should be talked about (e.g. Dunayer, 2001; Smith-Harris, 2004). Studies of this type tend to provide one "politically correct" (Stibbe, 2012: 4) way of describing animals. Effective as they may be, they shut down other possibilities in the meanwhile. This tendency of exclusiveness will probably lead to, as Fairclough states, "resentment even among people basically committed to antiracism, anti-sexism, etc." (2003: 25), and in this specific context, it will be harmful for people to creatively develop their consciousness of animal protection. In response, discourse-oriented approach attempts to explore how linguistic features cluster together to shape people's attitudes towards animals instead of concentrating on particular or individual lexical and grammatical features. Studies along the line work at raising people's critical awareness of existing animal discourses and advancing alternative discourses that promote more harmonious connections with animals. Studies as such welcome "any attempts to reform or call for change" (Mills, 2003: 90). Among these researches, of prominent importance is Stibbe's study on discursive erasure and animal representation.

2.3.2 Discursive erasure and animal representation

Discursive erasure is a popular concept in social science, denoting that "something important, something that we should be giving attention to, has been ignored, sidelined or overlooked within a text or discourse" (Stibbe, 2015: 146). Discursive erasure takes three major forms: "the void", "the mask" and "the trace" (Stibbe, 2015: 149). Of greatest use to ecolinguistics, as Stibbe points out, is "the mask". Drawing from Baudrillard's (1999) work on the hierarchy of representation, "the mask" refers to a way of erasure by which a profound reality is represented in a distorted and denatured way. In the context of animal representation, "the mask" foregrounds the instrumentality of animals, that is, animals are usually discursively constructed as objects or tools for exploitation. In this way, animals as subjective beings are implicitly erased.

This covert relationship between discursive erasure and animal representation is best revealed in Stibbe's (2012) *Animals Erased: Discourse, Ecology, and Reconnection with the Natural World*. In this book, Stibbe's inquiry into the erasure of animals in contemporary discourses is conducted upon the premise that "the discourses we use to construct our conceptions of animals and nature have important consequences for the well-being of the animals and the ecosystems that support life" (2012: 6). From this standpoint, he systematically criticizes the "suppression, backgrounding, exclusion, abstraction" (Stibbe, 2012: 146) of animals in anthropocentric mainstream discourses. His critical remarks on prevalent representation of animals tend to draw evidence from an extensive investigation into animal-related discourses in modern society. His findings suggest that most discourses under scrutiny are characterized by a tendency to objectify animals and to justify the utilization of animals via diversified linguistic means. For example, in discourses of meat industry, linguistic devices at various levels, such as nouns, pronouns, nominalization, passive voice, metaphor and metonymy, are deployed to construct animals as commodities or "unfeeling objects ready for oppression" (Stibbe, 2012: 6). These discursive strategies, as he asserts, will accurately help erase the agency of animals and lead to the creation and perpetuation of inhumane practices that are environmentally destructive. The underlying ideology contributing to the popularity of destructive discourses like these, he puts forward, is "a dominant human-centred ideology of mastery over an inferior sphere of animals and nature" (Stibbe, 2012: 15).

On the account that "anthropocentrism has merged into a powerful process of conceptual and moral legitimation" (Bowers, 2014: 27), Stibbe's critique is not just confined to destructive discourses. He also turns spotlight on animal representation in some counter discourses. By "counter discourses", he refers to the "mainstream discourses that explicitly aim to promote animal welfare or rights, ameliorate environmental destruction, conserve wildlife, or protect ecosystems" (Stibbe, 2012: 6). These counter discourses are supposed to offer sound alternatives to mainstream destructive discourses, yet they fail in their endeavors. Stibbe's study on counter discourses uncovers that animals are devalued as "specimens" or "resources" of instrumental value in most environmental, ecological and conservationist discourses which ostensibly convey environmental messages. Stibbe's critique of counter discourses is "as valuable and revealing as his critique of destructive mainstream discourses" (Tønnessen, 2013: 257). Nevertheless, challenging destructive and counter discourses is, in Stibbe's mind, far from enough to fulfill his aspiration of reconstructing the intimate interlacing between humans and animals. As an ecolinguist with a profound concern for the worsening environment, Stibbe attempts to tackle his duty with devotional enthusiasm and optimism: he commits himself to "reminding" people of the intrinsic value of animals as agents and subjects endowed with subjectivity and sentience. "Reminding" is the counterpart of erasure. They are a pair of complementary antonyms within the ecological and symbolic realms:

> Reminding is a linguistic act where an actor surveys the universe of elements that have been excluded from a particular discourse, declares that one of these elements is important, that the discourse is "erasing" it from consciousness, and demands that the discourse bring it back to mind. (Stibbe, 2015: 586)

As is defined, reminding is an attempt at bringing back to people's consciousness what is missing, or "erased", in contemporary discourses. One indispensable way of reminding, as Stibbe suggests, is to seek out "alternative discourses which represent animals, plants and nature in vivid and direct ways with the minimum of erasure" (2015: 597). To this end, he proposes alternative discourses to replace destructive and counter discourses. Alternative discourses, sharply different from destructive and counter discourses, are discourses that structure the world on the fundamental belief of "all things in the biosphere have an equal right to live and blossom" (Devall & Sessions, 1985: 68), and discourses that "encourage respect for animals and the natural world, and promote the fulfilling of human needs in ways that do not destroy the ecosystems that support life" (Stibbe, 2012: 10). Stibbe's proposal of alternative discourses are exemplified by his detailed analysis of two elements of traditional Japanese culture, namely, haiku and Zen.

Although there is nothing wrong to illustrate alternative discourses with these examples, the very model fails to prove its feasibility in other contexts, given that "as examples embedded in local culture, their appeal is quite naturally much stronger in Japan than elsewhere" (Tønnessen, 2013: 257). An ideal model of alternative discourses that has a wider applicability, in Tønnessen's (2013) mind, should be aimed at restoring the association between humanity and animality through language. Tønnessen's claim is strongly inspired by Abram's work of *Becoming Animal: An Earthly Cosmology*. Similarly using animals as points of reference, Abram's project is a parallel to Stibbe's—both deal with the role of discourse or language in the context of ecological devastation. Methodologically distinct from Stibbe's critical accounts, however, Abram favors a fairly modest reflection based on animistic sensibility. The concept of "becoming animals", which highlights "first and foremost the matter of becoming more deeply human by acknowledging, affirming and growing into our animality" (Deleuze & Guattari, 1987; cf. Tønnessen, 2013: 256), denotes the indispensable linkage between humans and animals. "Becoming animals" is inhabited by Abram's empathy with concrete, individual animals as depicted in his work. It is through the encounters with these animals that Abram strives to "recover or develop a sensuous and connected language, and likewise for perception (and thus help transform lifestyles and ways of being in the world)" (Tønnessen, 2013: 256). Abram's attempt to recall animality in human beings is experimental in advocating an alternative way of speaking, yet it is also inspirational in that it entails the assumption that "since we are animals, we should learn from other animals" (cf, Tønnessen, 2013: 259).

2.3.3 Discussion

To learn from other animals necessitates a good knowledge of animals, which presumes the importance of descriptions of animals, their behaviors in particular, for "they are constitutive of knowledge about animals" (Lederer, 2014: 834). With regard to the portrait of animal behaviors, animal narrative, which features cogent observation of individual animals, can be considered as a tangible medium to create the link between the human world and animal life. Thus, how the image of animals is constructed in animal narratives deserves serious attention. Nevertheless, so far, linguistic approach to studying the representation of animals in animal narratives remains limited. In China, even though scholars have shown an increasing interest in linguistic dimension of ecological issues (e.g. Fan & Chen, 2018; Feng, 2013; He & Zhang, 2017; Huang & Xiao, 2017; Xin & Huang, 2013; Zhou & Huang, 2017), few of them investigate linguistic or discursive construction of animals in animal narratives. Being alternative discourses, culture-specific as Stibbe proposes or new ways of speaking that move towards the convergence of animality and humanity as Abram advocates, Chinese animal narratives are of great significance for scholars in China to seek out Chinese-characteristic discourses that enhance a more equitable relationship between humans and animals. Among many animal narratives, Shen Shixi's works have gained enduring popularity in contemporary China. The next section will be dedicated to a review of previous studies on his works.

2.4　Studies on Shen Shixi's animal narratives

2.4.1 The issue of "authenticity"

The emergence of animal narratives is closely related to the progress of how people understand the relationship between human beings and nature. Human beings' awareness of their engagement with nature has undergone significant transformation since the industrialized age when modern science and technology seriously threaten their survival. People start to realize that human and human rationality are not omnipotent, and that man is only a part of nature. Accompanied by the awakening of ecological consciousness, the pursuit of harmonious inter-connection between human and nature permeates the field of literature. It is in this context that animal narratives came into being.

With an emphasis upon enhancing the subjective status of animals, animal narratives advocate green and harmonious ecological wholism. Animal narratives as such are under prosperous development worldwide, not excepting China. Although started late, Chinese animal narratives developed and matured gradually in the twentieth century. Since the 1980s, there has been a group of writers dedicated to producing animal narratives, represented by Shen Shixi, who is one of the first writers in the Chinese mainland to explore animal narratives. From the 1980s to the present, Shen Shixi has created hundreds of novels featuring animals. His animal novels, well-sold both at home and abroad, have won a number of literature awards. With considerable quantity and high quality of literary works on animals, Shen Shixi is known as "the king of Chinese animal narratives". Some critics also believe that Shen Shixi's works in the late 1980s "help to transform people's recognition towards the style of animal novels" (Shi, 1995: 76), and "open up a new artistic world" (Shi, 1995: 81). In addition, Shen has "made important contributions to the theoretical construction of animal novels" (Chen, 2018: 11).

The wide-ranging impact of Shen Shixi's animal narratives has attracted the attention of researchers in the field of literature study. Qu regards the writing style of Shen Shixi's animal narratives as pioneering in China for the reason that "it has developed a whole new perspective of animal narrative writing in the country" (2011: 129). She points out that different from fables which work on conveying moral sermons, Shen Shixi's writings provide readers with a clearer understanding of the nature of animal life and the diversity of animal world by presenting real animals. By "real", Qu refers to the fundamental principle of animal narrative writing: authenticity—"animal narrative takes authenticity as its first lifeline. In animal novels, animals' habits and behaviors should stand up to the test of biology" (Dong, 2011: 3). However, whether animals depicted in Shen Shixi's narratives follow their nature remains controversial. The authenticity of animal images in his works are questioned by scholars. It is argued that animals represented in Shen Shixi's writings go beyond the limitation of animals' natural properties and show a tendency to deviate from the prescribed principle of animal narratives (Yang, 2013). Researches suggest that in writing about animals, Shen Shixi is more inspired by the complexity of human society than the mysteries of animal world (e.g. Chen, 2018; Qu, 2011; Yang, 2013; Zhu, 2005). Therefore, anthropomorphic tendencies of animal representation have become "the fundamental artistic model of Shen Shixi" (Yang, 2013: 20). Critics hold that although animals in Shen's works retain their biological appearance and natural habits, their behaviors are humanized and socialized; moreover, animals are portrayed to possess cognitive abilities such as the abilities of rational thinking, causal judgment, ethical and moral concerns, and philosophical reflections on life. Thus, to a certain degree, the so-called "authenticity" of Shen's animal narratives is hypothesized. Commenting on the artistic model of Shen Shixi's novels, Zhu Ziqiang argues:

Shen Shixi's fictional stories of animals are fantasies that hover over both the realities of animal life and human life... When Shen Shixi invents the stories that are freed from the nature of the animal life, he gives up the opportunity to reveal another part of nature that is equally important as human beings—the mystery and the magic of animal world, and meanwhile a vast and precious aesthetic tendency that could not be approached by other genres but animal novel disappears… (2005: 363)

Zhu further points out critically that in Shen Shixi's narratives most animals are depicted in a state of "division"—partly revealing the natural laws of animal world and partly reflecting the moral laws of human society.

Rather, Qu views this way of representing animals as an artistic "integration"—human emotional appeal and animals' personality characteristics are effectively integrated:

> Apart from focusing on the introduction of biological properties of animals, in his works, Shen Shixi also highlights the expression of their social attributes. Shen Shixi believes that literature is created by human, and should be about human. We human beings more or less retain some kind of animality, so that humans may be able to discover both the good and evil of human nature from animal stories… (2011: 129)

For Qu, an appropriate word to describe the "integration" of human society and animal world in Shen Shixi's animal narratives is "mirror". Sun expresses similar concern:

> The depiction and disclosure of the seemingly unique world of animals will lead us to see what appears to be a very universal form of life. All this, like a mirror, makes people see their own spiritual world, the similarities between human society and animal world, as well as the basic rules of the universe. (2010: 3)

Shen Shixi himself, however, seems to have his own understanding. Upon defining animal narratives, he points out that one of the characteristics animal narratives bear involves ideological connotations, which should be artistic reflection rather than simply an analogy or a symbol of certain customs of human society. It is apparent that Shen Shixi's animal narratives embody his own artistic exploration, as he states, "… I am deeply aware that animal novels are more attractive than other types of novels, because they are most likely to puncture the shell of human culture, the whitewash of etiquettes, the bondage of morals and all kinds of hypocrisy of civilized society" (cf. Sun, 2010: 6).

2.4.2 Anthropomorphism in Shen Shixi's animal narratives

Diversified as interpretations may be, it is agreed that the intricate interweaving relationship between animal world and human society is creatively illustrated in Shen Shixi's animal narratives: ecological concerns and human reflections are converged in the animal images constructed in his works. Scholars name animal novels of this type as "humanoid animal novels". As an innovative variant of animal novels, humanoid animal novels demonstrate the writer's artistic pursuit, making unique contributions to the development of ecological literature (Sun, 2010: 159). Most of Shen Shixi's works have been categorized as "humanoid animal novels" (e.g. Dong, 2011; Sun, 2010; Zhu, 2005), which are characterized by anthropomorphic animal images.

Quite different from the instrumentalized animal images in fairy-tale-oriented animal novels, in which animals are just the symbols of human beings, anthropomorphic representation of animals in humanoid animal novels goes beyond the intuitive comparison of animal externality (look, behavior, etc.) and probes into the inner emotional and spiritual world, serving the dual purposes of calling for the return of animal subjectivity and triggering human's reflection of themselves. They represent a novel literary practice in that on the one hand they strictly follow the biological properties of animals while on the other hand they attribute human-like cognitive and emotional abilities to animals. As Shen Shixi realizes, while working on animal images, one should "strictly regulate the behaviors of the animal protagonists based on their biological attributes" and "sink into the inner world of animal characters and grasp the psychological characteristics of the animals" (cf. Sun, 2010).

This is well-justified by the fact that anthropomorphic construction of animal images in Shen Shixi's narratives is mostly achieved by detailed description of animal behaviors and their psychology, which concerns the reproduction of animals' external features and the speculation of their psychological activities (Chen, 2007). Dong (2011) points out that in creating animal images, Shen Shixi prefers to describe the "external" and "potential" behaviors of animals. Dong associates "potential" behaviors with the (sub)conscious activities and thinking mode of animals, which determines the way animals behave physically. She argues that it is the portrayal of the interaction between animals' external (physical) and potential (psychological) behaviors that makes animal characters slide away from their animal nature and demonstrate the unique trait specific to the human race (Dong, 2011: 8).

In a similar vein, Yang (2013), while studying animal representation in Shen Shixi's works, highlights Shen's description of animal psychology. He states that psychological portrayal of animals indicates the writer's efforts to reposition animals from instrumental into subjective status, because animals cannot "speak" for their subjectivity in human language. He further points out that even if the motivation is to bring out animals' subjectivity, when depicting animals' psychological activities, human thinking will inevitably seep into the writing, which makes obvious the anthropomorphic tendencies of animal description in Shen Shixi's works.

Scholars also recognize that the anthropomorphic way of representing animals can be a double-edged sword:

> Writing animal novels in the anthropomorphic way is like walking a tightrope—it is dangerous. However, if the writer can take the use of anthropomorphic techniques under control, it will not hinder the writer's description of animals' natural habits and inner feelings, but can add unique charm to animal novels. (Zhu, 2005: 362)

2.4.3 Discussion

A glimpse of the current literature on studying Shen Shixi's animal narratives suggests that most of the researches on his works concentrate on the construction of animal images. Opinions vary on the question of whether Shen Shixi's animal representation is authentic or not. At the core of all the controversies is the anthropomorphic tendencies of animal depiction in the novels. It is argued that anthropomorphic representation of animals could possibly help to restore the intrinsic value of animals or reaffirm their epistemologically symbolic status. Another important finding of these studies is that anthropomorphic animal representations are constructed mostly by elaborate depiction of the physical behaviors and psychological activities of animals. Insightful as the investigations are, there is still room for further exploration. Firstly, from a macro-perspective, researches on animal narratives in China, as Chen (2018) reviews, have not attracted due attention from academic circles, and thus are theoretically and methodologically under-examined. Secondly, with regard to the studies on Shen Shixi's animal narratives, the majority are conducted within the realm of (ecological) literature; therefore, an interdisciplinary paradigm, e.g. an integration with linguistic approach, is in need to boost the research. Thirdly, although agreements have been reached that animals in Shen Shixi's novels are represented anthropomorphically, there lacks a systemic and thorough inquiry into how anthropomorphic animal images are shaped by linguistic means as well as how they will act on readers' cognition.

2.5   Summary

This chapter is dedicated to reviewing literature relevant to the present study. Researches from three interdependent fields are cross-examined. Literature review of the researches reveals that animal narratives are always imbued with authentic and metaphorical depictions, which is best manifested in the paradox of anthropomorphism extensively used in portraying animals.

These previous researches, taken together, are imperfect in the following aspects. First, in China, explorations into the discursive animal representation in animal narratives remain underscored; there has not been a systemic study of animal representation in Shen Shixi's animal narratives. Second, although previous studies on animal representation in literature and studies on the linguistic dimension of animal representation have presented fruitful discussions from different perspectives, they rarely hold an integrational view. An interdisciplinary approach to studying animal representation in animal narratives, which tends to view animal narratives as a form of discursive practice and social practice, and therefore aims at uncovering the dynamics between human society, discourse and animal world, is necessary. Third, previous researches on anthropomorphic animal representation focus more on explaining anthropomorphism as a static structure and rhetorical device. There is yet to be an extensive study which views anthropomorphic animal representations as both the continuum between human and animal domains as well as the conceptualizing tool to evoke complicated continuity between humans and animals. There is a need for studies on the construction and construal of anthropomorphic animal representation from a dynamic dimension of relational networking and cognitive functioning. Fourth, there remains a question of whether the existing critical-oriented framework of ecological discourse studies, which is based upon Western ecosophy, is applicable, reliable and feasible in the Chinese context. Theoretical exploration is of necessity on the contextualized framework for exploring Chinese ecological discursive practice, which will shed light on animal representation study in China.

Built on these, the current study brings in a cognitive perspective to investigate anthropomorphic representation of animal images in Shen Shixi's animal narratives. It envisions anthropomorphic animal representation as a way of interpretation involving both meaning construction and construal, and attempts to explore the discursive strategies and cognitive processing underlying anthropomorphic representation of animal images. It also tends to approach the topic in the broad social and cultural context with an aim to reveal the dynamics between human beings, discourse and animals. To conduct the study, an ecological critical-cognitive analysis framework of animal representation as a modified model of Stibbe's (2012, 2015) is put forward in the next chapter.

Chapter 3 Theoretical Foundation

3.1 Introduction

This chapter is particularly devoted to establishing the theoretical and analytical framework of the study, under which anthropomorphic representation of animal images in Shen Shixi's animal narratives will be explored. It begins with a discussion of the dynamic and dialectical relationship between animal life, discursive representation and human society, paving the way for the integration of ecological dimension into critical discourse study. In particular, it focuses on the socio-cognitive approach to investigating the manipulative role of ecological "stories" constructed in discourse, i.e. the discourse of animal representation, in people's attitude toward ecological issues. Specifically, it addresses the function of discursive strategies performing in linguistic coercion and discursive manipulation. With an emphasis on the cognitive aspect of language, it delves into the conceptualizing mechanism of discursive representation, foregrounding metaphor as a way of conceptualization. On this basis, it attempts to bring up a three-dimension framework for the current analysis of animal representation in discourse.

3.2 Animal world, discursive representation and human society

Among various factors contributing to the intricacy of the relationship between humans and animals is language. The moderating role language exposes on human-animal relationship takes its root in the transformation of ways in which humans and animals interact in modern society (Cook, 2015; Jacobs & Stibbe, 2006; Stibbe, 2001, 2012). That is, with the increasing urbanization and changes in technology, nowadays animals are increasingly marginalized and even "erased" from human life, for which one of the major reasons is that interactions between humans and animals are mostly mediated through symbolic representation. This very stage of mediation deserves serious attention in that "representations necessarily are partial" (Jacobs & Stibbe, 2006: 1). As Crist points out, "language use is not a neutral instrument in the depiction or interpretation of animal life" (1999: 4). Divergent ways of linguistic representation configure distinctively different ways to witness and construe animal beings. Thus, investigation into linguistic and discursive representation of animals is of great necessity to maintain or subvert the relationship between humans and animals. However, it is as yet "an under-researched area" (Cook, 2015: 588). The situation is now improving with the rise of ecolinguistics. A number of scholars who are keen on studying how language can impact the ecosystem human beings depend on tend to show unprecedented interest on issues to do with animals and there have been substantial academic achievements on the linguistic analysis of discourse about animals (e.g. Cook, 2015; Cook & Sealey, 2018; Goatly, 2006; Sealey & Charles, 2013; Sealey & Oakley, 2013, 2014; Stibbe, 2012).

Of the studies on linguistic representation of animals so far, one central theme is to reveal and criticize the (potentially) devastating effect language makes on sustaining the harmonious connections between humans and animals. This critical tendency is evident in Stibbe's works. His linguistic inquiry into animal representation, as is clarified (Stibbe, 2001, 2012), adopts a discourse-oriented approach which centers around discourse rather than language system to examine "how particular groups in society select particular lexical items and grammatical structures from those available from the language system, and combine them in particular ways to tell stories about the world" (Stibbe, 2015: 56). To be brief, a discourse approach attempts to uncover the underlying ideology of discourses through analyzing a cluster of linguistic features. In this sense, the approach Stibbe employs to study linguistic representation of animals is in alignment with CDS, as is claimed, "the discourse approach is, of course, a form of Critical Discourse Analysis" (2015: 60).

Integrating CDS into ecolinguistic studies, linguistic analysis of animal representation in particular, is the consistent position Stibbe holds (Stibbe, 2012, 2014, 2015, 2018). He maintains the view that ecolinguistics and CDS in essence share common grounds. For example, both of them resort to discourse analysis to unveil a specific "worldview", and both of them aim at challenging the "common sense" encoded in discourses which sustains "unseen" power abuse and social inequality. For ecolinguistics, social inequality goes beyond the simplistic construction of the oppressed and the oppressors (Goatly, 2001). Ecological dimension of social inequality concerns the impact of ecological destruction on the present and future generations, on societies of someone's own and others, and on both humans and animals.

To raise people's awareness of ecological embedding and embodiment, one main task of ecolinguistics is to assert the prevailing role language and discourse play in ecological reality. As far as this is concerned, CDS as "dialectical reasoning" (Fairclough, 2018: 13) could provide solid and powerful support. Dialectical reasoning, "a way of reasoning from critique of discourse to what should be done to change existing reality" (Fairclough, 2018: 13), is a further extension of Fairclough's earlier account of the dialectical relationship between discourse and society (Fairclough, 2010). It is through dialectical reasoning that CDS makes its contribution to elucidating how discourse and other social elements or entities, e.g. power, ideologies and institutions, interact dynamically. Specifically, CDS views discourse as social practice, which is socially constitutive as well as socially conditioned. Being "socially conditioned" gives prominence to the constraints social structure imposes upon discourse—discourse is determined by social structure; being "socially constitutive" stresses "the constructive effects of discourses on the wider social reality" (Fairclough, 2018: 16)—discourse gives rise to social continuity or social change, as is stated:

> Discursive practices may have major ideological effects—that is, they can help produce and reproduce unequal power relations between (for instance) social classes, women and men, and ethnic/cultural majorities and minorities through the ways in which they represent things and position people. (Fairclough & Wodak, 1997: 258)

The dialectical view that entails the mutual construction between discourse and social reality is applicable in ecolinguistics, studies on animal representation included. When approaching the topic of "the erasure of animals" in contemporary human society, Stibbe foregrounds the Foucauldian interpretation of discourse as "ways of speaking and writing that construct or shape the objects being spoken of" (2012: 3) to call for an understanding of the mechanisms of discursive representation of animals.

Drawing on the concept that discourse "is a practice not just of representing the world but of signifying the world, constituting and constructing the world ideology meaning" (Fairclough, 1992: 64), Stibbe (2001, 2012) argues that how animals are discursively and socially constructed makes a profound influence upon how animals are construed and treated in human society. At the core of discursive representation of animals, as he repeatedly emphasizes, is the issue of power relation between humans and animals, which has been overlooked all the time for the reason that animals themselves are not involved in their own construction via language. The power in animals is "completely coercive" (Stibbe, 2001: 146), manipulated by a few people or institutions that use animals. Discourses produced by them reinforce the mainstream discourse of a commercialized society by justifying their utilization and oppression of animals. In these discourses, i.e. discourses of animal industry, animals are constructed as insentient objects and inexhaustible resources ready for domination. Representing animals in this way, from an ecological perspective, violates the natural law that all species as cohabitants of a larger ecosystem are interdependent, and hence contributes to an unfriendly and inequitable relationship between humans and animals, which is ecologically damaging. Discourses of this type is classified into "destructive" discourses (Stibbe, 2012: 6).

"Destructive" discourses are prevalent in societies that worship meat-eating culture. They can "go unnoticed and just be treated as 'the way things are'" (Stibbe, 2012: 6). It is through the implicit consent among the human population for the exploitation of animals that "destructive" discourses make hazardous effects on the treatment of animals in human society. In addition to these oppressive discourses, there are "counter" discourses. "Counter" discourses present a tendency to resist against human domination over animals with an aim of reconciling and improving the relationship between human and other species. However, it proves that they are not completely free from the mainstream ideological assumptions they criticize, and are prone to simply providing "alternative hegemonic discourses" (Stibbe, 2015: 15). A case in point is the discourses of animal liberation. Despite the fact that they seek to set free animals from human exploitation, they fail to promote a radical change in human-animal relationship in that just like "destructive" discourses, they "treat both human and other species of animals within socially-constructed realities, rather than engaging with the lived reality of the animals themselves" (Stibbe, 2015: 15). Therefore, to encourage an attitude of looking at animals with respect, it is advisable to bring back awareness to discourses which underline the intrinsic value of animal being. This kind of "alternative" discourses arises as the counterpart to "destructive" and "counter" discourses.

"Alternative" discourses refer to "discourses that represent humans as both part of and dependent on natural systems, encourage respect for animals and the natural world, and promote the fulfilling of human needs in ways that do not destroy the ecosystems that support life" (Stibbe, 2012: 10). In "alternative" discourses, e.g. haiku nature poetry, animals are attributed with individuality and subjective spirit, which encourages a positive attitude of humans towards animals and thus boosts a more equitable bond among different species. The proposal of developing "alternative" discourses made by Stibbe (2012), once again, echoes the fundamental belief in the dialectics and dynamics between discourse and society within the realm of CDS. More specifically, Stibbe's premise is, as he states, "if discourses construct society along inhumane or unsustainable lines, then it might be possible to discover and promote discourses that encourage more harmonious relations with animals and the natural world" (2012: 3-4).

The classification of discourses concerning animals lays the groundwork for a broader theoretical framework to deal with the complicated relationship between language, ecology and human life. In his book *Ecolinguistics: Language, Ecology and the Stories We Live By*, Stibbe (2015) establishes a unified ecolinguistic framework by bringing together multiple theoretical and methodological approaches. Under the proposed framework, discourses are categorized into three types, destructive, ambivalent and beneficial respectively, according to his ecosophy of "living"—the ecosophy which attaches equal importance to all the species. Destructive discourses go against the ecosophy; ambivalent discourses partially favor yet partially counter the ecosophy; beneficial discourses strongly advocate the ecosophy. Corresponding suggestions are offered for different discourses: destructive discourses should be resisted, ambivalent discourses should be improved and beneficial discourses should be promoted.

An ecolinguistic framework as such represents the continuum of ecolinguistics from CDS to positive discourse analysis. This is methodologically promising in that it is not only helpful in revealing linguistic patterns in discourses that normalize ideologies negatively impacting sustainability of ecology but also is good for examining positive texts that "inspire, encourage and hearten us" (Martin, 1999: 51-52). In line with the framework—an upgraded version of his earlier categorization of animal discourses, this study seeks to explore how animals are discursively represented via language means in Shen Shixi's animal narratives. A further step the study will take, drawing on Stibbe's model, is to determine whether they are destructive, ambivalent or beneficial. The ecosophy the study will refer to is traditional Chinese ecosophy, which can be of practical significance, as is emphasized as follows:

> The only criticism which we would make of this book concerns the small amount
> of information that it has on traditional Chinese ecosophy, which is well known for
> its abundance of ecological wisdom and its long influence on East Asian ecoculture.
> (Fan & Chen, 2018: 3)

It is based upon traditional Chinese ecosophy that discursive representation of animals will be judged and thus the relationship between animal world, discourse and human life can be exposed. If ideologies conveyed by discourses of animal representation run (partially) counter to the traditional Chinese ecosophy, these discourses will give rise to people's negative attitudes toward animals, and hence they'll be harmful for developing sustainable and ecological connection between animal world and human society. Otherwise, they'll be beneficial to raise ecological awareness and will aid in restoring the harmonious bond between humans and animals. What matters after all is, in Stibbe's words, the "stories" that "are embedded deeply in the minds of individuals across a society and appear only indirectly between the lines of the texts that circulate in that society" (2015: 5). It is through the mediation of the "stories" that animal world, discursive representation and human society link and interact with each other. To understand how "stories" play their roles in the interaction among animal world, discursive representation and human society, the next section will explore the mechanism in which discursive representation, social cognition and manipulation establish their link.

3.3   Discursive representation, social cognition and manipulation

3.3.1 Ecological "stories" and mental models

Language plays a fundamental role in the connection between animal world and human society. It is through language that animals are constructed as either exploitable objects or living subjects, and it is through language that people can be led to despise or respect animals, as is claimed, "(linguistic) representation increasingly will become the site where the future of many species of animals is determined" (Jacobs & Stibbe, 2006: 2). The dialectical dynamics between animal world, discursive representation and human society is mediated by, as Stibbe (2015) proposes, "stories" from the perspective of ecolinguistics.

The term "story" here is not employed in its traditional sense to refer to a recognizable narrative which is characterized as a way of interpreting the reality. Stories in Stibbe's words "exist behind and between the lines of the texts that surround us" (2015: 3). This kind of stories generally remains imperceptible in that they are disguised as "common sense". They tend to exert invisibly formative influence upon the way people view the world, and the way people view the relationship between human and nature. In effect, stories can be considered as "cognitive structures in the minds of individuals which influence how they perceive the world" (Stibbe, 2015: 6). Cognitive structures of this type are termed as "mental models". Mental models are representations of personal experience, knowledge and opinions in cognition (van Dijk, 1990), which entails two layers of meanings. Firstly, mental models are originally supposed to be personal, individual and subjective representations of certain situations and events; secondly, cognitively, mental models involve schematic conceptualization of events, consisting of schematic structures such as setting, participants and actions. Schematic mental models perform a crucial function in producing and understanding a meaningful discourse. As specific instances of social representation, they act as the indispensable medium for the manifestation of social representations in discourses. It is through the activation of mental models in a specific event or situation that social representations are expressed in discourses (van Dijk, 1998). To some degree, it can be said that "the direct communicative intention of much discourse is the transmission of the mental model of speakers/writers" (van Dijk, 2018: 30). In this sense, understanding discourses concerns "the construction or updating of a mental model of the event" (van Dijk, 2018: 30). With the aid of mental models, readers are able to construe their own interpretations of discourses, and then take proper actions.

In addition to the above-mentioned personal and semantic aspects, the social and pragmatic perspectives of mental models cannot be ignored. The pragmatic aspect of mental models highlights the contextual parameters which restrain the ongoing cognitive process of both the production and consumption of discourses. Mental models of "the very communicative situation *in which* they (language users) ongoingly participate" (van Dijk, 2018: 31) are termed as "context models" (van Dijk, 2008, 2009). Context models are composed of schematic categories specified for communicative ends. They function to assure the appropriateness of discourses in given communicative situations. In the process of discourse production, context (pragmatic) models determine how semantic mental models should be expressed, as is claimed, "producing discourse, thus, not only consists in forming or activating a semantic model of an event we want to speak or write about, but *before that* of planning, construing and dynamically adapting a context model" (van Dijk, 2018: 31).

Taken together, semantic and pragmatic mental models constitute the whole of personal cognition which significantly affects the coding and decoding of discourses. What deserves attention is that the impact of personal cognition upon the construction and construal of discourses acts largely on social dimension. It is attributed to the reason that although personal mental models work at an individual level, "they can also become socially widespread and become stereotypes" (Stella, 2014: 22). In view of this, mental models become the interface "between the personal and the social, and between discourse and society" (Stella, 2014: 22). The influential role mental models play in mediating discourse and society is highlighted particularly by van Dijk. He stresses that the collectively naturalized mental models, namely "social cognitions", function as an interface between discourse and society, which is a great contribution he has made to the development of CDS (van Dijk, 1990).

3.3.2 Socio-cognition and discourse

CDS, along the line of Critical Linguistics, attempts to uncover the veil of the ideological power of discourses and reveal how "social power abuse, dominance, and inequality are enacted, reproduced, and resisted by text" (van Dijk, 1993: 283). CDS analysts view language use as "social practice" which suggests "dialectical relationship between a particular discursive event and the situation, institution and social structure, which frame it: the discursive event is shaped by them but it also shapes them" (Fairclough & Wodak, 1997: 258). Being the theoretical cornerstone of CDS, such a claim has been criticized as "mechanic" (You & Chen, 2009: 45) in that there lacks a link between discourse and society and the role of language users and readers in the process of producing and interpreting discourses is overlooked (Widdowson, 2004; Hart, 2010). As is pointed out, "social or political structures can only affect text and talk through the *minds* of language users" (van Dijk, 2018: 28). In a similar vein, the counterproductive effect of discourses upon social structure can only be undertaken through the minds of discourse recipients. A possible reason is that both social and discourse structures pre-exist mentally in social members' minds and these mental models can be more easily related to the structures (either social or discourse) being expressed in actual communication (Stella, 2014).

The very "missing link" between discourse and society is referred to as "social cognition" by van Dijk. As an advocate for the generic view of discourse as language use "essentially involving three main dimensions, namely language use, cognition, and interaction in their socio-cultural contexts" (van Dijk, 1997: 32), van Dijk introduces the socio-cognitive approach which provides the necessary interface to theoretically investigate the relations between discourse and society. Grounded in the work of social constructionism, the socio-cognitive approach of CDS deals with "the social construction of cognition" (Condor & Antaki, 1997: 321) and seeks to enunciate "not only how cognition is involved in (the processing of) actual talk or text, but also why it is needed in the very description and analysis of many discourse structures" (van Dijk, 2018: 32). At the core of socio-cognitive approach, the concept of "social memory" (van Dijk, 2002) is closely connected to the operating mechanism of social cognition. Memory is an "abstract mental structure" (van Dijk, 2002: 207), consisting of short-term memory (STM) and long-term memory (LTM). STM, also named working memory, involves online processing of information acquired. The outcome of the processes, usually taking the form of knowledge or beliefs, will be stored in LTM, which can be further broken down into episodic and semantic memory. Episodic memory is idiosyncratic by nature and is prone to store information derived from personal experience while semantic memory, also called "social memory" (van Dijk, 2002: 208), contrastingly tends to deposit more abstract and socioculturally-shared knowledge, such as attitudes, norms and values shared by members belonging to the same epistemic community (van Dijk, 2002, 2018). It is the semantic/social memory where social cognition is kept in reserve. Social cognition researchers (e.g. Moscovici, 1981, 1984, 1988; Moscovici & Duveen, 2000) attempt to approach human thought from a collective/ macro perspective and stress the impact of society and culture in cognitive processes. Therefore, social cognition is characterized as "the manner in which we interpret, analyze and remember information about the social world" (Baron & Byrne, 1997: 12)，and concerns "people's representations of their world or their social knowledge" (Livingstone, 1998: 26). It is to some degree in parallel to "consensual universe" (Moscovici & Hewstone, 1983: 98), that is, common-sense knowledge integrated into daily social practices and "collective representation" (Durkheim, 1995: 15) which serves the function of establishing and maintaining social solidarity.

Following the line, van Dijk defines social cognition as "the system of mental representations and processes of group members" (1995: 18), which is, in its basic sense, values, norms and ideologies widespread among social actors. Here "ideologies" are metaphorically referred to as "group-specific 'grammars' of social practices" (van Dijk, 1997: 28), which "form the basis of knowledge, attitudes and other, more specific beliefs by a group" (van Dijk, 1997: 28). The interpretation of "socio-cognition" as "ideologies" highlights not only the dimension of social schemas but also of social representations in explaining socio-cognitive processes, both of which are considered indispensable to socio-cognition study. In addition, van Dijk (1990) goes a crucial step further to point out that the discourse dimension also deserves serious consideration in researching cognitive structures, in agreement with what Moscovici and Duveen suggest, "there are no social representations without languages, just as without them there is no society. The place of the linguistics in the analysis of social representations cannot, therefore, be avoided" (Moscovici & Duveen, 2000: 159). Van Dijk (1987) argues that the acquisition, application and adaptation of social representation, "a general concept that specifically applies to organized clusters of social beliefs (knowledge, attitudes, etc.) as located in social memory" (cf. Stella, 2014: 46), are mediated through discourse, and hence discourse analysis will be helpful in disclosing the underlying mechanisms of socio-cognition (van Dijk, 2001).

Within the realm of discourse studies, given that "any account of discourse and its features… needs to integrate the two [social and cognitive] functions" (Koller, 2005: 207), there is also an urgent need for the introduction of cognitive perspective (e.g. Chilton, 2005a, 2005b; O'Halloran, 2003; Hart, 2010). For these discursive researchers, language is the "socially constitutive force of cognition" (Stella, 2014: 20). It thus makes sense to utilize discursive resources as "interpretative repertoires" (Stella, 2014: 20) to understand social reality. In an effort to reconcile discourse and cognition, van Dijk (1995, 1998, 2002) proposes a triangle model which establishes the connection between texts (as the micro-level notion), socio-cognition (as the mediating interface) and social structures (as the macro-level notion). The proposal of socio-cognitive model emphasizes the crucial role of language in the (re)production of ideologies which in turn perform the critical function in creating and sustaining social identities and inequalities (Wodak, 2001), and hence it helps to "[bridge] both the individualism and social constructivism associated with text-consumption" (Hart, 2010: 16) and yield enlightening insights into both the fields of cognitive and discourse study. As van Dijk puts forward, it "not only makes explicit the fundamental role of mental representations, but also shows that many structures of discourse itself can only (completely) be described in terms of various cognitive notions, especially those of information, beliefs or knowledge of participants" (2018: 28).

Under the socio-cognitive framework, discourse understanding goes beyond merely the construal of semantic representations and involves nothing less than referring to creating cognitive structures, which conjures up discourse recipients' attitudes in their minds. Construing discourses, in this respect, is unavoidably connected to "constructing cognitive metarepresentations of the linguistic representations in text" (Hart, 2010: 16). Thus, linguistic representations intended by discourse producers perform critical function in manipulating discourse readers in their formations of knowledge, attitudes and ideologies by means of creating and transmitting cognitive models. As is stated, discourses "play a fundamental role in (this kind of) ideological manipulation by the symbolic elites" (van Dijk, 2018: 41).

3.3.3 Discourse and manipulation

The underlying mechanism in which discourse exerts power and domination upon readers has long been one of the most appealing subjects for CDS researchers (e.g. Chilton, 2004; Hart, 2010; van Dijk, 1997). Drawing on his triangulated approach to disclosing the interconnection between discourse, cognition and society, van Dijk develops his "triangulation" framework to study discourse and manipulation, under which manipulation is viewed as "a form of social power abuse, cognitive mind control and discursive interaction" (2006: 359). To be specific, discourse manipulation involves three dimensions: it is fundamentally a social practice which concerns the exertion of elite power over the dominated social actors; it is essentially a cognitive phenomenon which occurs mostly in people's mind; it is basically a discourse practice by means of which mind control is made possible. This three-dimensional interpretation gives a comprehensive and systematic insight into the notion of "discourse manipulation" in that it attempts to answer what manipulation is by nature, where manipulation takes place and how manipulation is exercised. More importantly, it brings into the public's awareness that discourse manipulation implies "the exercise of a form of *illegitimate* influence" (van Dijk, 2006: 360) which tends to be operationalized without notice.

The operation of discourse manipulation is undertaken implicitly in people's cognitions, comprising the process of STM-based and LTM-based manipulation. STM-based manipulation is concerned with online control of discourse understanding. Discourse understanding in STM involves ongoing processing of various (e.g. phonological, syntactic and semantic) components of discourses, which can be manipulated by means of strategic language use. Thus, STM-based manipulation "affects strategic processes of the understanding of specific discourses" (van Dijk, 2006: 367). Notably, the results of discourse processing in STM reside mostly in the more stable schematic structure called "episodic memory", a forming part of LTM. In this sense, discourse manipulation is also associated with manipulative construction of personal mental models in episodic memory, which contributes significantly to personal interpretations of discourses: the manipulators will facilitate the formation and activation of certain mental models in episodic memory to make sure that discourse recipients will comprehend discourses as they expect; otherwise they are going to hinder the process of discourse understanding.

For the reason that personal mental models represent the "instantiation" of social beliefs, manipulating personal models is not only essential to affecting how individuals acquire episodic personal knowledge, but also vital to impacting how members of social groups develop socially-shared ideologies or attitudes, namely, "social cognition". In other words, cognitive dimension of manipulation involves controlling both subjectively-based personal construct of everyday experience and more stable beliefs widespread among social communities, the latter constituting semantic memory in the mechanism of LTM. Compared to personal mental models, these social representations stored in semantic memory appear to be more abstract and meaningful. Concentrating on the creation and modification of preferred representations about social issues that can be socially shared, discourse manipulation of "social cognition" is regarded as "the most influential form of manipulation" (van Dijk, 2006: 368) since "the general goals of manipulative discourse are the control of the shared social representations of groups of people because these social beliefs in turn control what people do and say in many situations and over a relatively long period" (van Dijk, 2006: 369). Hence if discourse production is geared toward making recipients interpret discourses as discourse producers expect, the key step manipulators should take is to control the generation of semantic mental models and the formation of social cognition. Remarkably, manipulation of social cognition is indispensably concerned with "the very basis of all social cognition: general, socioculturally shared *knowledge*" (van Dijk, 2006: 371).

The management of knowledge in discourses is complicated (van Dijk, 2014). A socio-cognitive approach to studying knowledge reveals that knowledge can be manipulated, that is, selectively made either explicit or implicit, emphasized or hidden by or in discourses. Knowledge, as well as attitudes, is learned instead of being innate. The conveyance and acquisition of knowledge involves the transmission of certain social representations among different social actors. To convey specific knowledge, for example, to disseminate scientific knowledge among the general population, is associated with "an introduction of social beliefs of special (e.g. scientific) SR [Social Representation] groups into the general knowledge system of the community" (van Dijk, 2014: 107), which once being adopted can be further transformed into "taken-for-granted" everyday common sense.

Knowledge transfer of this kind is unavoidably congested with ideological manipulation by the symbolic elites, which is especially true in the contemporary information society. The modern society, as Giddens points out in *The Consequences of Modernity*, is characterized by "trust vested in abstract systems which by its very nature is filtered by the trustworthiness of established expertise" (1991: 84). Being the "established expertise" of modern time, those "representatives of abstract systems" (Giddens, 1991: 85), symbolic elites in other words, are admittedly responsible for the reproduction of elite power via knowledge transmission which can be largely realized by offering general clients (e.g. readers) access to public discourses (narratives included). More specifically, knowledge transmitters, either being speakers or writers, who perform their role as "member[s] of a dominant collectivity" (van Dijk, 2006: 364), are supposed to produce knowledge that could be partial or biased to best serve the interests of the dominant institutions. Potentially critical knowledge that could pose a threat to the dominant power thus will be deliberately eliminated. In this sense, discursive manipulation, exemplified by knowledge distribution, is essentially "the discursive social practices of dominant groups geared towards the reproduction of their power" (van Dijk, 2006: 363).

The reproduction of power via discursive manipulation could be strategic. Strategies involved in manipulation tend to be geared towards activating or generating "preferred" mental models, which mostly go unnoticed. The "preferred" mental models are fundamentally the cognitive structures that are identical with the interests of the dominant groups. To subtly control the minds of the dominated community, discursive strategies that may better represent and recall the intended models will be employed in manipulative discourse use.

3.4 Discursive strategies, linguistic coercion and conceptualization

3.4.1 Manipulation as linguistic coercion

Linguistic expressions are perspectivated by nature because "language use is subjective" (Danler, 2005: 46). In this vein, manipulation should be inherent to language communication. Despite its semantic complexity, manipulation in language communication, e.g. discourse production and interpretation, can be regarded as deliberately deceiving targeted recipients into accepting the ideologies ("preferred" mental models) that favor the interests of the dominant group. Notably, it is "when an ideology is at variance with the basic experience of the world, or with the basic needs, desires and moral values of people" that "the need for manipulation arises" (Rocci, 2005: 96). Ideological imposition signifies asymmetrical relationship between different parties, and thus its manipulating process involves coercion—the most basic form of power exercise. In addition to unequal power allocation, ideological manipulation in contemporary communication also features the discursive/linguistic medium through which manipulation is realized. To be specific, in the information age, when knowledge and public discourse become the foremost resource to control the minds of others, the reproduction and inculcation of ideologies are largely processed via symbolic means. Supposedly, groups and institutions which are endowed with symbolic and discursive power are capable of coercing the dominated into complying with the dominant ideologies. In this sense, manipulation in modern society can be deemed as linguistic coercion.

Different from other forms of coercion, linguistic coercion attempts to persuade people to adopt an ideology through manipulative use of language. It aims at evoking emotional sharing and cognitive consensus between discourse producers on one end and addressees on the other end. As is pointed out, the macro-strategy of coercion involves cognitive and emotive effects (Hart, 2010). Thus manipulation as linguistic coercion is primarily concerned with manipulating "some aspects of human cognition, notably reasoning, checking for likeliness, emotions, etc." (Saussure, 2005: 134). To control the minds of addressees, manipulative discourse is intentionally deceiving and strategically persuading. By "strategically persuading", it means that manipulators tend to lure discourse recipients to be in alignment with their ideologies through covert use of language devices, which will otherwise be challenged by "generally acknowledged critical standards of reasonableness" (van Eemeren, 2005: xii). Therefore, manipulative discourse is fundamentally "a type of language use" (Saussure, 2005: 118). It is about using a certain strategy or device to produce "take-for-granted" common sense which to a large extent could be unreliable and biased by social prejudices.

3.4.2　Linguistic coercion and discursive strategies

Manipulation in the context of language use can be understood as a kind of "lexicalized metaphorical derivation" (Saussure, 2005: 134). More accurately, it is about applying constraints to individuals by means of linguistic devices or hidden strategies. These constraints will act on the addressee's information processing and further affect their beliefs and actions. It goes without saying that in manipulative discourses, it is through manipulative use of language that coercion can be realized. Recognized as "an ultimate goal for strategic text-producers" (Hart, 2010: 6), coercion is a strategic function which concerns "Machiavellian intelligence and tactical deception" (Hart, 2010: 64), and is motivated by "an intention to cause addressees to act in a way that otherwise they would not have chosen" (Chilton, 2004: 47). To exert control upon discourse consumers, discourse producers perform coercively in the text world, i.e. dictating the topics under discussion, and presenting information as they wish. In this way, they attempt to frame coercively the ideational meaning of language, that is, to influence how reality is represented in the minds of discourse consumers. In so doing, discourse consumers can decide and act in alignment with the interest of discourse producers.

Given that "decisions and behavior are motivated by knowledge and affect" (Hart, 2010: 64), coercion in manipulative discourses involves emotional and cognitive dimensions (Chilton, 2004). Cognitive coercion should be propositional and is about yielding "cognitive effects" to discourse recipients. Cognitive effects specifically produced by coercion can be understood as "forced inference" (Chilton, 2004: 119) in terms of speech act theory (Austin, 1962; Searle, 1969), involving presupposition, implicature and presumptions. It is concerned with modifying existing mental representations. The modification of representations could be "adding new representations or strengthening, weakening or deleting existing ones" (Hart, 2010: 64). To be specific, manipulative effects of discourses upon readers' cognition can only be achieved when background knowledge or "primitive belief" (Chilton, 2004: 119) is activated, which helps to "provide a cognitive context against which text is interpreted" (Hart, 2010: 64). And knowledge is always in the form of mental models (representations), including cognitive frames, image schemata and conceptual metaphors, which tend to be evoked, maintained or modified in discourse production. Once established in the process of discourse comprehension, the cognitive models will not be easily challenged.

Notably, "the cognitive representation might be linked with affective valuation" (Chilton, 2004: 119). When cognitive associations are constructed intentionally by discourse producers, namely, when cognitive coercion is operated, emotive coercion occurs simultaneously. As is argued, "cognitive associations activate text-consumers' social intelligence and emotion modules, eliciting emotive decisions and actions intended by the text-producer" (Hart, 2010: 87). Emotive coercion tends to induce emotional effects upon discourse addressees. It involves the emotional appeal stimulated by certain cognitive representations which can be activated by the use of language. For example, in political discourses, the conceptualization of one nation as a closed container implies that the nation could be penetrated, which triggers fearful response on emotional dimension. Emotive effects, on the other hand, can also "prompt further cognitive effects" (Hart, 2010: 64). They can be ideological and manipulative (Hart, 2010). In other words, particular language usages intended by discourse producers elicit specific affective responses and further impel cognitive processing, which in turn produces biased behavioral outcomes. From this perspective, emotions navigate cognition and behavior in important ways (Cosmides & Tooby, 2000; Damasio, 1994; Pinker, 1997). Therefore, although cognitive and emotive coercions are "analytically separable" (Hart, 2010: 64), they arc interactive in the practice of discourse manipulation, which can be identified in single text units as well as in some smaller structures.

The interaction of cognitive and emotive coercion is realized by various discursive strategies. The interpretation of discursive strategies is closely related to the Hallidayan sense of language as meaning potential. Language as meaning potential allows for a variety of possible ways to demonstrate the messages language users aim to convey. It corresponds to the fact that language use is subjective—it depends largely on the speakers to decide what should be discussed and how the intended meaning should be expressed by linguistic means. It is through subjective use of language that ideologies of language users are mapped on various levels and dimensions of discourse, characterized by different structures or strategies. In this sense, linguistic coercion as "a macro-level strategy" (Hart, 2010: 7) to implant language users' ideologies takes place in either higher or lower levels of discourse, constituted by more or less efficient micro-level linguistic strategies. Discursive strategies of all levels act on the process of information treatment to achieve linguistic coercion. The manipulators use these strategies to conceal their own manipulative intentions on the one hand, and on the other hand they aim to block "*truth, likeliness* and *acceptability* checking, as well as *consistency* checking" (Saussure, 2005: 126) of discourse recipients.

Discursive strategies used by manipulators cover a wide range, including resorting to active/passive voice, employing impersonal construction, or using deverbal nouns, to mention just a few. These strategies can be further organized into strategies of "vagueness, polarization, manipulated communicative relevance, mystification, or genericity" (Danler, 2005: 46). Saussure (2005) proposes a more general classification of discursive strategies. For him, discursive strategies are of two categories: local strategies and global strategies. Taking manipulation as the device to impose constraints upon the addressees, he refers to the strategies that are used to "constrain the interpretation at the level of utterance processing" (Saussure, 2005: 126) as local strategies, while strategies that are "used to create adequate social and psychological conditions to obtain irrational consent" (Saussure, 2005: 126) are considered as global strategies, which bear direct relevance to his interpretation of manipulation as the mechanism to block one's rational device. In practical sense, the boundary between local and global strategies is blurred since "meaning is 'situated', bound to one's own position in the cultural and physical context of interpretation" (Hart, 2018: 79). To be specific, the strategies of different categories function at various structures of discourse to manipulate the process of discourse comprehension, that is, to "affect processing in STM, the formation of preferred mental models in episodic memory, and finally and most fundamentally the formation or change of social representations" (van Dijk, 2006: 372), and hence to "implement the usual ideological square of discursive group polarization" (van Dijk, 2006: 374). Foregrounding the ideological basis of discursive strategies, CDS researchers identify some specific discursive strategies, reference, predication and legitimization in particular (e.g. Cap, 2006; Chilton, 2004; Chilton & Schäffner, 1997; Reisigl & Wodak, 2001). Hart (2010) takes a step further to classify these strategies into two types—representation and legitimization, both of which are in service of linguistic coercion, the macro-level speaker strategy.

Representation strategies are deployed to communicate representations of the world, involving referential and predication strategies. Adhering to the ideological nature of discursive strategies, referential strategies entail "intentions to promote dichotomous conceptualizations of social groups" (Hart, 2010: 8). One typical example is that pronoun variations applied to the syntactical level of discourse can perform the social function of group polarization such as strengthening ingroup membership or producing outgroup distance. The pronominal pair of "us" and "them", for instance, is ideologically-loaded to manage the social positioning of discourse insiders and outsiders, with first-person pronouns being a prototypical exponent of the speaker-group and third-person pronoun as the group exclusive of discourse participants. Given pronouns "can be used to induce interpreters to conceptualize group identity, coalitions... and the like, either as insiders or as outsiders" (Chilton & Schäffner, 2002: 30), and as most of the other referential strategies, they are considered to act as an important device to express and manipulate social relations, status and power.

The manipulating force of these referential strategies in distinguishing ingroupness and outgroupness is closely linked to evolutionary psychology (Hart, 2010). It is suggested that biologically human beings are "evolutionary ready" to build up cognitive representations which take referential strategies into effect and help to explain the psychological impact of the strategies. Such an account is evidenced by the claim that "discourse is expected to be used strategically on evolutionary grounds" (Hart, 2010: 185) and "[linguistic] coercion may be an inevitable evolutionary outcome of cooperative communication" (Hart, 2010: 185).

It should be noted that referential strategies alone are not a sufficient condition for linguistic coercion. Successful referential strategies are affected with the functioning of predication strategies (Hart, 2010). Predication strategies are concerned with ascribing qualities and quantities to members of social groups. In communicating cognitive representations and arousing emotional resonance, predications can be coercive when they are engaged in activating certain "evolved modules" (Hart, 2010: 9) that are available for exploitation. Once activated, these modules will play a great role in guiding cognition and reproducing ideologies.

Similar to referential strategies, predication strategies are effective in ideological reproduction. Predications tend to act as premises that implicitly presuppose the conclusion and thus justify certain social practices. Referential strategies and predications, although considered independent of each other categorically, are connected. Rather than referring exclusively to predicates, predications also comprise elements of semantic, syntactic or pragmatic levels. Referential and predication strategies work in collaboration to reinforce existing representations or construct novel ones, serving the purpose of imposing cognitive and emotional coercions upon discourse consumers. Referential and predication strategies, together known as representation strategies, are effective and affective only when "the representations realizing them are accepted as true" (Hart, 2010: 88).

To achieve this, legitimization strategies are significant. Legitimization is a "prominent function of language use and discourse" (van Dijk, 1998: 255). The legitimization function tends to establish "legitimacy", that is, the right the speaker is granted to make an assertion, and hence to persuade the readers to accept the claim without any doubt. In this sense, it is closely related to linguistic coercion. Nevertheless, different from representation strategies, legitimization doesn't directly contribute to coercion. To be specific, legitimization is not about manipulatively constructing representations of the world or altering the existing ones as is the case with referential and predication strategies. Rather, the primary aim of legitimization focuses on endorsing representations and involves "getting text-consumers to accept cognitive representations as true and retain them in long-term memory" (Hart, 2010: 65). To this end, linguistic expressions imprinted with evidence and authority are used to confirm the truth of utterances and pragmatically presume the felicity conditions that take control of illocutionary act of assertions.

Furthermore, legitimization presupposes justifiable grounds, either morally or legally, of ideologically-biased claims, which attempt to naturalize the hierarchical distinction made between Us and Them (van Dijk, 1998: 257). That means in discourses, legitimization strategies can help to get discourse recipients to accept intended cognitive representations as true and store them in LTM. From this perspective, linguistic coercion is dependent on legitimization. As Hart states, "coercion can only be successful when legitimization is simultaneously achieved" (2010: 87). Legitimization can be achieved largely by means of "internal" and "external" coherence, with the former referring to grammatical cohesion and the latter being some semantic categories such as evidentiality and epistemic modality (Hart, 2010). Legitimization strategies, in addition to representation strategies, comprise the overall micro-strategies contributing to the macro-strategy of coercion in discourses.

3.4.3. Conceptualization and metaphor

Coercion realized by linguistic strategies in discourses—representation and legitimization strategies as illustrated above—fundamentally occurs in the minds of human beings (Chilton, 2005a; Hart, 2010). It is argued that linguistic coercion involves imposing intended mental representations upon the targeted addressees by discourse input and language means to invoke certain cognitive and behavioral responses. And it can be said that language-induced coercion "is propositional and involves producing 'cognitive effects' in text-consumers" (Hart, 2010: 64). The acknowledgement of the role of cognitive factors in linguistic coercion is attributed to the view of language as "a resource for reflecting on the world" (Halliday & Matthiessen, 1999: 7) and as "the means by which we describe our experience" (Langacker, 1991: 294). Choices of language structures and discursive strategies thus are perspectivated and give rise to particular conceptualization of the world. This is best captured in a further claim held by Langacker—"grammar is conceptualization", which particularly points out that grammatical devices are available as "alternate means of coding a given conception" (Langacker, 1991: 294). The discourse producers, therefore, are able to promote the intended construal of a given reality, which is bound to be ideologically-controlled, by resorting to language means.

Associating the ideological dimension of linguistic phenomena with general conceptual principles constitutes the essence of Cognitive Linguistic Approach (CLA) to critically studying discourses. The role of cognition has been addressed by van Dijk in his socio-cognitive approach to CDS. Socio-cognitive approach tends to reveal the mediating function that social cognition performs between discourse and society. Nevertheless, "cognitive theories of meaning in discourse have been neglected by mainstream approaches to critical discourse analysis (CDA)" (Hart, 2008: 91). The necessity of introducing cognitive approach into meaning reproduction in discourse has been increasingly stressed by some discourse researchers (e.g. Billig, 2003; Chilton, 2005a, 2005b; Hart, 2010; Stubbs, 1997; O'Halloran, 2003; Widdowson, 2004). Consensus has been achieved that conceptual structures and cognitive process invoked by linguistic constructions are of primary importance in motivating, supporting and legitimating social action (Chilton, 2005a, 2005b; Hart, 2010; van Dijk, 1993), which further helps to shape and sustain social structures. For this reason, the incorporation of Cognitive Linguistics into CDS should be on the agenda.

Cognitive Linguistics is "one framework which provides the systematic theory of language and cognition that critical discourse analysis (CDA) seems to need and can be directly aligned with the socio-cognitive approach" (Koller, 2005; cf. Hart, 2010: 23). Viewing meanings as conventionalized conceptualizations, it delves into exploring "the *internal* semantic resources of ideological discourse... in terms of historically specific *external* relations between conceptualizations (social consciousness) and social practice (social being)" (Jones, 2000: 243). More specifically, the cognitive approach to discourse study is able to account for meaning construction at both ends of discourse production and interpretation: on the one hand, it presents a cognitive account of ideology in discourse, which "is made possible by the choices a language allows for representing the same material situation in different ways" (Haynes, 1989: 119); on the other hand, it concerns the extent to which alternative linguistic structures have any (measurable) effect on our cognition of the situation or event being described (Hart, 2010, 2014a, 2014b). At the center of the cognitive approach to CDS sits an important notion— "conceptualization".

Conceptualization is "the dynamic cognitive process involved in meaning-making as discourse unfolds" (Hart, 2010: 167). Instead of cognitive models stored in LTM, conceptualization is "an 'online' cognitive process of meaning construction" (Hart, 2010: 25). In the process of meaning production, language structures and discourse strategies can trigger "an array of conceptual operations and the recruitment of background knowledge" (Evans & Green, 2006: 162) whereby the conceptual import of discourse representations is realized. Conceptualization, taking place during discourse and prompted by language resources, is inherently ideologically-constrained in that it is always motivated by the interest of discourse producers. In this way, choices of discursive strategies significantly impact how a given situation is mentally represented, or conceptualized, and finally make a difference in readers' construal of the reality, given that "conceptualization always encodes 'construal'" (Hart, 2010: 10). The effect conceptualization has upon discourse addressees' construal is operated via processes of entrenchment.

Equally important as conceptualization, entrenchment is another key notion which deserves attention in the cognitive approach to CDS. Entrenchment refers to the cognitive process through which conceptual structures built online can "become entrenched in Long-term Memory and available to be activated all at once"

(Fauconnier & Turner, 2002: 103). Meanwhile, its cultural and social dimensions concern the issue of ideological "naturalization"—it is the mechanism which helps to normalize and conventionalize ideologies embedded in discourse "by making what is social seem natural" (Kress, 1989: 10). The significance of entrenchment, as Hart maintains, "may reconcile the individual mentalism often associated with Cognitive Linguistics on the one hand and the social constructivism associated with CDA on the other" (2010: 124). From this perspective, entrenchment, in combination with conceptualization, serves to "provide the missing link between linguistic representations in text and ideologies or cognitive models which CDA needs in order to explain how discourse can be constitutive of society" (Hart, 2010: 25). This particularly justifies the reason why "Cognitive Linguistics seems to sit quite comfortably in CDA" (Hart, 2010: 24). The penetrating ability of cognitive approach to disclosing the interaction among discourse, cognition and society is well-informed by its giving insights into "the pervasiveness and persuasiveness of metaphor" (Hart, 2008: 92). Metaphor is recognized as "a special although all-pervasive subtype of conceptualization" (Dirven et al., 2003: 4). Long been regarded as a semantic or pragmatic phenomenon, the cognitive nature of metaphor is brought into awareness especially upon Lakoff and Johnson's publishing of *Metaphors We Live By*, in which metaphor is viewed as being "among our principal vehicles for understanding our physical, social and inner world" (Lakoff & Johnson, 1980: 159). From then on, there has been a consensus that metaphor and its related mental processes comprise the basis of language and cognition.

In addition to being conceptual in essence, metaphor also contributes to creating social realities in so far as it "define[s] in significant part what one takes as reality" (Chilton & Lakoff, 1995: 56), corresponding well to the nature of ideology which involves "a systematically organized presentation of reality" (Hodge & Kress, 1993:15). Metaphor as a cognitive mechanism of ideology (Balkin, 1998) is increasingly being recognized. For instance, Dirven et al. (2003) point out that conceptual metaphors are the cognitive basis of ideology. The ideological function of metaphor plays a great role in the mental processes it entails, which has consequences for further social actions. "Such actions will, of course, fit the metaphor. This will, in turn, reinforce the power of the metaphor to make experience coherent" (Lakoff & Johnson, 1980: 156). Considering that metaphor concerns forming a coherent standpoint of reality, it should be viewed as the structure that "is central to critical discourse analysis" (Charteris-Black, 2004: 28), which mainly deals with the manipulative and mystifactory nature of language. As is highlighted, "it is evident that such a perspective on metaphor as a conceptually significant, even central, cognitive mechanism matches the research interests of CDA to a large extent" (Musolff, 2012: 302) in that it helps to "add to CDA's account of meaning constitution in the social context" (Musolff, 2012: 301).

Within the paradigm of CDS, a considerable number of studies on metaphor resort to Conceptual Metaphor Theory proposed by Lakoff and Johnson (1980), which is confronted with challenges from Hart (2008, 2010) and O'Halloran (2007). Both of them question the appropriateness of applying Conceptual Metaphor Theory to CDS. Holding that Conceptual Metaphor Theory is discordant with interpretation-stage analysis (Hart, 2008), they suggest that the process of meaning construction in metaphor should be studied in terms of Conceptual Blending Theory. Conceptual Blending Theory, firstly proposed by Fauconnier and Turner (2002), is considered to be a theory of conceptualization accounting for the online conceptual process of various linguistic phenomena. It involves representing mental spaces and conceptual blending patterns in diagrammatic notations. Mental spaces, similar to "text worlds" (Werth, 1999) or "situation models" (van Dijk, 1990), are "conceptual packets constructed as we think and talk, for purposes of local understanding and action. They are interconnected, and can be modified as thought and discourse unfold" (Fauconnier & Turner, 1996: 113). A mental space is constructed to create the "reality space" for the discourse participants when discourse comes into being. To promote particular representations of reality, mental spaces can be blended. The blended spaces, "conceptual blends" in other words, "are sites for central cognitive work: reasoning, drawing inferences and developing emotions" (Fauconnier & Turner, 1996: 115). Once entrenched, "they become our new construal of reality" (Fauconnier, 1997: 168). Conceptual blends, thus, are ideologically-imbued. This is especially true with the conceptual blends invoked by metaphors in discourse.

In light of Conceptual Blending Theory, metaphor is treated as "four-space model" (cf. Hart, 2010: 118) involving a dynamic construal operation. Specifically, metaphor in discourse functions as "a space-builder" (Hart, 2010: 115) to construct a number of mental spaces. As discourse unfolds, these spaces "undergo a conceptual blending operation whereby they are manipulated in an integrated network, producing inferential structure" (Hart, 2010: 115). Thus, in terms of Conceptual Blending Theory, metaphor is treated as a conceptual projection which concerns projecting a conceptual structure from (at least) two mental spaces into one blended space which helps to generate new emergent structure. In this way, Conceptual Blending Theory provides an alternative account to metaphorical expressions in discourse, which are defined as "a strictly directional phenomenon" (Hart, 2010: 118) from the perspective of Conceptual Metaphor Theory. In Conceptual Metaphor Theory, metaphor is regarded as a conceptual representation concerning asymmetrical mapping in two distinct domains, a "source domain" and a "target domain" (Lakoff & Johnson, 1980). The conceptual associations between the two domains are unidirectional, stable, and experientially-grounded. Thus, metaphor in this sense—"pre-discursively established source-target mappings" (Musolff, 2012: 305)—is more of cognitive organization instead of conceptualization as the cognitive process of online meaning construction. Conceptual blends invoked by metaphorization, however, pertain to conceptualization (Hart, 2010).

Metaphorical extension as conceptual blending refers to the dynamic construal operation triggered by linguistic choice in discourse rather than the deterministic mapping process motivated by experiential comparison. This account of metaphor as language-invoked conceptual blend implies the ideological orientation of metaphorical expressions in discourse considering language system "provides wide margins of choice for which items are motivated in which ways" (Chilton, 1988: 49). Therefore, metaphors engineered by strategic language choice allow for manipulation. The conceptualizations that metaphors prompt could to a large extent give rise to rich scenarios, compressing complicated social events into comprehensible cognitive models. Steered by groups with strategic interest, models like these tend to represent and evaluate actions and events in a particularly ideologized way, yielding consequences for further cognitive processes. That explains how metaphor in discourse comprises the cognitive basis of ideology (Dirven et al., 2003), and hence "can contribute to a situation where they privilege one understanding of reality over others" (Chilton, 1996: 74).

3.5   Toward an ecological critical-cognitive discourse analysis model of animal representation

Representation of animals has become the site where the relationship between humans and animals can be constructed. The mediating effects of animal representation may be twofold: on the one hand, representations offer the human population growing opportunities to have contact with animals indirectly in an age when actual animals are increasingly excluded and marginalized from human experience; on the other hand, given "representations necessarily are partial" (Jacobs & Stibbe, 2006: 1), distorted representations of animals, i.e. animals are addressed in mere categories of usefulness, could probably further devastate the connection between humans and animals. The contradictory roles representation plays in the existing and potential human-animal relationship have attracted the scholars dedicated to the interaction between language and ecological issues. When it comes to the topic of animal representation, they attempt to explore the dynamics between language, power and social construction of animals. It is admitted that representation of animals in discourse is closely linked to the sense of utilitarian anthropocentrism embedded in daily language usage. One grave consequence of "linguistic anthropocentrism"—the erasure of animals, has been highlighted in Stibbe's study—*Animals Erased: Discourse, Ecology, and Reconnection with the Natural World*.

Taking focus on animals, Stibbe seeks to restore the connection between language and the larger ecosystem. In this endeavor, he proceeds to work on another monograph entitled *Ecolinguistics: Language, Ecology and the Stories We Live By*, with the aim to establish a unified and cohesive ecolinguistic framework to approach the role of language and discourse in the context of ecological destruction. These two works constitute tangible cornerstones on the way stepping towards the new language of a more harmonious Earth. Noteworthily, they provide a model that studies of animal representation can take as reference. Firstly, the unified and comprehensive framework set up in Stibbe's texts is a breakthrough initiative to ecolinguistics which has long been confronted with critiques for "its lack of cohesion" (Poole, 2017: 1); thus it provides inspirational significance to studies on language and ecology, studies of animal representation in particular. Secondly, the framework is, methodologically, CDS-oriented. A CDS approach has become "core texts in ecolinguistics" (Poole, 2017: 1). Stibbe's study well justifies that "the normative orientation of ecolinguistics is quite closely aligned with CDA" (Poole, 2017: 1). The framework draws upon the insights of critical studies to inquire the implications of human's disconnection from the natural (animal) world, which brings about enlightenment on animal representation study. Thirdly, the framework, extending the reach of CDS to explore the role of language and discourse in human domination over other species, is not restricted to disclosing ideological bias disseminated through discourse, but also involves providing hopeful and practical avenues for change, that is, promoting greater parity between human and other species and building resilience for sustainable living. Under the framework, based on the ecosophy of "Living" which emphasizes the wellbeing of all species, three types of discourse are identified: destructive, ambivalent and beneficial discourses. As such, the categorization of discursive practices in relation to an ecosophy in Stibbe's works "gives clear form to the field of ecolinguistics" (Poole, 2017: 2) and provides procedural instruction for ecolinguistic research of animal representation study. By making possible the implement of "broad notion of ecology" and furnishing the field with desirable unity, the framework remains a significant contribution to ecolinguistic research of animal representation study. However, there is still room to be improved.

Stibbe's accounts are, as Tønnessen argues, "strongest when they are at their most systematically critical" (2013: 257). Nevertheless, his endeavors to provide alternatives for replacing mainstream anthropocentric discourses seem to be less successful—"Stibbe's weakest point, in my judgment, is his treatment of the third category of discourses, which he presents as alternative discourses" (Tønnessen, 2013: 257). His probe into alternative models draws exclusively on the practices and customs found in traditional Japanese culture, which is less than convincing to discourse on nature and the living in general. As examples rooted in local culture, it is quite natural that their appeal is much stronger in Japan than elsewhere. Additionally, in Stibbe's framework the ecosophy particular discourses are measured against draws from "deep ecology" (Naess, 1955), which is not necessarily the most suitable one for every ecolinguistic exploration. Analysts are allowed to have their own angles counting on their deepest intuitions:

> An individual ecolinguist will survey the wide range of possible ecosophies described in the literature, consider them carefully in light of available evidence and their own experience of human communities and the natural world, and build their own ecosophy through combining them, extending them or creating something entirely new. (Stibbe, 2015: 15)

Given the framework concerns little about traditional Chinese ecosophy, an integration of Chinese ecological philosophy is in need for ecolinguistic analysis conducted in Chinese context, which corresponds perfectly to what Stibbe calls for—"(more) voices... from traditional and indigenous cultures from around the world" (2015: 193). Plus, although his framework of ecolinguistic analysis highlights the role of cognition—"stories" in his words—as the link between language and ecology, i.e. a variety of approaches are clustered together in the framework to study ideologies, metaphors, frames and a diversity of other cognitive and linguistic phenomena, there still lacks a systematical and cohesive interpretation from the perspective of critical-cognitive discourse studies. Therefore, to uncover the stories underlying animal representations in Chinese literature, it is advisable to make modifications to Stibbe's framework on the premise of absorbing the essence.

The modified framework attempts to approach animal representations in Chinese literature from three dimensions. On the macro-level, it delves into studying animal representations under the global framework of ecolinguistics. In terms of macro-level ecolinguistics, different discursive representations of animals in Chinese context can be, as Stibbe suggests, classified as destructive, ambivalent or beneficial discourses, or some other types of discourse that go beyond Stibbe's classification, judged against the principle of Chinese ecosophy. On the meso-level, it resorts to the main angles from CDS: the dialectical perspective and the social cognition perspective. The dialectical perspective helps to explain how animal world, linguistic (discursive) representation and human society are interacted. The social cognition perspective attempts to elucidate how the intersection is mediated through social cognition. On the micro-level, it counts on cognitive linguistics to dig out the "stories" implied between the lines of animal representation. Cognitive description of language use in animal representation in combination with cognitive explanation for the effects is provided in this stage: specific discursive strategies in animal representation, including representation and legitimization strategies, are identified; the conceptualizing process of animal imagery is uncovered; moreover, the cognitive effects of discursive representation of animals are revealed. To summarize, the three-level model of animal representation study can be shown in Figure 3.1:

Ecolinguistics
    identifying the ecological attribute of discourse in terms of Chinese ecosophy

    CDS
            dialectical perspective
            social cognition perspective

        Critical-Cognitive Discourse Studies
            discursive strategies: representation

                            (referential / predication)

                        legitimization

            (grammatical cohesion / evidentiality / epistemic modality)

            conceptualization & cognitive models

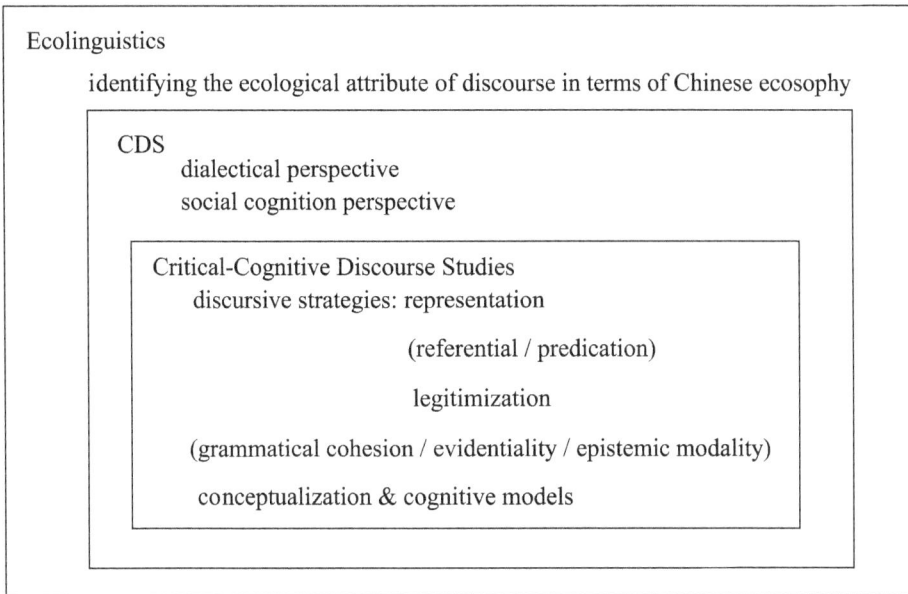

Figure 3.1 A three-level model

A more elucidated model can be shown in Figure 3.2.

As the model suggests, how animals are represented in discourses and how animals are treated in real life are dialectically-related. The dynamics between discourse and animals are mediated by social cognition. Discursive representation of animals can be realized through a diversity of representation strategies, naturalized by various legitimizing devices. The ecological attribute of these animal representations can be identified, e.g. destructive, ambivalent or beneficial as proposed by Stibbe (2015) in terms of Chinese ecosophy. Different types of discourse are conceptualized not merely in individual's mind but also in the widespread social cognition held by a majority of social members, which takes effect in manufacturing the consent within the human population for the treatment of animals.

In line with the model, the study, focused on the anthropomorphic representation of animals in Shen Shixi's animal narratives, probes into the constructing and constituting role discourse plays in the interaction between humans and animals. The main purpose of the study is to disclose how language

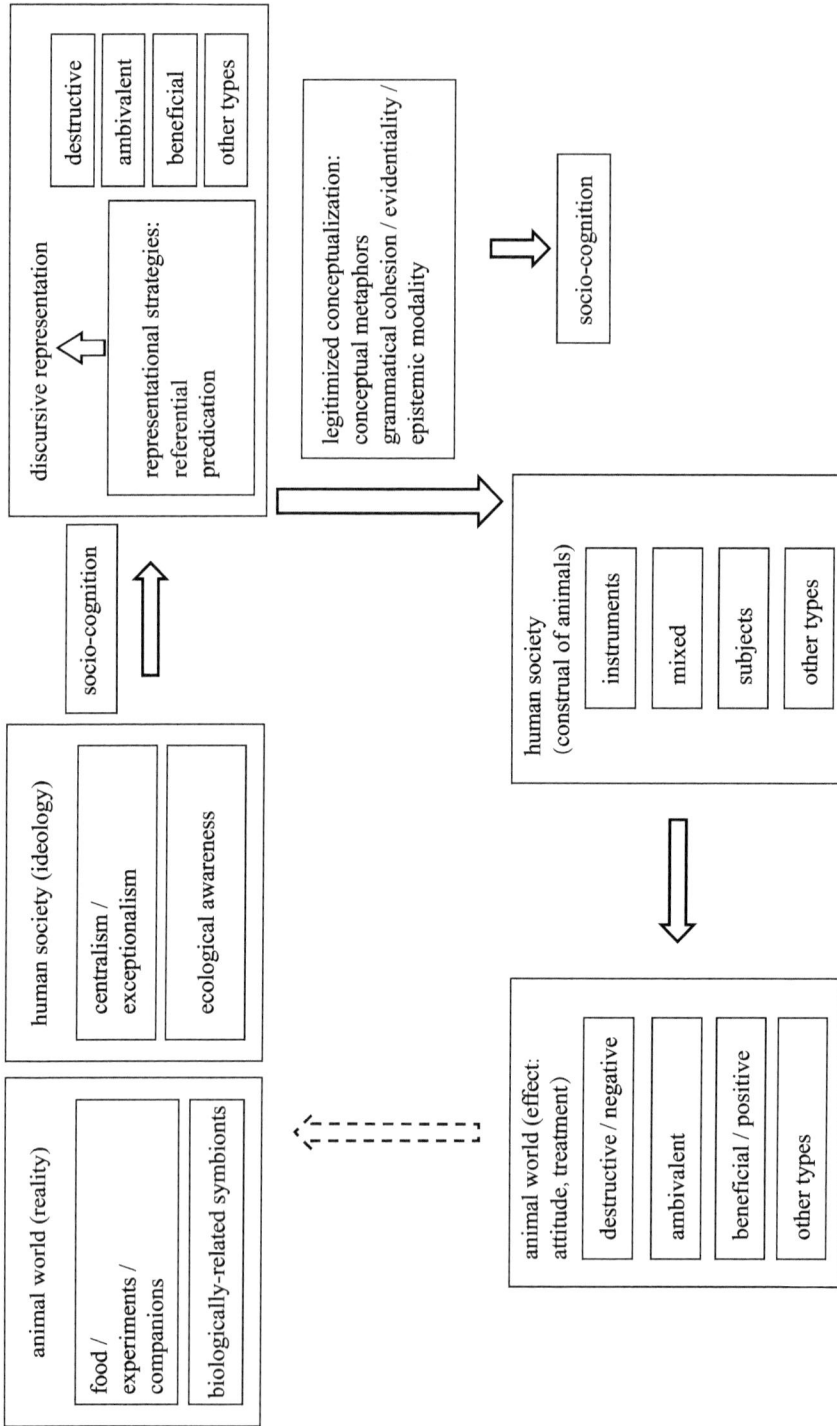

Figure 3.2   Elucidation of three-level model of animal representation study

functions to bring about discursive representation of anthropomorphized animals and the cognitive mechanism of animal representation. Furthermore, it aims at catching a glimpse of Chinese ecosophy embedded in and disseminated through anthropomorphic representation of animals in the narratives.

3.6   Summary

This chapter is dedicated to setting up a solid theoretical framework for the present study. The dialectical relationship between animal life, discursive representation and human society is first and foremost discussed. Conclusion has been drawn that how animals are represented in discourse bears direct relevance to how they are treated in reality, which will in turn influence the human society significantly. It is also highlighted that the interaction between animal life, discourse and human society is mediated by social cognition. Therefore, this chapter proceeds to clarify the interconnectedness between discursive representation and social cognition, particularly pointing out that discursive manipulation is largely processed in cognition. Furthermore, regarding discursive manipulation as linguistic coercion, it turns to nail down the question of how linguistic coercion can be realized, bringing into focus the issue of discursive strategies. It introduces representation and legitimization strategies in the service of linguistic coercion. In addition to illuminating discursive strategies contributing to linguistic coercion, it tends to address how discursive representation can be conceptualized, and hence how linguistic coercion can go into effect. Based on these discussions, it attempts to put forward an ecological critical-cognitive discourse analysis framework of animal representation as a modified model of Stibbe's (2012, 2015).

Chapter 4　Representation Strategies in Anthropomorphic Representation of Animal Images

4.1　Introduction

In the previous chapter, an ecological critical-cognitive discourse analysis framework has been proposed for animal representation study. Under the analysis framework, it is highlighted that discursive representation of animals is ideological and manipulative by nature, realized by strategic choices of language structures. As is postulated, representation strategies, referential and predication strategies in particular, play a crucial role in constructing animal images in discourse, affecting people's attitude toward animals. This chapter is dedicated to unveiling representation strategies in anthropomorphic representation of animal images in Shen Shixi's animal narratives. It attempts to disclose the way in which referential and predication strategies are employed to represent animals in an anthropomorphized way in Shen Shixi's animal narratives. It also attempts to reveal the potential effects produced by these strategies in constructing and construing anthropomorphic animal images.

4.2　Referential strategies

Among various representation strategies, referential strategy is the most basic one to achieve discursive manipulation by drawing the line of group boundaries. In a narrow sense, referential strategies can be defined as "intentions to promote dichotomous conceptualizations of social groups" (Hart, 2010: 8). Explicit and deictic noun phrases, pronouns, possessive determiners are referential strategies that have often been employed in discourse practice (Hart, 2010: 56). The fundamental nature of referential strategies in the communication of prejudice, e.g. in the racist discourses, has been highlighted (e.g. Reisigl & Wodak, 2001; Wodak, 2001). Nevertheless, their role in representing animal images has not been fully investigated. Given that referential strategies constructing group boundaries presuppose binary conceptualization, it is not difficult to understand why they are employed to anthropomorphic representation of animals, which connotes binary interpretations. The referential strategies used in Shen Shixi's narratives include individualization and assimilation.

4.2.1 Individualizing animals as subjective beings: Names and naming in *The Seventh Hound*

Names and naming practices have long been considered as a major theme of philosophical and linguistic enquiry. So far, there has been an extensive literature on studying names as referential device—names are primarily used to refer to specific entities. Prioritizing the identifying and deictic function of names scholars from different epistemological backgrounds are keenly interested in the interconnection between names and referents. It is agreed that using names or naming is an efficient way to individualize the referents with a concentrated linguistic expression. It is argued that the individualizing function of naming is closely linked to a series of related propositions about names. Firstly, names are definite noun phrases with a fixed denotation, which suggests the unique existence and prototypical occurrence of referents in the universe, as is stated, "we regard a name as a nominal expression that denotes a unique entity at the level of established linguistic convention to make it psychosocially salient within a given basic level category" (van Langendonck, 2007: 125). Secondly, names can be meaningful—"names are not only practical labels, instead they are packed with meaning in many senses" (Nyström, 2016: 58). The meaning names have involves various aspects, including lexical meaning, proprial meaning①, categorical meaning, associative meaning and emotive meaning (Nyström, 2016). Besides, names act as abbreviated descriptions that can be evaluated as true or false (cf. Smith, 2016: 338). In this sense, naming is helpful in giving rise to connotations, and thus "can be exploited in discourse to identify or to characterize the name-bearer" (van Langendonck & van de Velde, 2016: 49). Thirdly, names are regarded as semiotic resources to construct identity of the referents and "naming is always a question of assigning identity" (Aldrin, 2016: 424); it is recognized that one of the main functions of names is to make identifiable the referents within a certain community, and therefore names to a great extent index the referents' identity, which is considered to be "an essence, a personal property belonging to an individual" (Aldrin, 2016: 426).

The fundamental reason why names can function to individualize entities is that "the labels used to denote entities in the world are indicative of our perceptions of them—and of our stance toward them" (Sealey & Charles, 2013: 486). This is especially true when it comes to labeling living creatures. Abundant literature has concentrated on how people belonging to particular social categories are named and how the naming patterns serve to make a difference upon the public's perception of the referents, e.g. of migrants, females, or the disabled (e.g. Aldrin, 2016; Erwin, 1995; Lawson, 1996).

Name-based stereotypes, namely, generalized (positive or negative) views towards individuals aroused by names, can also be found in naming animals. How animals named in different discourses are differently perceived has always been the focus of cross-disciplinary researches on naming practice (e.g. Fill & Mühlhäusler, 2001; Russell, 2010; Smith, 2012; Stibbe, 2012). Recent literature has revealed that people's direct experience of animals and the linguistic resources

---

① In Nyström's words, "proprial meaning" refers to the meaning of a word when used in a proprial function. "Proprial" means being namelike. For more details, see Nyström (2016).

available for naming them are highly interconnected. It is established that "all human groups respond to the diversity of... animals in their habitats by grouping them into labeled or named categories of greater and lesser inclusiveness" (Brown, 1984: 1). For example, in English animals that are a culturally acceptable source of meat are usually referred to with specific words (Sealey & Charles, 2013). Another piece of notable evidence can be found in that pets tend to be labeled in the singular while most animals categorized as "livestocks" are named in plural form (Stibbe, 2012). In addition, the naming of pets in most cases are "beyond generic words for species and cultural category" (Sealey & Charles, 2013: 500).

It is worth noting that not all animals in close relationship with humans are labeled with an individual name. Leibring (2016) lists out the requisites for making feasible the naming of animals. Some of them are:

> the animal is regarded as an individual by the carer/handler/owner; the animal is treated as an individual (being milked, ridden, etc., or lives in the family home); there is a need for identification of the animal—or for communication with it; the animal is one of several in a herd or flock; the animal is in some way distinctive in its outer appearance (e.g. by colour, markings etc.).

Not surprisingly, among various reasons animals are given names, individualization, or "singularizing function" (cf. Leibring, 2016: 664), is of the greatest significance. The role of naming in individualizing animals is particularly magnified in literature.

The writing of animal novels, which are defined as a literary form, involves "how language communicates human experience (with animals) and gives some aspects of experience a particular significance, and thereby meaning" (Smith, 2016: 338). For the reason that naming represents the elemental way in which people use language (Smith, 2016: 338), at the heart of literary writing on animals is the practice of labeling animals. Naming practice in animal novels, in conformity with most other namings, acts primarily to foreground the individuality of animals referred to, thus to highlight their intrinsic value as subjective beings. The fictional animal names, better viewed as semiotic signs in terms of C. S. Peirce's (1955) semiotic approach, are intended to evoke varied yet thematically relevant associations.

According to Peirce, the potential associations names can activate are classified into three basic types: iconic, indexical and symbolic. The iconic type stresses the associative relationship based on visual or aural similarity between a name and the signified; the indexical type infers the associative relation between names and referents on the basis of contiguity or correlation; the symbolic type concerns the connection between two or more indices, implying the higher-ordered indexical references between names and referents realized "by virtue of a law, usually an association of general ideas" (Peirce, 1955: 102).

In literature, these general types of semiotic associations elicited by names function in varying degrees to achieve artistic prominence and thematic coherence. Animal novels are no exception. In Shen Shixi's animal novels, it seems that the indexical as well as symbolic associations names evoke matter more to animal representation. A well-illustrated example is the naming practice in Shen Shixi's *The Seventh Hound*, one of his masterpieces awarded three times in the Children's Literature Prize of the China Writers Association. This novel is dedicated to the story of a hunting dog.

- **Obscuring the other six hounds: Indexical associations evoked by names in *The Seventh Hound***

Indexical associations are "the most dominant type of name associations" and are "most obviously and easily subject to manipulation for artistic ends" (Smith, 2016: 351). Names, as "rigid designators" (Kripke, 1980: 48), act primarily to refer to definable entities and can be indexically interpreted. In literature, animal novels for example, names can be granted to bring to the fore the name-bearer, or "a name might also be delayed to create a special interest in a character, or characters may function without names, to indicate their unimportance, to create psychological distance" (Smith, 2016: 351).

Dogs are more readily picked up as heroes in Shen Shixi's writing. *The Seventh Hound* begins with a brief introduction about the hounds raised by the human protagonist—Zhao Panba, a veteran hunter living in Plantain Village:

(1)芭蕉寨老猎人召盘巴在四十余年闯荡山林的生涯中，前后养过七条猎狗。第一条猎狗腿长得太短，撵山追不到麂子，被牵到街子上卖掉了；第二条刚满五岁就胖得像头猪；第三条猎狗长得笨头笨脑，第一次狩猎时就被豹子咬死；第四条猎狗是母的，长大后被一条公狗拐走了；第五条猎狗满身疥疮；第六条猎狗糊里糊涂踩上了猎人铺设的铁夹子。一个猎人，得不到一条称心如意的猎狗，就像骑兵没有一匹好马一样，召盘巴常常为此唉声叹气。(Shen, 1999: 1)

In his more than forty years' life in the mountains and forests, Zhao Panba, a veteran hunter of Plantain Village had respectively kept seven hounds. The first one's legs were too short to chase muntjaks in the mountains and was taken by him to the country fair and sold away; the second was already as fat as a pig at the age of five; the third was dull and clumsy and so it was killed by a leopard on its first hunting trip; the fourth was a female one and was seduced away by a male dog when she grew up; the fifth got scabies all over its body; the sixth foolishly stepped onto a hunter's iron clasp. A hunter, without a satisfactory hound, is like a cavalryman without a good horse. Zhao Panba often sighed about it. (Shen, 1999: 1)[1]

Concise as it is, this beginning paragraph presents readers with the background of the story. Dogs here are referred to with common nouns modified by sequential order numbers. Rather than designating a single individual, common nouns "specify sets of common attributes among all items in the class of things named" (Smith, 2016: 339). In this sense, the individual peculiarities of these dogs are somehow obscured because of the naming practice. Meanwhile, the rough descriptions about them substantiate their marginalized role in promoting the

---

[1]   The English version of the novel *The Seventh Hound* is quoted from: Shen, S. X., 1999. *The Seventh Hound*. Cheng, Q. (trans.). Taiyuan: Hope Publishing House. Translations of the excerpts from the other four novels in the current study are mine.

development of the story. Readers will be highly impressed by the fictional fact that the six hounds fail to meet the demand of their owner, which is unsurprisingly the common trait they share. In the meantime, naming hounds in this way helps to create an expectation for the animal protagonist—"the seventh hound", as is suggested, "in literature the indexical function of names helps to stimulate our curiosity and lead us forward in our reading" (Smith, 2016: 350).

- **Foregrounding the seventh hound as a subjective individual: Symbolic associations evoked by names in *The Seventh Hound***

In addition to indexical references, names are able to elicit an array of meaningful associations. In particular, names in literary works, of which people's understanding mostly stems from the symbolic nature of language, "are apt to evoke symbolic associations" (Smith, 2016: 351). Symbolic references triggered by names in fictional stories help to construct the "imaginary universe" (Peirce, 1955: 103), making possible literary creation. Smith (2016) explains why names in literature tend to be interpreted symbolically. One possible reason, as he points out, is that they arise from previous context and thus are able to evoke pre-existing associations in the minds of both writers and readers. The other determinant factor is attributed to their lexical potentialities: just as other types of words, names "have potential lexical meanings" (Smith, 2016: 351), which can be either explicitly descriptive or figurative. As such, names of characters in literature can invite interpretations that are abundant in symbolic associations. The specific name given to the seventh hound in Shen Shixi's work is a case in point.

　　(2)三年前，召盘巴六十大寿时，曼岗哨卡的唐连长作为贺礼送给他一条军犬生出来的小狗。三年来，召盘巴情愿自己顿顿素菜淡饭，也要让这第七条猎狗餐餐沾着荤腥。在他的精心抚养下，小狗长大了，背部金黄的毛色间，嵌着两条对称的浅黑花纹，身材有小牛犊那么大，腰肢纤细，十分威武漂亮。它不愧是军犬的后裔，攀山快如风，狩猎猛如虎。有一次，一只秃鹫俯冲到院子里捉鸡，它从花丛中猛蹿上去，一口咬断了秃鹫的翅膀。召盘巴给它起了个名字

叫 "<u>赤利</u>" （傣族传说中会飞的宝刀）。(Shen, 1999: 2)

Three years ago, captain Tang of the Mangang sentry post gave him <u>a gift puppy of an army dog</u> when he celebrated the sixtieth anniversary of his birthday. For the past three years, he had willingly had a vegetarian diet for every meal, but had fed the puppy with some meat at each feed. Owing to his careful fostering, the dog grew up with two symmetrically blackish stripes inlaid into his golden fur on his back. He was as big as a calf but with a long thin waist, looking heroic and handsome. He was worthy of being <u>a descendant of army dogs,</u> running on the mountainsides in chasing animals as fast as a strong wind and hunting as ferociously as a tiger. Once when a vulture swooped down on a hen in the yard, he sprang up from the flowers and tore down one of its wings at one bite. Thus Zhao Panba named him <u>Chili</u> (meaning a flying treasure sword in legendary stories of the Dai nationality). (Shen, 1999: 2)

Following a sketchy depiction of six unsatisfactory hounds raised by Zhao Panba, this paragraph turns to introduce the animal protagonist of the story—the seventh hound. As a descendant of army dogs, the seventh hound is wildly different from the other six. A detailed elaboration of its external appearance and physical capability well exhibits its talent as a hunting dog, hence a satisfactory hound in the eyes of its owner. Nevertheless, it is not until the dog is endowed with a specific name that its image as an individual with subjectivity is shown forth. Chili is the name that Zhao Panba gives to the seventh hound.

As is illustrated in the work, the name Chili is connotative, meaning "a flying treasure sword in legendary stories of the Dai nationality". The name provokes meaningful associations it used to have in the heroic legends passed down from ethnic minorities and the associations arising from legendary context enrich the lexical connotation of Chili. With its literal meaning as "a flying treasure sword", when used to refer to the seventh hound, it is imprinted with metaphorical implications: firstly, a flying sword is expected to unleash virulent attacks on the battlefield, so is the seventh hound when going hunting; secondly, a flying sword is supposed to be obedient and loyal to its owner, and the same is true with the seventh hound to Zhao Panba; thirdly, a flying sword and its bearer are vitally bound up with each other, so are the seventh hound and Zhao Panba.

By naming the seventh hound as Chili, the above symbolic references are called into the mind of the addressees as the unique attributes the seventh hound possesses. Apart from inviting figurative interpretations, the name Chili is also helpful in achieving the artistic unity of the story owing to its thematic richness. As "part of a deliberately crafted sample of language" (Smith, 2016: 340), names in literature have thematic relevance, and symbolic associations provoked by names are assumed to be thematically relevant. The name Chili in *The Seventh Hound* helps to set the keynote of the story. Figuratively interpreted as "a flying treasure sword", Chili, the seventh hound, is unsurprisingly brave, fierce, loyal and hence treasured by its owner, as is narrated at the very beginning of the story, "he was worthy of being a descendant of army dogs, running on the mountainsides in chasing animals as fast as a strong wind and hunting as ferociously as a tiger", "fond of his hound like any hunter, he (Zhao Panba) regarded the dog as the second apple of his eye". These attributes the name Chili grants to the seventh hound seem to become the main clue of the story even though something accidental occurs as the story develops.

The unexpected incident is that one day Zhao Panba perceives chili as "an evil creature, an ominous beast", and tries to kill chili on the account that in his eyes chili acts cowardly in the face of a brutal solitary boar, because of which chili almost loses his life. Chili is saved and set free by Zhao Panba's grandson and becomes a wild dog from then on. Time elapses quickly. When one day Zhao Panba and his cows run into more than twenty hungry jackals, Chili turns up and sacrifices its life to protect them.

A twist in the plot is that Zhao Panba's presumption of Chili as a coward is proved to be a misunderstanding. The truth turns out to be that at the very moment when Zhao Panba aims at the boar with his gun, ready to shoot, a black brown cobra gazes at his naked arms from behind, ready to bite. It is Chili who dauntlessly preys on and takes hold of the snake, which goes unnoticed by the hunter. In one word, Chili is wronged in being beaten up by the owner and forced to flee into the forest. The story ends in Chili's death and Zhao Panba's waking up to his mistake. It is through the series of episodes and emotional collisions that the meaningful associations the name Chili acquires are strengthened and highlighted. As a "semi code" (Barthes, 1975: 17), the symbolic associations of Chili run through the whole story to link up every individual fragment, hence giving birth to the thematic unity of the story.

The seventh hound is flashed out in the story as a subjective individual because of the symbolic name. Readers are likely to be impressed by the anthropomorphic image of the seventh hound constructed in this story by naming, and begin to realize the intimate connection between humans and animals, as the moral awakening of Zhao Panba signifies.

4.2.2 Blurring the boundaries between humans and animals: The pronoun use of "you" in *The Old Hark*

Pronouns, functioning as part of the deictic system, have appealed to researchers from various fields, linguistics, semiotics and discourse studies in particular. Making pronouns as the object of careful attention, studies have stressesed the formative capacity of pronouns, addressing "their crucial role in shaping communicative and referential structures of discourse… and anchoring utterances in wider communicative contexts" (Grishakova, 2018: 193). To play their formative role, pronouns as indexical signs perform referential and identifiable functions in discourse by "calling up deictic centres, signaling communicative roles and aligning them with different deictic set-ups" (Grishakova, 2018: 194).

The deictic flexibility of pronouns not merely accounts for its rhetorical potential, but also helps to yield ideological effects. It is suggested that power relations are embedded and exercised in the selective employment of personal pronouns (Fowler & Kress, 1979). The exhibition of power and ideology in the use of personal pronouns is made possible in that pronominal use indicates self versus other focus, and thus produces group boundaries. As Chilton postulates, pronouns "can be used to induce interpreters to conceptualize group identity, coalitions, parties, and the like, either as insiders or outsiders" (2004: 56). Cramer (2010) also argues that alternative uses of pronouns give rise to aligning speakers with or distancing them from different social groups. Hence the emergence of ideological allegiances.

The ideological importance of pronouns have been well documented in a wide range of discourses. Studies on political discourses find that polarized distinction produced by personal pronouns contributes significantly to the presentation and transmission of ideologies, as well as the power negotiation underlying discourses (e.g. Chilton, 2004; Maitland & Wilson, 1987; van Dijk, 1998). Similarly, the inferential fashion of ideological manipulation in literary discourse, which is perceived as a form of "inventive discourse" (Nielsen, 2018: 217) as well as "a rhetorically manipulated linguistic product" (Kragh & Lindschouw, 2013: 172), has won extensive attention.

Regarded as "inventive discourse", literature signifies a special medium committed to seeking a new language for representing social processes. In the process of constructing social processes in literary works, pronouns in literary works are one linguistic means that is crucial to determining the perspectives characterizing mental simulations (e.g. Bergen & Chang, 2005; Herman, 2002). Positioned perspective generated by pronouns functions as the focalizing window which delineates a narrator's subject position in relation to others, and hence makes a difference in readers' perceptions of the positions of other characters in relation to that narrator's role and locus. It is acknowledged that readers may either mentally simulate events and objects in literary works from an internal "actor" perspective or embody an external "onlooker" perspective owing to the focalizing function of a particular pronoun-designated position. Relevant literature has revealed that compared to third-person pronouns, which is usually bound up with an external perspective, first- and second-person pronouns are conducive to evoking an internal perspective from the readers, and establishing their identification with a character in a story (e.g. Brunyé et al., 2009, 2011;

Hartung et al., 2016). It thus can be said that pronoun variations mediate the degree of embodiment experienced during narrative perception, and manipulate the readers' comprehension of the fictional world—"pronouns can therefore affect readers' empathetic, emotional and ideological relations with and responses to narratorial, poetic and other speaking voices and characters in literature" (Gibbons & Macrae, 2018: 3).

- **Epistemological transfer: Second pronoun "you" in perceptual coding**

The ideological functioning of the pronoun use is also evident in animal narratives. In most of Shen Shixi's animal narratives, animal characters are referred to with the pronoun "it". The pronoun use of "it" in animal-related discourses has been extensively investigated. Literature has found that referring to animals as "it" in discourses tends to construct animals as objects, corresponding with "the commonsense assumption that animals are property" (Stibbe, 2012: 25). In contrast to objectifying animals, "the same pronoun could be used as part of a quite different discourse of empathy and respectful distance" (Stibbe, 2012: 5). The widespread employment of the pronoun "it" in most of Shen Shixi's animal stories is a case in point.

Rather than representing animals as insentient objects, Shen Shixi is committed to depicting animals as subjective beings in his works. The pronoun "it" is mainly deployed to foreground the realistic tendency of the writings, which admittedly comprises the lifeline of animal narratives. Nevertheless, an exception can be found in *The Old Hark*. *The Old Hark* is a piece of work dedicated to portraying Hark—the king of the deer herd living on the prairie, who sacrifices its life to protect the herd from being hunted by a haunting wolf.

In this story, the old Hark is constantly referred to with the second-person pronoun "you". And *The Old Hark* is the first second-person narration among all of Shen Shixi's works so far. Of all the second-person narrations, scholars postulate that, reader involvement is a typical characteristic (e.g. Mildorf, 2016; Ryan, 2002). The special effect of involvement literary second-person narration exerts upon readers is realized to a great extent by the potential ambiguity and complexity of "you", which goes beyond the narrator–protagonist–reader distinction. As Rembowska-Płuciennik argues, "the narrative 'you' places the capacities of declarative pointing, social referring and adopting another's viewpoint at the very core of the transmission and processing of narrative information" (Rembowska-Płuciennik, 2018: 167). In other words, nothing parallel to mere inferences about others or self-consciousness, the second-person narration involves "a self-and-other conjugation" (Rembowska-Płuciennik, 2018: 166). By employing direct address, second-person narratives activate the identification mechanism and thus stimulate the "we-mode" agency among narrative existents, namely, the narrator, protagonist and reader.

The protagonist in Shen Shixi's second-person narratives, the old Hark, is the king of its herd. To help the deer herb survive from the wolf infestation, the old Hark, who in the narrator's words is outstandingly brave and brilliant, makes a tough yet bold decision to wage a life-and-death battle with the wolf. Being depicted as capable of making decisions, Hark is represented anthropomorphically. And this anthropomorphic tendency is furthered especially when Hark is addressed by the second pronoun "you". Given the gross disparity in strength between wolf and deer, a choice like this appears to be solemn and tragic, which brings the question of individualistic heroism to the foreground of the novel.

(3)但你却感觉到了巨大的压力，这压力来自于你的内心。你是鹿王，你有责任也有义务保护种族，令它生存和繁荣。生存和繁荣的首要条件就是和平和安宁。一种鹿王才有的神圣使命感驱使你做出一个非凡的决定，临死之前同老狼较量一番，但愿能消灭这个祸根，为你所挚爱的鹿群除害。你明白，这将是一场力量悬殊的搏斗。首先你要克服鹿的自私和怯懦的天性，但动物要改变天性谈何容易，简直比登天还难，人类也不例外。(Shen, 2017: 16)

However, you feel a lot of pressure, which comes from your heart. You are the deer king, and you have a responsibility and an obligation to protect the herd so that it can survive and prosper. The essential presupposition for survival and prosperity is peace and tranquility. A sense of sacred mission that deer kings are endowed with drives you to make an extraordinary decision—to fight against the old wolf before you die, in the hope that you can kill the wolf and protect your beloved deer herd from being killed. You know that it's going to be a tough fight, considering the great disparity in strength between wolf and deer. First of all, you have to overcome the selfish and cowardly nature of the deer, but how difficult it is for animals to challenge their nature—it is a lot harder than it looks. Human beings are no exception.

By employing direct address, "you" in the fictional story world of *The Old Hark* is able to elicit affective-emotional involvement from readers and to activate identification mechanisms. The intention to portray the old Hark as a hero who is determined to sacrifice its life to save the deer herb shows forth in the beginning of the story. In the above paragraph, the identity of the old Hark is revealed in a forthright manner, which serves as a hint foreshadowing later development in this story. The identity of being a deer king justifiably accounts for Hark's choice, which can never be an easy one, exposed by a detailed presentation of Hark's psychological operations.

The extended use of perceptual encoding is characteristic of second-pronoun narration, one possible reason for which is that the author wishes to describe "a veritable progress of consciousness" (Parker, 2018: 98). Thus, in explaining why Hark decides to fight with the wolf, the protagonist's mental state is reported, both by means of the predictive verbs "feel" and "know" and by what could be regarded as free indirect thought presentation such as "you have a responsibility and an obligation to protect the herb", "a sense of sacred mission that deer kings are endowed with drives you to make an extraordinary decision" and "in the hope that you can kill the wolf and protect your beloved deer herd from being killed". It is through these psychological descriptions that readers are allowed an insight into Hark's thoughts, and can be possibly invited to assume the position of that "you" to some degree. As Linhares-Dias suggests, the psychological encoding of subjectivity can be viewed as "a text-induced process of *epistemological transfer* such that the recipient will decode the perceptual information source as something he might have experienced" (Linhares-Dias, 2006: 7).

- **Emotional resonance: Second pronoun "you" in highlighting moral qualities**

In addition to the collocation of "you" with psychological portrayal, similarities between the protagonist and readers in second-pronoun narration also contribute to evoking a sense of proximity and empathy from readers. In the process of storytelling, Hark is confronted with a "to-be-or-not-to-be" question, that is, whether it should risk its life to combat with the wolf, which contradicts with the natural instinct of deer. The third voice "human beings are no exception" is helpful in creating a sense of experientiality by highlighting the resembling experiences or circumstances between Hark and readers (human beings). A narrative technique as such, in particular when combined with the deployment of second pronoun *you*, is conducive to triggering emotional responses from the addressees and therefore leading to their greater identification with the character. By doing so, the narrator, narratee and character interact as *I* and *you* in a dynamic process, producing the effect of we-mode thinking: the heroic and idealistic choice made by Hark seems just like a narrate-protagonist decision.

More examples can be found in the following paragraphs:

(4)你不甘心就这样普普通通地死去。你虽然是鹿，但你不是一般的鹿，你是勇敢的智慧出众的鹿王。你希望自己生的与众不同，死的时候也与众不同。(Shen, 2017: 5)

You don't want to die like this. Although you are a deer, you are the distinguished one—you are a brave and intelligent deer king. You want to be different, and you want to be different when you die.

(5)你毫不怀疑自己能卫冕成功，但你再也没有力量去对付那匹老狼了。你只是成功地死在鹿王的位子上，却亲手毁掉了自己辉煌的理想。(Shen, 2017: 36)

You have no doubt that you can defend your title, but you have no power to deal with the old wolf. You may succeed in dying in the throne of the deer, but you could personally destroy your own faith.

(6)你心里出现一架天平，价值就是重量。王位固然有其特殊价值，但种族的生存和繁荣无疑要比王位的价值大得多。你痛苦地发现心里的天平倾斜了。(Shen, 2017: 37)

There is a balance in your heart, and value is weight. The throne has its special value, but the survival and prosperity of the herd is undoubtedly much greater than the value of the throne. You find in pain that the balance in your heart is tilted.

The indexical pronoun "you" "does not operate in a discursive vacuum" (Mildorf, 2016: 146). Lexical items with positive connotations, such as "distinguished", "brave" and "intelligent", function together to construct the image of an adorable deer king who is "different" from the rest of its companions. More accurately, these attributes are nothing parallel to the specificities of the deer herd; instead, they are closer to the merits human beings hold in high esteem. Highlighting the character's moral quality while overlooking the uniqueness of its physical appearance in second-pronoun narration will give rise to the empathetic, emotional and ideological connections between readers and the protagonist. Moreover, readers become more immersed in the story world especially when these moral qualities are elaborated with minute depiction of Hark's reflection— "the second-person address may be more effective (i.e. more engaging) if the *you*-narrative is presented in the reflectoral mode" (Mildorf, 2016: 153).

- **Embodied experience: Second pronoun "you" in joint actions**

Upon reading the mental process of Hark in you-mode, empasized by human-oriented words such as "faith" and "value", readers are stimulated to adopt an internal perspective of the active agent (Brunyé et al., 2009), and feel the same sense of agency in decision-making as Hark. Thus it is no wonder a shared identity between readers and Hark can be assumed. In addition to rendering the consciousness of a blurring "you", readers' identification with the protagonist in second-pronoun narration is activated by recorded actions of the character, linguistically signaled by verbs.

(7)猛地，你觉得臀部一阵剧痛，你听见自己的鹿皮被狼牙咬破、肌肉被狼牙嚼碎的嚓嚓声，听见血液从伤口流出来的潺潺声。碧绿的草地上洒下一窜鹿血，像红罂粟。你发疯般地狂蹦乱跳，但根本没用，老狼的牙已经触到你的后腿骨，发出嘎嘎的啃咬骨头的噪音。(Shen, 2017: 74)

Suddenly, you feel a sharp pain in your hips. You feel your deer skin bitten by the wolf's teeth and your muscles chewed up by the wolf's teeth. And you also hear the sound of blood coming out of the wound. A splash of deer blood, like a red poppy, is sprinkled on the green grass. You jump madly in an attempt to shake the wolf off, but it's no use—the wolf's teeth have touched your hind leg bone, making a rattled, bone-biting noise.

(8)你忍住剧痛，观察四周地形。你看见左侧不远有一片密密匝匝的灌木丛，荆棘纵横，毒藤纠缠，毒藤上布满了一根根鱼钩似的倒刺。你有了主意，驼着老狼奔向灌木丛，一头钻了进去。毒藤上的倒钩划破了你的鼻子和脸，也同样刺进了狼皮。你听见狼发出一声呻吟，"咕咚"一声从你背上摔了下来。(Shen, 2017: 76)

You hold back the pain and observe the terrain around you. You see a dense bush not far to the left, with crisscrossing thorns and poison rattan entangled and covered with a root hook-like sting. You have an idea, hunching the old wolf into the bushes, and drilling in. The hook on the poison rattan pierces your nose and face, and also pierces the wolf's skin. You hear the wolf moaning and falling down to the ground.

The interplay between "you" and verbs in the above passages may lead to readers' taking the protagonist's perspective and simulating its bodily state and actions in the bloody fight with the old wolf from an internally embodied position. Previous researches suggest that readers mentally simulate the first character's perceptual state and motoric actions when directly addressed as the subject of a sentence (Brunyé et al., 2009; Fischer & Zwaan, 2008; Glenberg, 2007). The perceptual verbs (or verbal expressions), like "feel", "hear", "see" and "have an idea", on the one hand signal the perceptual subjectivity of Hark, and on the other hand when combined with "you" can activate a perceptual unity or whole between readers and the deer king—they share the same perceptual field and have the same focus of attention, as if the readers feel being there. Nevertheless, "the palpable sense of 'being there' during reading does, in fact, involve the perceptual and motoric mental simulation of described discourse elements" (Brunyé et al., 2009: 31). Therefore, apart from sensory identification with the protagonist, readers, upon reading and comprehending the above passage, can be engaged in joint action with Hark. Action verbs (or verbal expressions), such as "jump", "shake off", "hold back", "observe", "hunch into" and "drill in", are put in chronological and causal sequence to report Hark's bodily actions during its battle with the old wolf. In this way, readers are able to embody the described actions and have a sense of sensorimotor engagement in that "reporting or imagining—step by step—somebody else's actions in a form of second-person narration stimulates bodily marking of the same activity" (Rembowska-Płuciennik, 2018: 164). And, "engagement in joint action can transform a sense of self-agency into a sense of 'we-agency'" (Pacherie, 2014: 25-27).

In this sense, over the course of reading the second-pronoun narration of Hark's heroic battle with the old wolf, readers co-participate with the protagonist as a collective subject in the enactment of the sequences of the actions. The act of reading is thus converted into the act of fighting. At this moment, the interdependence and the interconnection between readers and the first character seem to reach the climax: they share the common weal and woe when confronted with the common enemy. There is no doubt that the second pronoun "you" plays its role in eliciting both direct and perceptually mediated effects of transcending the boundaries between human readers and animal characters.

4.3　Predication strategies

In addition to referential strategies, predication strategies are also extensively employed in anthropomorphic representation of animals. Basically, predication strategies represent the way of linguistic identification, which involves ascribing specific qualities and traits to the referents, the latter being either members of social groups in political discourses or animals in animal narratives. Previous investigations into predication in discourse reveal that strategic predication can be stereotypical and evaluative by nature, given that the strategies "aim either at labelling social actors more or less positively or negatively, deprecatorily or appreciatively" (Reisigl & Wodak, 2001: 46). It is admitted that predications with affirmative or negative deontic-evaluative connotations are effective in framing "people, objects, events, processes and states of affairs in terms of quality, quantity, space, time and so on" (Reisigl & Wodak, 2001: 46).

The coercive function of predication strategies is performed throughout the whole process of constructing and communicating representations, realized by an array of linguistic means. Discursively-utilised predications, explicit or implicit, comprise a wide range of linguistic resources, i.e. syntactic, semantic or pragmatic reflexes. Most commonly-acknowledged predications include adjectives, prepositional phrases, relative clauses, numerals, verbs, norminalizations, implicatures, presuppositions and nouns (Hart, 2010; Reisigl & Wodak, 2001). Linguistic components of different dimensions could work interactively and interdependently to realize predication strategies. Nevertheless, diversified as predication might be, the central role of predicates exerting in Shen Shixi's animal narratives is apparent. Predicates and other strategic predications effected by diversified linguistic means work together to construct anthropomorphic images of animals: animals as affectionate and their behaviors as meaningful and authored.

4.3.1 Animal behaviors as meaningful and authored: The use of action verbs in *The Last War Elephant*

In Shen Shixi's animal narratives, the depiction of animal behaviors is foregrounded. The portrayal of animal behaviors, in accordance with the fundamental principle of animal narration which demands a high conformity between the writing of animal life and the physical reality, embraces both the realistic and aesthetic orientation in animal narratives. Profoundly different from mechanomorphic imagery—the mechanical icon which features the abstract portrayal of typified animal behaviors, Shen Shixi's realistic approach to describing animal behaviors emanates from a commitment to disclosing the agency of animals as sentient beings. When it comes to behaviors and actions, the subjectivity of animals encompasses "the meaningfulness of experience" and "the authorship of action" (Crist, 1999: 5). Shen Shixi's representation of animals displays his perception of subjectivity in the animal world, based on the premise that their behaviors are experientially meaningful and their actions are authored. And his focus on meaningfulness of animal behaviors is well-justified by narrating the detailed nuances and variations of animal actions in concrete behavioral events and specific episodes. That is, when portraying the meaningful and authored actions of animals, Shen Shixi consistently relies on episodic description.

Episodic description refers to the depiction of "an actual and specific sequence of observed behaviors of notable though varying duration" (Crist, 1999: 67). It is through episodic description that the uniqueness as well as the holistic feature of animal behaviors can be revealed, thus giving insights into the meaningfulness and authorship of animal actions. With regard to the concept of "meaningfulness", Crist highlights its experiential dimension, which means that the actors are able to "experience objects and events, as well as actions and relations, as phenomena imbued with import and repercussions" (1999: 6); as for "authorship", it refers to the state that actors are imparted with the power to decide whether to experience or not and how to experience events in their world as a matter of agency. "Meaningfulness" and "authorship" are intertwined closely with each other. They are meticulously interwoven into the display of animal behaviors in Shen Shixi's narratives through the use of verbs. To take a few illustrations:

(9)嘎羧的神志突然间清醒过来。虽然它的身体仍然衰弱不堪，但精神却处在亢奋状态中，两只眼睛烧得通红，见到波农丁，欧欧短促地轻吼着，鼻子一弓一弓，鼻尖指向象房堆放杂物的小阁楼，象蹄急促地踢踏着地面，好像是迫不及待想得到小阁楼上的什么东西。开始波农丁不想理它，它发起脾气来，鼻子抽打房柱，还用庞大的身体去撞木板墙。(Shen, 2008b: 11)

Gasuo suddenly came to consciousness. Though it was still weak, it was in a state of great excitement. Its two eyes burned red. Upon seeing Bonongding, it roared shortly, moving its nose up and down. The tip of his nose constantly pointed to the attic filled with piles of debris. Its feet hastily kicked and stepped on the ground, as if it couldn't help wanting to get something in the little attic. Knowing that Bonongding had no response, it lost its temper, using its nose to beat the column again and again, and its huge body to hit the wooden wall.

This is an episode described in Shen Shixi's *The Last War Elephant*. Gasuo is the last surviving war elephant from the War of Resistance Against Japanese Aggression. When it was about to reach the end of its life, it put on the elephant saddle again, walking to the bank of Dalo—the battlefield where it used to fight with its fellow soldiers during the war, musing over the past. After that, it buried itself in a pit next to the elephant mound where its companions had been interred. The above example is a narration of Gasuo's determination to face death as a war elephant, indicated by its strong will to get its saddle back and put the saddle on again.

- **Animal actions imbued with experiential meaning: The use of ordinary language**

Instead of a portrayal of its psychological activities, to display Gasuo's intense desire of wanting its saddle back, a succession of actions is presented. How actions are illustrated in language can "work as a gateway to see actions in particular ways" (Crist, 1999: 34). It is notable that the lexical set of verbs used to describe Gasuo's action here is "ordinary language" rather than technical terms. By "ordinary language of actions", Crist (1999) refers to the everyday language of human life. It can be found that in portraying Gasuo's behaviors, most of the verbs are applicable in the context of describing human activities. The ordinary language of representing animal actions presupposes and reaffirms a strong alignment between animal actions and human activities. In using ordinary language to account for animal actions, its logical dimension in regard to human actions can be witnessed in the case of animals as well. In other words, given that "meaning is internal to human conduct, being constitutive of the production, form, and reception of action in specific circumstances" (Crist, 1999: 5), in deploying this language, animal actions are imbued with experiential meaning. In this way, perception of animal behaviors is led to understanding the intrinsic meaning of the actions—the subjective experience the behavior embodies, and therefore subjectivity of animals can be perceived.

- **Animal agency: Animals as authors of material process**

The perception of agency in animal life is also realized by representing animals as authors of action—"animals are also frequently activated by being represented as Actors of material processes, i.e. as involved in purposeful activity" (Stibbe, 2015: 176). In episode 9, the last elephant, Gasuo, appears to be the agent of the processes of "roared", "moving", "pointed to", "kicked and stepped", "using", "beat" and "hit", which are regarded as material processes in active sentences, constructing it as a sentient being actively engaged in purposeful activities. Authorship of Gasuo, therefore, is embedded in the representation of the action as performed by, rather than happening to, the elephant. In addition, Gasuo's strong will to get back the saddle, indicated by the sentence "as if it couldn't help wanting to get something in the little attic", is presented as the cause of the actions, further justifying its behaviors as evidently embodying an experientially meaningful dimension. The internal cohesion of the successive actions is thus created. In the scene described above—"it roared shortly, moving its nose up and down. The tip of his nose constantly pointed to the attic filled with piles of debris", the sequential link can be found between verbs including "roar", "move" and "point to", signifying that Gasuo is yearning for something.

- **Subjective cohesiveness: Animal actions in the organizational continuity**

Gasuo's strong desire of wanting something is made visible when continuous actions are depicted—"using its nose to beat the column again and again, and its huge body to hit the wooden wall". In deploying the adjacent verbs "use", "beat" and "hit" to depict the more intense activities, the continuity of the elephant's actions in their sequential tightness is descriptively preserved. And the organizational continuity of the actions contributes to disclosing the eagerness of Gasuo to get something, as is stated, "awareness surfaces in virtue of the way an action, or a sequence of actions, is perceived and depicted" (Crist, 1999: 78). In so doing, the subjective cohesiveness and the meaningfulness of animal behaviors are foregrounded. The meaningfulness of the actions is particularly highlighted when Gasuo's responses to having the saddle returned are narrated.

(10)奇怪的事发生了，嘎羧见到那破玩意儿，一下安静下来，用鼻子"呼呼"吹去蒙在上面的灰尘，鼻尖久久地在破玩意上摩挲着，象眼里泪光闪闪，像是见到了久别重逢的老朋友。(Shen, 2008b: 11-12)

Strange things happened. Upon seeing the worn-out saddle, Gasuo calmed down. With tears standing in its eyes, it used its nose to blow away the dust on the surface of the saddle, the tip of the nose stroking gently the saddle for a long time. It looked as if it had encountered an old friend after a long separation.

In the similar vein, verbs of ordinary language are employed to describe how Gasuo behaved differently as soon as it had its saddle returned. In contrast to its strenuous efforts to getting back the saddle, Gasuo behaved calmly and unhurriedly upon seeing the saddle. In using verbs (verbs phrases) "blow away" and "stroke" in accounts of Gasuo's actions—"blow away the dust on the surface of the saddle" and "stroking gently the saddle for a long time", together with other predication strategies—the attribute in the form of prepositional phrases such as "with tears standing in its eyes" as well as the rhetoric figure as demonstrated in "it looked as if it had encountered an old friend after a long separation", the inner life of the elephant emerges as a natural and viewable facet of the behavioral scenery. The sentimental attachment of Gasuo to the saddle, a memento of the war it experienced years ago, is linguistically manifest.

In alignment with the depiction of Gasuo's demeanor of wanting the saddle, the portrayal of its actions after getting back what it wanted in the narration preserves the organizational continuity that comprises the holistic character of a complete and self-contained act. As continuous components of an unfolding act, the successive actions in their specific integrity are meaningfully interconnected and authored, which lead to a delivery of subjectivity to the animal protagonist.

4.3.2 Animals as sentient beings: The use of mental predication in *Dream of the Wolf King*

Understanding animals as subjects with an experiential perspective and authoring force allows for the possibility that animals are endowed with inner life. Anthropomorphic representations of animals in Shen Shixi's animal narratives rest mostly on his depictions of animal mind (Chen, 2007; Chen, 2018; Zhu, 2005). Shen intends his portrait of animals, descriptions of mental activity included, as realistic representation of animal life rather than mere metaphorical extension of language from the human to the animal dimension. This is closely related to his understanding of "animal narratives", of which a distinctive characteristic is that they should be committed to revealing the inner life of the animal characters and making the display of animal psychology believable.

Another inexorable factor is his recognition and appreciation of subjective life of individual animals, which characterizes his writing. Shen remains consistent in stressing individual variability with respect to the mental characteristics of animals displayed in specific episodes. Animals in his narratives are represented as having as complex thoughts and emotions as those of human beings. They are attributed with "mental faculties" such as reasoning, self-consciousness, moral sense and aesthetic sensibility. The disclosure of animals' mental life could be achieved explicitly or implicitly, by means of either "the ascription of particular mental predicates" or "the more diffuse sense of mindfulness in the animal world" (Crist, 1999: 78). Direct ascription of mental predicates is more easily accessible to laying bare animal psychology. In the light of three-subtyped mental process within the realm of systemic functional linguistics (Halliday, 2000), mental predicates can be categorized into predicates of feeling, thinking and perceiving. Different forms of mental predicates are applied to reflect a regard for animals as sensors, or conscious subjects. In addition, mental attributions can be scenically presented, that is, they can also be observed in behavioral and contextual evidence. It is claimed that "behavior and mental states are a single, fused totality" (cf. Crist, 1999: 23). And behavioral episodes are deemed as most effective to prove the existence of animal mind. In behavioral anecdotes, mental phenomena emerge when actions are embodied in verbs that are semantic composite of physical action and mental attitude, i.e. verbs delivering the emotional or intentional constituent of an action.

Both explicit and implicit mental predications are generously used in Shen Shixi's *Dream of the Wolf King*, which is a story about how a female wolf is determined to cultivate the wolf king. In this story, female wolf Zilan and male wolf Heisang were a couple. Heisang was physically strong and had huge potential to be the next wolf king. Unfortunately, Heisang lost its life in a fight against a rhino. Grief-stricken as Zilan was, it vowed to fulfill Heisang's unfinished wish by raising and training one of their wolf cubs into the wolf king. Centering on Zilan's determination to cultivate a real wolf king, the author attempts to portray Zilan's psychological activities at great length. Extensive use of mental predications to describe Zilan's mind can be seen in Table 4.1.

Table 4.1   Mental predication in *Dream of the Wolf King*

Explicit	Perception: feel (体会/感到); see (眼看); perceive (觉得); sense of hunger (饥饿感)
	Affection: disappointed (失望); happy (幸福); worried (担忧); concerned (忧虑); is crazy about (痴迷); distressed (忧伤); heartbroken (心疼); thrilling (激动); satisfied (惬意); indignant (愤慨); sad yet stirring (悲壮); pride (自豪); guilty (愧疚)
	Cognition: think (想到/以为); know (知道); reflect (回想); understand (晓得/明白/懂得); ambition (野心); plan (计划); long for (渴望); idea (主意); envisage (设想); regret (后悔); manage (设法); deduce (推断); speculate (推测)
Implicit	Emotional action verbs: prefer (偏爱); tease (逗弄); sigh (叹气); hesitate (踌躇); frown (皱眉); groan (呻吟); stand still (伫立); tremble (战栗)
	Intentional action verbs: intimidate (威逼); coerce (胁迫); incite (怂恿); wait (等待); observe (观察); keep watch on (监视); show off (卖弄); give up (放弃); make a sneak raid (偷袭)

Far from exhaustive as the mental predications shown above are, they provide a general picture of how the mental state of Zilan is revealed by various forms of mental predications in *Dream of the Wolf King*. To illustrate that in more details, the following is an example:

(11)紫岚在洞里躺了许久，也无法入睡。一种<u>强烈的饥饿感</u>折磨着它。要是仅仅为了自己的口腹，它紫岚也许还能<u>忍受</u>。但它现在肚子里有了小狼崽，作为母狼，它无法<u>忍受</u>小宝贝跟着自己倒霉，和自己一起挨饿……紫岚心疼极了，难受极了。它用前爪<u>摸摸</u>自己胸前的乳房，既不结实也不丰满，因消瘦和营养不良而显得有点干瘪。这样下去，它怎么能哺养好自己的宝贝呢？……它<u>内心深处还有个野心</u>，让自己生下的狼崽中有一个将来能当上地位显赫的狼王。(Shen, 2009: 16)

Zilan lay in the cave for a long time, unable to sleep. <u>A strong sense of hunger</u> tormented it. If it was alone, it might be able to <u>endure</u> the hunger. But now it had a little wolf cub in its belly, and as a mother wolf, it couldn't <u>bear</u> the little baby following its own bad luck and starving with itself... Zilan was very <u>distressed</u> and <u>uncomfortable</u>. It <u>touched</u> the breasts with its front paws, which were neither firm nor plump, and appeared a little shriveled due to emaciation and malnutrition. If this continued, how could it feed its own babies?... It also <u>had an ambition in its heart</u>, that is, one of the wolf cubs it gave birth to could become a prominent wolf king in the future.

The above paragraph depicts the scene of Zilan's suffering from hunger when it lost Heisang and was pregnant. To expose what is going on in Zilan's mind, an array of mental predications is deployed. Explicitly, words such as "hunger" indicate the perceptual constituent of Zilan's mentality; "distressed" and "uncomfortable" suggest that the female wolf is affectionate. Implicitly, emotional action verbs such as "bear", and conceptually composite verbal expressions like "had an ambition in its heart", which imply the imbrication of motion, intention, and affect, charge the actor with a sense of awareness, exhibiting its determination in cultivating its babies into the wolf king. As such, the connection between bodily expressiveness and the perception of mentality can be found in the action verb "touch" in "touched the breasts with its front paws, which were neither firm nor plump, and appeared a little shriveled". Contextual conceptual link is established among "hunger", "touch" and "shriveled breasts", and thus conceptual environment is created, paving the way for the emergence of Zilan's subjectivity. In this way, the ascription of cognition to the animal character Zilan is made reasonable. As Crist states, "subjectivity comes first, and then the tacit or direct ascription of mental predicates, naturally, supervene" (1999: 6).

As the story develops, narrative focus is on how Zilan implements its plan to cultivate the wolf cubs. The image of Zilan as being both a sensible instructor and an affectionate mother is constructed through abundant depictions of its psychological activities. Taking the episode of its rearing Heizai as an example:

(12)自己下手下得太重了些，紫岚想。作为母狼，看到自己的宝贝被揍出血来，未免有点心疼，但它不<u>后悔</u>。它是狼，它不能有怜悯之心，它就是要打掉黑仔对它的依恋和温情。(Shen, 2009: 48)

Too heavy a blow it was, Zilan <u>said to itself</u>. As a female wolf, seeing her baby being beaten and bleeding, Zilan hurt a little, but didn't <u>regret</u> it. As a wolf, it was not allowed to have mercy. It had to cut off Heizai's emotional attachment.

For the reason that Heizai resembles Heisang in appearance, Zilan expects a lot from it. Heizai becomes the first wolf pup to be trained as a future wolf king. Clinging to the idea that a wolf king is supposed to be ferocious and cold-hearted, Zilan adopts tough parenting. One important step is to "cut off Heizai's emotional attatchment", for which Zilan beats up Heizai over nothing. The above depiction vividly shows Zilan's mental activities after bashing Heizai, distinctly signified by the mental predicate "said to itself". As Halliday (2000) illustrates, "say to oneself" is often used to recognize the fact that one can think in words. Similar to other mental predicates like "think", "wonder", "reflect" and "surmise", this expression can be regularly deployed to quote one's thought. In quoting, the projected element, the animal's thought, has independent status, and thus is "more immediate and lifelike" (Halliday, 2000: 256).

Directly quoted thought like this places special emphasis on disclosing the affection constituent of animal mentality, representing Zilan as an affectionate mother who cares about its baby, while indirect reported speech focuses more on displaying animal's cognitive ability. For example, the other evident mental predicate "regret" in "[Zilan] didn't regret it" tends to indirectly report what is going on in the female wolf's mind, constructing the wolf as a sensible and rational instructor who is determined to cultivate a future wolf king by every conceivable means. Either by quoting or reporting, that animals as sentient beings is shown forth in Shen Shixi's writing through the use of various mental predicates.

4.4   Summary

In this chapter, different strategies functioning in anthropomorphic representation of animal images in Shen Shixi's animal narratives are under scrutiny. Special attention is paid to exploring referential and predication strategies in animal representation. Referential strategies used to construct animal images in Shen Shixi's narratives include individualization and assimilation. Individualization refers to the referential strategy of names and naming aimed at individualizing animals as subjective beings. It is suggested that the naming practice in animal novels, in conformity with most other naming, acts primarily to foreground the individuality of animals referred to, thus to highlight their intrinsic value as subjective beings. Assimilation involves the referential strategy of the pronoun use of "you" which blurs the boundaries between humans and animals. It is revealed that the second pronoun "you" plays its role in eliciting both direct and perceptually mediated effects on transcending the boundaries between human readers and animal characters. In addition to referential strategies, predication strategies, which concern ascribing specific qualities and traits to the referents, play a critical role in anthropomorphic representation of animal images. The predication strategies of using verbs tend to construct animal behaviors as meaningful and authored in Shen Shixi's animal narratives. His focus on meaningfulness of animal behaviors is well-justified by narrating the detailed nuances and variations of animal actions in concrete behavioral events and specific episodes. The predication strategy of using mental predication shapes animals as sentient beings in Shen Shixi's animal narratives. Animals in his novels are represented as having as complex thoughts and emotions as those of human beings either by ascribing animals with particular mental predicates or by evoking the more diffuse sense of mindfulness in the animal world. Taken together, referential and predication strategies in anthropomorphic representation of animal images in Shen Shixi's animal narratives construct the constituted reality about animals in discourse, which can only be brought into effect when messages are accepted as true. With regard to this, legitimization strategies are exploited to enable coercion.

Chapter 5   Legitimization of Anthropomorphic Representation of Animal Images

5.1   Introduction

In anthropomorphic representation of animals, referential and predication strategies can only be effective when legitimization strategies are at work. Legitimization is a remarkable function of language use and discursive practice. It is commonly agreed that legitimization involves enacting the "rightness" of the speaker's claim (van Leeuwen & Wodak, 1999; Cap, 2006; Chilton, 2004; Sperber, 2000; van Leeuwen, 2007). To be specific, legitimization is concerned with using "linguistic expressions to imbue utterances with evidence, authority and claims to truth and/or presumptions about the felicity conditions which give the speaker the right to make an assertion" (Hart, 2010: 90). It's a multi-level phenomenon that is heterogeneous, presuppositional and ideological in essence. The heterogeneous essence of legitimization takes its root in the duality of language which "makes possible evoking or reinforcing various dichotomous representations in accordance with speakers' goals" (Cap, 2013: 49).

In speeches or discourses, the central objective of legitimization is to persuade the addressees or readers into the speaker or writer's assertion of what is good or evil, right or wrong, acceptable or unacceptable. In line with this assertion-directive orientation, the communicative act of legitimization presupposes norms and values, implicitly or explicitly laying legal and moral foundation for certain claims and actions. The presuppositional power of legitimization is pragmatically related to "implicature", of which the pragma-rhetorical capacity is to evoke possible inferences in terms of different pre-expectations as a result of contextual developments (Cap, 2013). The pre-expectations of the addressees are parallel to the notion of taken-for-granted knowledge that can be presupposed. Not explicitly stated, this presupposed knowledge penetrates into new statements as common-sense assumptions that are unconsciously taken as true by people. Common sense is "just another term for the set of social beliefs" (van Dijk, 1998: 103). It is essentially shared lay-knowledge among members of social groups, "responsible for enacting credibility that is needed to legitimize actions/policies" (Cap, 2013: 53). Notably, common sense is "possibly biased by social prejudices and illusions" (van Dijk, 1998: 104). It is not surprising that naturalization and the generation of common sense is in the service of ideological manipulation. That is, ideologies can be implanted into discourses as matters of common sense and taken for granted. As Fairclough suggests, "relationships between things which are taken to be commonsensical may be ideological" (1989: 109).

The fact that common sense is inherently ideological determines that the commonsensical legitimization is ideological by nature and "is one of the main social functions of ideologies" (van Dijk, 1998: 255). In other words, the functioning of ideology is premised upon the recognition of its legitimacy. Once recognized, the legitimated ideologies, norms and values can serve as the general base of presupposed beliefs to justify actions and arguments. Ideologies, at the very best, provide the foundation for legitimization. This is the way ideology and legitimization interact in the control of social relations, such as those of power, dominance and resistance (van Dijk, 1998).

Linguistically, the processing of ideologies as the background assumption in discourses is achieved through a wide range of legitimization strategies, which "get more or less relative to the demands of the context" (Cap, 2013: 31). Generally, they involve "displays of internal and external coherence" (Hart, 2010: 187). Internal coherence is manifested by grammatical cohesion (Halliday & Hasan,

1976); external coherence is particularly expressed in evidentiality and epistemic modality. It is through these specific legitimization strategies that authors of animal narratives attempt to "textualize" (van Dijk, 1998) the animal world and make possible the automatic "fitting" of animal representation in narratives to the reality.

5.2   Legitimizing anthropomorphic representation of animals through implication, presupposition and inferencing: The use of grammatical cohesion

5.2.1 Grammatical cohesion and ideological coherence

In anthropomorphic representation of animals, in addition to displaying propositional content, authors of animal narratives are also dedicated to exhibiting continuity between propositions, making the discursive construction of animals more coherent and convincing. The continuity between propositions, or internal coherence, as Hart (2010) proposes, has relevance to the textual function of language. It is enhanced by using logical connectors and items indicating inferential relationships (Gough & Talbot, 1996). These cohesive devices can be generally divided into lexical type and grammatical type (Halliday & Hasan, 1976). Of special interest to legitimization is the kind of grammatical cohesion.

According to Halliday and Hasan's (1976) categorization, grammatically cohesive devices can be specified into additive, adversative, temporal, and causal conjunctions. Besides, Hart (2010) suggests the conditional "if-then" construction as an addition to the category of causal conjunctions. Among them, additives are exemplified by words such as "and", "or" and "furthermore"; adversatives are signified by "but", "nevertheless" and "however", to name a few; temporal conjunctions comprise lexical items like "since", "after" and "when"; causal conjunctions indicate causal relations, including conjunctions like "because", "so" and "therefore" as well as "if-then" constructions in which "the antecedent 'if-clause' is conventionally inferred as the cause of the situation in the consequent 'then-clause'" (Hart, 2010: 92). Referred to as "logical connectors" (Fairclough, 1989: 109) or "quasi-logical forms" (Hart, 2010), these cohesive markers are deployed for reasoning and reflection. Moreover, the (para)logical vocabulary can be used as adaptive devices for persuasion (Fairclough, 1989; Hart, 2010; Cap, 2013). For Sperber, persuaders "cannot do better than displaying the very consistency—or at least the appearance of it—that their audience is likely to check for" (2000: 136). In the case of discourse production and interpretation, both considered as being "creative, constructive interpretative processes" (Fairclough, 1989: 63), discourse producers are responsible for exhibiting internal coherence of their interpretation of the world in order that the addressees are able to "accept ideational information and accommodate inferences" (Hart, 2010: 92); while discourse recipients are supposed to draw upon socially/discursively constituted knowledge in the top-down processing of discourse interpretation—assumptions and expectations of discourse producers (Gough & Talbot 1996: 225), in order to interpret coherently the interpretation constructed by the addresser. In other words, the coherence of a whole discourse is generated in what Fairclough called "a sort of chemical reaction" between discourse producers and recipients when they share "members' resources" (1989: 65), that is, presupposed social beliefs and ideologies. It is through the cohesive markers that the discourse addressees can trace the cues of the ideologies taken for granted by discourse producers and reproduce the ideologies in the process of interpretation.

5.2.2 Legitimizing anthropomorphic representation of the hound by the use of adversatives in *The Seventh Hound*

The ideologically manipulative effect of cohesive devices is evident in that even if the logical reasoning involved is fallacious, it may still "overcome the logico-rhetorical module on the appearance of rationality" (Hart, 2010: 91). The ideologically relevant property of cohesive markers, which are conducive to achieving "local and global coherence" of discourse, are also recognized by van Dijk (1998). In his words, coherence, realized explicitly by grammatical cohesion, is "both contextually and socially relative, and depends on our ideologically controlled interpretation of the world" (van Dijk, 1998: 206). This is also true when cohesive devices are applied to animal representation in narratives which "provide an important means for constructing social reality in line with one or another group's view of the world" (Hodges, 2018: 680). One example can be found as follows:

(1)召盘巴瞅准这个机会，一个箭步冲上来，举起棍子对准赤利的鼻梁骨砸去。这时赤利如果纵身一跳，可以一口咬定召盘巴的手腕，但它没那样做，而是一偏脑袋，待木棍擦着耳朵落地时，一口咬住木棍不放。(Shen, 1999: 16)

Seizing the opportunity, Zhao Panba took a sudden big stride forward, and aiming at Chili's nose he struck with the stick. At this moment Chili could have jumped up and snapped Zhao Panba's wrist through at one bite, but it did not attack. Instead, it turned its head aside and snatched the stick with its mouth tightly when the stick swished by its ear to the ground. (Shen, 1999: 16)

The above example depicts an episode occurring between the animal protagonist and its master in *The Seventh Hound*. When Zhao Panba found Chili, the descendant of the army dog, he thought he had found a most valuable treasure and expected Chili, the seventh hound, to behave heroically. However, to his disappointment, once when he was in the danger of being attacked by a boar, Chili seemed to shrink back, which turned out to be a misunderstanding though. Filled with an ungovernable rage, Zhao Panba wanted to beat the hound. The excerpt above is a description of how Chili reacted to the unjust treatment from its master. Adversative conjunctions "but" and "instead" in this example help to establish the local coherence of the propositions based on the inference that once a dog is being attacked, no matter whether it is deserved or not, it can be expected that the dog will deliver a counterattack. As such, when attracked, "Chili could have jumped up and snapped Zhao Panba's wrist through at one bite", which is thought to be the mechanically perfect instinct of a dog, an animal endowed with the ability to fight back. A further implicit assumption can thus be drawn from the contrast that the dog went against its biological instinct in that it had a strong affection for its master. In this way, the anthropomorphic representation of dogs as affective and sentient beings is naturalized and legitimized.

5.2.3 Legitimizing anthropomorphic representation of the dog by the use of causal conjunctions in *Dream of the Wolf King*

Discursive construction of this sort is substantially ideological in presupposing a view of the world that is common sense for people. The ideological role of implication inferred by adversatives in this instance is in providing a common-sense reasoning framework in the interest of language users. It can be said that "coherence is based on the interpretation of events as represented in the mental models of the language users, and may therefore also be ideologically influenced" (van Dijk, 1998: 206). That is, strategic use of grammatical connectors to realize coherence depends on language users' ideological orientation, which can be contextually constrained and modified. For example, in narratives, a specific technique is commonly employed that favorable presentation of the animal character could be ideologically inconsistent. Specifically, "in one story, a likeable character may indeed be the carrier of a positive value system, while in another story likeability may incorporate all kinds of negative values" (cf. Herman & Vervaeck, 2005: 122). This is evidenced by another example:

(2)按常理，一条狗是对付不了一匹狼的，狗之所以能在凶猛的野狼面前骁勇善战，那是<u>因为</u>依仗着主人的势力。俗话说狗仗人势。一旦主人没在身旁，狗的威风立刻锐减，由勇敢的斗士变成夹紧尾巴逃命的懦夫。(Shen, 2009: 18)

Normally speaking, a dog is unable to fight against a wolf. The reason why the dog stands in front of a ferocious wolf and appears to be brave and skillful in battle is simply <u>because</u> it has the owner at its back. As the saying goes, "a dog threatens others on the strength of its master's power". Once the owner is not around, the dog's courage immediately fades away. It would turn into a coward with its tail clamped to escape rather than a brave fighter.

At the very beginning of the story *Dream of the Wolf King*, the animal protagonist Zilan suffered from the loss of its spouse when it found itself pregnant. In order to survive together with its unborn baby wolves, Zilan risked hunting red deer raised by human beings. Unfortunately, it was caught and chased by a dog. The example above presents the psychological activity of Zilan after an exhaustive flight from the dog. The causal relation between the two clauses "the dog stands in front of a ferocious wolf and appears to be brave and skillful in battle" and "it has the owner at its back" is explicitly constructed by the casual conjunction "because". Here "because" acts as "reversed causal" conjunction, cueing "the information in the second clause as the cause of the condition in the first" (Gough & Talbot, 1996: 220). Coherence in this case requires the assumption that there is great disparity between dogs and wolves in strength and the inference that dogs are crafty and coward. The positive image of dogs as being courageous and loyal as represented in *The Seventh Hound* is thus subverted.

In animal narratives, it is not unusual to read propositions involving comparisons between dogs and wolfs. These propositions can "cohere cotextually or intertextually and interact cognitively to create further inferences with ideological, argumentational or affective attachments" (Hart, 2010: 11). Similarly, in the story *Dream of the Wolf King*, taking Zilan as the protagonist, discursive construction of dogs aims to serve the purpose of foregrounding positive attributes of wolves by means of implicit or explicit comparison. This is the way how discourse producers manipulatively shape the semantic representation of animals "following a number of strategies that allow the differentiation of importance, focus, foregrounding" (van Dijk, 1998: 238), in addition to the construction of minimal local coherence. Readers are hence manipulated to bring together assumptions and inferences into the process of interpretation, accordingly modifying their mental models and altering their attitudes towards dogs.

5.2.4 Legitimizing anthropomorphic representation of the wolf by the use of "if-then" construction in *Dream of the Wolf King*

Another notable point concerning the ideologically-legitimizing function of internal coherence in shaping the image of dogs is the presupposition of hierarchical relationship between dogs and human beings. Whether the dog is discursively constructed as being loyal or servile is premised upon the idea that dogs are subordinate to people, and the readers are led to interpret the intended message through a speculation based on the accepted premise. Represented as such, dogs are cumulatively stereotyped and meanings that can be attached to them are therefore constrained. The process both embodies and reproduces "human centralism"—discoursal common sense that contributes to sustaining unequal power relations between animals and human beings. Likewise, propositional relationships embodying ideological presupposition and entailment are also expressed in conditional conjunctions to legitimize animal representation.

> (3)假如狼不是自幼便割弃那种强烈的恋母情结，便会削弱它们的独立精神，软化它们桀骜不驯的野性；而狼就是靠这种独立不羁的嗜血本性才得以在充满激烈竞争的环境里生存下来的，这是物竞天择适者生存的结果。(Shen, 2009: 46)
>
> If wolves do not abandon that strong maternal complex from an early age, then their independent spirit will be weakened and their wild nature will be effaced; whereas wolves rely on this independent and wild nature to survive in an environment full of fierce competition, which is the result of natural selection.

Coherence is "a condition of continuity and reproduction" (van Dijk, 1998: 94). In the above portrait of wolves, the conditional "if-then" construction works to establish semantic coherence on the premise that being independent and wild are recognizable attributes of wolves and maternal attachment is detrimental to the qualities. Presuppositions like these provide a common-sense reasoning framework against which specific inferences can be drawn. In view of this, in this example, the situation in the antecedent "if-clause" can be conventionally inferred as the cause of the situation in the consequent "then-clause". Moreover, by using the adversative conjunction "whereas", the consequent "then-clause" coheres with the subsequent proposition which presupposes being independent and wild as vital to the survival of wolves. Thus, the inference that wolves should abandon maternal complex from an early age is legitimized, which in turn reproduces and naturalizes the existing knowledge of wolves that prevails among people.

As is elucidated in these examples, in Shen Shixi's animal narratives, grammatical cohesion is deployed to realize the internal coherence of propositions, and hence to legitimize anthropomorphic representation of animals. Cohesive devices, such as adversatives, "if-then" constructions and casual conjunctions, play a critical role in creating semantic coherence of animal representation, mostly by the way of presupposition, implication and inferencing. The process is substantially ideological, for the reason that "coherence rests on ideologies taken for granted by the text-producer, and which the text-consumer is forced to at least entertain for communicative purposes during the discourse event" (Hart, 2010: 94).

In the same way, legitimizing anthropomorphic representation of animals is also ideologically influenced. On the one hand, animal representation in discourse is context-dependent. Animals can be "deliberately" and "justifiably" represented as the writer requires, leading to specific attitudes readers take towards animals. As Hunston points out, legitimization can be taken as "persuasion of the readership to accept the writer's claim" (1993: 116); on the other hand, legitimization of animal representation is stamped with the ideology of human-centralism which takes its root in acknowledged categorical differences among different species.

5.3 Legitimizing anthropomorphic representation of animals through objectification: The use of evidentiality

5.3.1 Evidentiality and epistemological stance

Apart from displays of internal coherence, the demonstration of external coherence is also crucial to legitimizing anthropomorphic representation of animals in narratives. External coherence indicates "relations of commitment and support for propositions" (Hart, 2010: 10), linguistically expressed by evidentiality and epistemic modality in discourse. Evidentiality and epistemic modality are a pair of different yet closely related concepts, both contributing to the credibility and legitimacy of information provided in discourse. Evidentiality, in its narrow sense, is the linguistic category pertaining to the source of information whereby the language user feels justified to make a factual claim (Anderson, 1986; Marín-Arrese, 2011; Marín-Arrese et al., 2017). More broadly, evidential semantics is extended to cover "its perceptual basis, reliability of knowledge, or the speaker's attitude toward the validity of information" (Langacker, 2017: 18). Even so, it is invariably agreed that encoding the source of information is the default and unmarked interpretation of evidentiality, "evidentiality concerns the speaker's indication of the nature (the type and quality) of the evidence invoked for (assuming the existence of) the state of affairs expressed in the utterance" (Nuyts, 2001: 27). Therefore, even though evidentiality is similarly intended to invoke an epistemic evaluation in discourse consumers in the process of legitimization, different from epistemic modality which is more prone to the explicit operation, evidential strategies incline to achieve legitimization by means of "objectification" (Hart, 2010: 11). It can be said that the use of evidentials "correlates with clarity and transparency in how one knows things" (Aikhenvald, 2018: 35). That is, a major motivation for having evidentials in discourses is to validate the intended knowledge in the communicate proposition. Thus, while using linguistic marking of evidence, discourse producers aim at qualifying the truth of assertions by acknowledging the status of communicated information. To this end, it is a common practice for them to consult an objective authority and make a recourse to "sources of information or bases of knowledge independent of themselves" (Hart, 2010: 173).

The objectiveness of evidentiality is also acknowledged by Givón (2001). As he puts it, "rather than pertaining directly to subjective certainty, ... evidential systems code first and foremost the *source* of the evidence to back up an assertion, and only then implicitly, its *strength*" (Givón, 2001: 326). At the core of evidentials' objectifying epistemic assessment, the degree of credibility of the source as well as mode of access to the information, both of which are considered as fundamental components of evidentiality (Chafe, 1986; Mushin, 2001; Marín-Arrese, 2011; Boye, 2012), matter the most. The two dimensions are closely interwined with each other. It is the dependence on the modes of knowing (direct or indirect) that different types of evidence are designated, triggering varied degrees of reliability of the information source—as Chafe points out, "mode of knowing implies something about reliability" (1986: 266). Evidentiality indicating direct or attested access to source mostly encodes sensory information, including visual, auditory and other sensory types; evidentials implying indirect mode of knowing can be further subdivided into reported information and inferential statements (Willett, 1988). Under the rubrics of indirect evidentiality, reported information "indicates that the speaker has learned about the facts s/he is talking about through communication with others" (Nuyts, 2017: 67), composed of hearsay evidence (secondhand, thirdhand) and folklore; inferential category involves the evidential marking that "has been inferred or deduced through logical reasoning, either from other bits and pieces of information which s/he did perceive directly or from general background knowledge and assumptions" (Nuyts, 2017: 67).

Distinction between indirect and direct evidentiality is also made by Bednarek's (2006) classification of evidentials into perception, proof, obviousness and general knowledge, which is highlighted in the study of Hart (2010). Among these bases of knowledge, "perception" provides attested evidence which can be acquired directly through various perceptual processes, expressed linguistically as "it seems/appears/looks like/sounds like that" or "visibly". Hearsay information drawing upon "general knowledge" is "marked as based on what is regarded as part of the communal epistemic background" (Bednarek, 2006: 640), conventionally indicated by evidential markers such as "as is known to all", "have been said to", "widely-held (opinions)", "everyone knows" and "is supposed to". Apart from "general knowledge", "proof" and "obviousness" represent the indirect means of knowing as well. "Proof" refers to the evidence inferred from results (of studies), statistics, reports which are aimed to "reveal" or "disclose" the facts. "Obviousness" is provoked as reasonably inferred evidence in discourse by indicating "the obviousness or self-evidence of what is modified" (Bednarek, 2006: 641), typically suggested by some lexicalized markers like "obviously", "clearly" or "apparently". Overall, the subdivisions of evidential semantics can be shown in Figure 5.1.

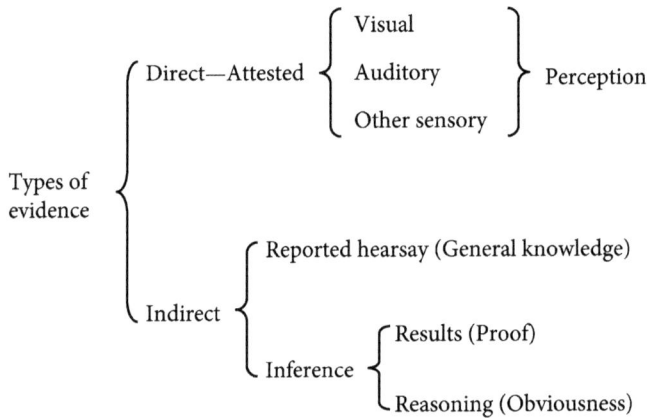

Figure 5.1   Categorization of evidential semantics (Hart, 2010: 95)

These bases of knowledge, relying on the source of evidence and mode of knowing (direct or indirect) accessible to the discourse producers, entail high, medium or low validity (Marín-Arrese, 2011) in the service of providing legitimacy to propositions in different ways. The very legitimizing role of both direct and indirect evidential markers in discourses—their persuasive function to enhance source reliability and information credibility has been stressed in a vast literature (Bednarek, 2006; Hart, 2010; Marín-Arrese, 2011; van Dijk, 2014). It is postulated that evidentiality is of particular importance in strategic discourse, e.g. media and political discourse, in that discourse addressees are able to recognize the strength of evidence "even if they have no confidence at all in the communicator" (cf. Hart, 2010: 94). To put it in another way, evidentiality is subject to creative manipulation, as is claimed, "a speaker can manipulate evidentials, depending on the effect they wish to achieve" (Aikhenvald, 2018: 30). In the expression of evidentiary justification for assertions, evidentials pertaining to the sources of knowledge can be deployed as epistemic resource to "legitimize claims of authority, and to mark explicitly their stance" (Hidalgo-Downing, 2017: 246), and thus exert coercive consequences upon discourse recipients.

As in print news media and political discourse, the correlation of evidentiality and epistemological stance in narratives has got extra attention as well. Storch (2018) emphasizes that manipulating evidential expressions in narratives makes it possible for writers to create multiple perspectives; Mushin states that in narrative retelling epistemological stance "provides the conceptual basis for the distribution of evidential phenomena" (2001: xii). Notably, in exploring the extralinguistic and discourse factors that motivate evidential use in narrative retelling, Mushin (2001) summarizes five types of epistemological stances which are hypothesized to be universal, namely, personal experience (private and perceptual), inferential, reportive, factual and imaginative. All these different types of epistemological stance "involve the representation of knowledge that is the speaker's construal of information acquired in the real world (e.g. representations of actual events) according to its manner of acquisition and the degree to which it is represented as publicly or privately knowable..." (Mushin, 2001: 95). It is at this point that the typologies of epistemological stance and evidentiality correspond with each other: a personal experience epistemological stance concerns the representation of information as the outcome of the conceptualizer's perceptual experience, indexed by the perception type of evidentiality; an inferential epistemological stance is adopted when discourse producers use a range of information acquired by means of reasoning and inferencing evidentials of inference type; a reportive epistemological stance represents knowledge of information as having "become known after the fact" (Mushin, 2001: 88), identical with another kind of indirectly acquired evidentiality—evidentiary support deriving from general knowledge. The slight difference is that factual and imaginative epistemological stances cannot find their clearly defined counterparts in the dimension of evidentiality: factual epistemological stance is reflected in "the *absence* of any representation of the source of information (and its status) in the construal" (Mushin, 2001: 93); imaginative epistemological stance, unique to the genre of fictional story, is a blend of personal experience and factual stances. Overall, the close correspondence between evidentiality and epistemological stance is shown in Table 5.1:

Table 5.1   Correlation of evidentiality and epistemological stance

Types of epistemological stance	Types of evidentiality	Evidential markers
Experience	Perception	it seems/appears/looks like/sounds like that; visibly
Reportive	General knowledge (reported hearsay)	as is known to all; have been said to; widely-held (opinions); everyone knows; is supposed to
Inferential	Proof & obviousness (inference from results or reasoning)	obviously; clearly; apparently
Factual	Absence	—
Imaginative	Blend	once upon a time; other expressive devices

As is shown, evidentiality and epistemological stance are closely related: the adoption of a particular epistemological stance determines the appropriate linguistic coding of information source; the choice of evidential expressions reflects the epistemological stance of discourse producers towards the information. When verbally representing a piece of information in narratives, discourse addressers necessarily take a stand on how to acquire the knowledge, based on which specific evidential strategies will be selected, so as to provide justifiable evidence for the propositions.

5.3.2 Evidential marker "seem" and personal experience stance in legitimizing animal representation

It can be said that discursive legitimization as such involves the pairing of subjectivity (subjective by nature) and objectification (objectified operationally). This is true with legitimizing the anthropomorphic representation of animals in animal narratives. To illustrate with one example:

(4)象冢由于世世代代埋葬老象，每一个象冢里都有几十根甚至上百根象牙，毫不夸张地说，找到一个象冢就等于找到一个聚宝盆。聪明的大象<u>好像</u>知道人类觊觎它们发达的门牙，生怕遭到贪婪的人类的洗劫，<u>通常</u>都把象冢选择在路途艰险人迹罕至的密林深处，再有经验的猎人也休想找得到。(Shen, 2008b: 14-15)

Because generations of elephants have been buried in elephant mounds, each of which has been left with dozens or even hundreds of tusks. It is no exaggeration to say that finding an elephant mound is equivalent to finding a treasure pot. Smart elephants <u>seem</u> to know that humans covet their well-developed teeth. To save their teeth from being ransacked by greedy humans, they <u>usually</u> locate the elephant mounds in the depths of dense forests so that even experienced hunters are not able to find them.

The Last War Elephant depicts the image of a war elephant as a sentient being who plans to bury itself in the place where its fellow soldiers rest in peace. The focal prominence of elephants' subjectivity, one important dimension of anthropomorphic animal representation, is justified and legitimized by the evidential marker "seem". Evidential meaning of "seem" is context-dependent (Lampert & Lampert, 2010). Although predominantly considered as perceptual evidential (Sanders & Spooren, 1996; Hart, 2010), "seem" "often participate[s] in developing non-visual evidentials" (Aikhenvald, 2004: 303). For example, "seem" can indicate "inductive inference" (Chafe, 1986), which is not provoked by visual evidence. Biber et al. (1999) also state that "seem" can be explained in terms of semantic compatibility with "likelihood". Thus, in the case of representing elephants as sentient beings that are cognitively able to "know that humans covet their well-developed teeth", by means of "seem" construction, the writer does not "directly acknowledge experiential role in the acquisition of knowledge" (Mushin, 2001: 99). Rather, he acknowledges the cognitive effort that is applied to develop his construal of the information, making the readers infer that he has evidence to prove the validity of his assertion, which triggers a certain inferred version of reality, thus the resulting belief state can be constructed and "the commitment to the validity of the information is shared or at least potentially shared by the speaker/listener (writer/reader) and other participants" (Sanders & Spooren, 1996: 246).

5.3.3 Evidential marker "usually" and inferential epistemological stance in legitimizing anthropomorphic animal representation

In a similar vein, the word "usually" signals the adoption of an inferential epistemological stance, indicating the acquisition of knowledge via inferencing. Inferencing, a fundamental component of the construction of knowledge representations, "allows people to access 'background' information which is not overtly present either in the immediate physical environment" (Mushin, 2001: 68). As such, the evidential marker "usually" in this example, triggered by an inferential epistemological stance, invites the inference of a causal interpretation: once confronted with potential threat, it is reasonable for one to take precautions. Hence it is not uncommon for elephants to "keep the elephant mounds in the depths of forests". In this way, meaningfulness of elephants' action is foregrounded, which helps to provide evidentiary justification for anthropomorphic representation of elephants as subjective existence with consistent agency.

5.3.4 Reportive evidentials and reportive epistemological stance in legitimizing anthropomorphic animal representation

Another type of commonly seen evidentiality contributing to legitimization of animal representation in Shen Shixi's narratives is evidentials encoding reportive epistemological stance. The adoption of reportive epistemological stance tends to represent knowledge of information "that is not part of the speaker/conceptualizer's direct experience of the information but rather information that has become known after the fact" (Mushin, 2001: 88). Discourse addressers who adopt a reportive stance are regarded as the recipients of the information rather than the origin of knowledge, which brings about the rhetorical effect of "distancing" or "detaching" discourse producers from the information, hence allowing for a relatively objective construal of information. Linguistic coding of reportive epistemological stance is conventionally found in hearsay contexts, embodying general knowledge "based on what is regarded as part of the communal epistemic background" (Bednarek, 2006: 640). In Shen Shixi's writing, to legitimize anthropomorphic representation of animals, information constituting general knowledge is expressed in evidential markers such as "generally speaking" (通常来说), "as the saying goes" (俗话说), "normally speaking" (按理说), "it is known that" (要知道), to name but a few. Four examples are illustrated in the following:

(5)<u>一般来说</u>狗是不敢惹毒蛇的。可是，在这危急关头，赤利不顾一切地蹿上去，一口咬住眼镜蛇的脖颈。(Shen, 1999: 28)

<u>Generally speaking</u>, dogs dare not offend poisonous snakes. However, at this critical moment, Chili dauntlessly preyed on it, gripping the cobra's neck at one bite. (Shen, 1999: 28)

(6)<u>按常理</u>，一条狗是对付不了一匹狼的，狗之所以能在凶猛的野狼面前骁勇善战，那是因为依仗着主人的势力。<u>俗话说</u>狗仗人势。一旦主人没在身旁，狗的威风立刻锐减，由勇敢的斗士变成夹紧尾巴逃命的懦夫。(Shen, 2009: 18)

<u>Normally speaking</u>, a dog is unable to fight against a wolf. The reason why the dog stands in front of a ferocious wolf and appears to be brave and skillful in battle is simply because it has the owner at its back. <u>As the saying goes</u>, "a dog threatens others on the strength of its master's power". Once the owner is not around, the dog's courage

immediately fades away. It would turn into a coward with its tail clamped to escape rather than a brave fighter.

(7)你望着气势汹汹的杰米，心里突然觉得很悲凉。老狼的血腥的恐怖笼罩着鹿群，杰米竟然还有心思来同你争夺王位。<u>要知道</u>，内讧只能加快整个鹿群的灭亡。(Shen, 2017: 29)

You look at the mighty Jiemi, and suddenly feel very sad. At the critical moment when the bloody horror of the old wolf still hangs over the deer herd, it's unexpected that Jiemi has the mind to compete with you for the throne. <u>As is known</u>, internal strife will definitely speed up the demise of the entire herd.

(8)<u>我听说过</u>关于象冢的传说。大象是一种很有灵性的动物，除了横遭不幸暴毙荒野的，都能准确地预感到自己的死期，在死神降临前的半个月左右，便离开象群，告别同伴，走到遥远而又神秘的象冢里去。(Shen, 2008: 12-13)

<u>I've heard</u> *legends* <u>about</u> elephants. Elephant is an animal with internal intelligence. Except for the unfortunate death in the wilderness, they can accurately predict their own death half a month before, then they will leave the elephant herd, say goodbye to their companions, and set out to the distant and mysterious elephant mound.

With evidentials identified in the above examples, the writer's processing of reported information results in reference to an established and reliable state of affairs which is accessible to the readers as well. Based on shared access to the existing and universally accepted knowledge about dogs, elephants and the disastrous effects that internal strife yields, representation of animals can be perceived as most reliable—"the information is considered to be most reliable when it is based on 'the shared (intersubjective)' access to the evidence and when it refers to states of affairs that have already happened" (Usonienė & Šinkūnienė, 2013: 283). Legitimization like this caters to "conformity authorization" (van Leeuwen & Wodak, 1999: 105), resting upon the *ad populum* fallacy that something is true if everybody believes it (van Eemeren et al., 2002: 131).

5.3.5 Evidential-absent assertions and factual epistemological stance in legitimizing anthropomorphic animal representation

A different type of legitimization strategies deployed in Shen Shixi's animal narratives is motivated by factual epistemological stance and corresponds with what van Leeuwen and Wodak refer to as "theoretical rationalization" (1999: 105), that is, legitimization by reference to "the fact of life" (1999: 105). Though closely linked to legitimization-oriented evidentiality, a factual epistemological stance is reflected in the absence of evidential markings. This is mainly because language users can be "motivated to adopt a particular epistemological stance partially on the basis of their source of information, but also on the basis of their rhetorical intentions, [and] on how they want their own utterance to be understood and treated in the moment of the interaction" (Mushin, 2001: 77). The rhetorical purpose of adopting a factual epistemological stance in discourse is to claim authority over the information even though there lacks representation of the source of information (and its status) in the construal. The reason is that adoption of a factual epistemological stance typically entails that the information is assumed to be universally accepted world truth within the speech community. This is particularly evident in the examples representing wolves:

(9)野心勃勃才是狼的本色。只有狗才逆来顺受，才安于现状。(Shen, 2009: 41)

Being ambitious is the nature of wolves. Only dogs meekly submit to oppression and are content with existing state of affairs.

(10)而狼就是靠这种独立不羁的嗜血本性才得以在充满激烈竞争的环境里生存下来的，这是物竞天择适者生存的结果。(Shen, 2009: 46)

It's owing to the independent spirit and unruly bloodthirsty nature wolves depend on that they can survive in an environment full of fierce competition, which is in accordance with the divine law of the survival of the fittest.

(11)狼象征着力量，象征着残暴，狼代表着毁灭和死亡。狼生来就是用强

者的姿态去征服弱者的。(Shen, 2009: 159)

Wolves are the symbols of power, cruelty, destruction and death. Wolves are born to conquer the weak with the posture of the strong.

Epistemological stance "may be expressed by linguistic means which go beyond the traditional definitions of evidential forms" (Mushin, 2001: 100). As is shown in the above three examples, a factual epistemological stance is reflected in evidentials-absent assertions, representing information as if it were describing facts about the wolves. It is precisely based on the premise of a shared epistemic ground about the distinctive traits of wolves that the factual epistemological stance can be adopted, disassociating the writer from the representation and leading to a maximally objective construal. Discursively constructed in this way, images of wolves as being independent, powerful, ambitious and sentient are considered to be credible and unchallengeable. Representations of deer and gorals are legitimized likewise:

(12)由于繁衍后代的强烈本能，在适者生存的遗传规律下，鹿角的第一功能往往胜过第二功能——鹿角趋向于更高大更壮观更漂亮更艺术化，而战斗性能却被削弱了。(Shen, 2017: 17)

With the strong instinct to reproduce the next generation, under the genetic law of survival of the fittest, the first function of a deer's antlers is often better than the second function—antlers tend to be bigger, more spectacular, more beautiful and more artistic, while their lethality in combat is impaired.

(13)斑羚虽有肌腱发达的四条长腿，极善跳跃，是食草动物中的跳远冠军，但就像人跳远有个极限一样，在同一个水平线上，再健壮的公斑羚最多也只能跳出五米的成绩，母斑羚、小斑羚和老斑羚只能跳四米左右。(Shen, 2008a: 66-67)

Gorals had well-developed tendons and four long legs. Also, they were leaping specialists and long-jump champions among all herbivores. Even so, just like humans, they had their limits in how far they could jump. On the same level surface, a strong male goral could at most jump five meters while four meters would be the limit for female/young/aged gorals.

Adoption of factual epistemological stance may not only be purported to be grounded in universally acknowledged "facts" but also be aimed at strategically constructing and transmitting new knowledge. As Sun points out, "evidentiality is ultimately about knowledge packaging and sharing" (2018: 118). The propositions exemplified above focus on presenting "expert knowledge" concerning biological characteristics of gorals and deer which readers supposedly have not been exposed to. In spite of downplaying the nature of the source of information and the way the writer acquires the information, the writer creates "expressive effects" (Hanks, 2014: 7) by means of detailed expressions such as "with the strong instinct to reproduce the next generation, under the genetic law of survival of the fittest", "well-developed tendons", "leaping specialists and long-jump champions", in an attempt to implicitly claim authority over knowledge that is communicated in discourse. In so doing, the writer is able to stand back from the assertion and allow the knowledge they present to "speak for itself". In the meanwhile, he expresses his epistemological stance to "guide the target audience on a topic which is not part of the expert background knowledge of the audience" (Hidalgo-Downing, 2017: 225).

5.4   Legitimizing anthropomorphic representation of animals through subjectification: The use of epistemic modality

5.4.1 Epistemic modality as epistemic resource to evaluate the probability and reliability of propositions

Epistemic legitimization of animal images is principally realized by evidentiality and epistemic modality, depending on "the speaker's claim to have better knowledge, recognition of the 'real' facts" (Chilton, 2004: 117). Evidentiality and epistemic modality are admittedly interwined as expressions of legitimization, which can be used by discourse producers to serve the strategic functions of coercion (Chilton & Schäffner, 1997; Chilton, 2004). Similar to evidentiality, epistemic modality also provides external coherence to assertions and thus makes effective legitimization strategies through displays of epistemic commitment. Nevertheless, in the process of co-constructing legitimization, although both evidentiality and epistemic modality are aimed to invoke an epistemic assessment in discourse addressees, "only epistemic modality involves an explicit evaluation on the text-producer's part" (Hart, 2010: 173). A more clarified distinction between evidentiality and epistemic modality dwells in that they are argued to "serve two different legitimization strategies: 'objectification' and 'subjectification' respectively" (Hart, 2010: 173). Subjectification is defined as "the historical pragmatic semantic process whereby meanings become increasingly based in the speaker's subjective belief state, or attitude toward what is said" (Traugott, 1989: 31). As well, it is succinctly described as "a semantic shift or extension in which an entity originally construed objectively comes to receive a more subjective construal" (Langacker, 1991: 215). In this sense, the notion of subjectification is helpful in explaining how an epistemic proposition can be subjectively construed and manipulatively legitimized.

When it comes to legitimization effected by epistemic modality, subjectification involves foregrounding the discourse producer's role in evaluating the probability and reliability of propositions. Rather than consulting an objective authority, discourse producers tend to "construct themselves as an authority" (Hart, 2010: 173) in epistemic modality. As is pointed out, "the significance of modality is that it 'suggests the presence of an individual subjectivity behind the printed text, who is qualified with the knowledge required to pass judgment" (Fowler, 1991: 64). The subjectivity of epistemic modality entails that the epistemic modal proposition should be perspectival in the very strong sense and is used to convey discourse producers' stance. Stance concerns a subjective component of attitude and assessment; epistemic stance is adopted "on the basis of their (discourse producers) rhetorical intentions, [and] on how they want their utterance to be understood and treated in the moment of interaction" (Mushin, 2001: 58).

As one type of stance resource, epistemic modality deals with one's attitude and estimation of the likelihood of an event and reflects a commitment to the truth and veracity of the proposition designating the event. To be precise, epistemic modality is a category of linguistic meaning embodied by the expression of either possibility or necessity. Epistemic possibility and necessity signal varying degrees of language users' certainty toward the assertions. Epistemic possibility involves "the speaker's logical inference and lack of confidence about the possibility of actualization of propositions" (Silva-Corvalán, 1995: 82), and hence implies a low degree of certainty; epistemic necessity conveys a conventional implicature of strong commitment to propositions, suggesting a high degree of certainty. They can be placed on the two ends of epistemic scale, conceptualized metaphorically in terms of epistemic distance to deictic center (Chilton, 2004; Langacker, 1991). Deictic center refers to "the individual's notion of what is CERTAIN or known reality" (Hart, 2010: 167) in the epistemic modality schema.

Epistemic modality schema is a dynamic cognitive model of the deictic construal operation in which "propositions are conceptualized as located at different points on a reality-irreality scale" (Hart, 2011: 187). In this model, known reality refers to the state of affairs conceived to be real by the conceptualizer (C), and irreality is on the contrary. Immediate reality involves the state of affairs that carry the greatest potential to be perceived as true in that conceptualizer "has perceptual access at the time of the discourse event" (Hart, 2011: 187). This shows that immediate reality can be discursively constructed and contextually determined, functioning as the interface between discourse and known reality. It can be said that immediate reality mirrors reproduced known reality. In discourse, representation of immediate reality counts upon the use of modalized expressions. Strategic use of modality by discourse producers tend to position propositions at more or less distal points relative to known reality, and thus yield intended cognitive effects upon discourse consumers.

As such, deictic construal operation under epistemic modality schema on the one hand presupposes that reality is ever evolving; on the other hand it provides cognitive basis for justifying the very nature of reality as being constructed. As shown in Figure 5.2, known reality depicted as the cylinder keeps growing along the axis indicated by the arrow:

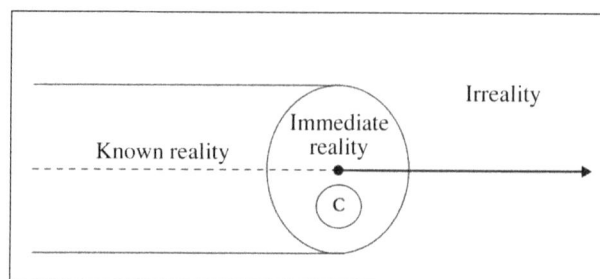

Figure 5.2   Epistemic modality scheme (Hart, 2011: 187)

Therefore, epistemic modality "is a matter of degree" (Hart, 2010: 167), and notions of epistemic possibility and necessity can be conceptualized in terms of remoteness, signifying different degrees of certainty. Epistemic possibility encodes discourse producers' reservations about asserting the truth of the proposition (Coates, 1983: 18-20), thus positioned "far from certain", while epistemic necessity suggests language users' commitment to the validity of the proposition, and thereupon is "close to certain".

5.4.2   Epistemic possibility modals in legitimizing anthropomorphic animal representation

Both epistemic possibility and necessity can be manifested in a wide range of linguistic forms, ranging from the modal auxiliaries, modal adverbs to discourse markers. Paraphrased as "possible that...", epistemic possibility is marked by epistemic modal auxiliaries such as "may", "might" and "could", and the modal adverbs such as "perhaps" and "possibly", which are assessment-sensitive to the likelihood of the proposition and usually used to hint at doubt. Taking "may" as an example. In anthropomorphic representation of animals, the use of "may" is conducive to invoking an epistemic reading which indicates a little less certainty about the possibility of assertions:

(14)狼习惯于用这样的观念对待生与死：活着就是一匹狼，死了就是一堆肉。对死者废物利用，拯救众多的活着的生命，也许还是一种慈悲呢。(Shen, 2009: 37)

Wolves get used to the idea of life and death: one is a wolf only if it is alive; once dead, it is a pile of meat. It may be a kind of compassion to use the waste of the dead and save many living lives.

In the novel *Dream of the Wolf King*, the protagonist Zilan is a female wolf who is determined to groom one of its wolf pups into the next king of wolves. This is bound to be a rocky road especially when its life partner passed away and it has to raise the wolf pups alone. The above example depicts an episode that in order to save itself from starvation and stay alive, Zilan decided to merely treat the dead body of its beloved wolf pup as food. It is never easy to make such a decision, and mental suffering appears to be unavoidable. Though started with the objective knowledge "wolves get used to the idea of life and death", the word "compassion" in the following sentence functions to shift the objective representation to subjective portrait of Zilan's mental activity. This is particularly evident when "may" is deployed to damp down the truth value of the proposition "it is a kind of compassion to use the waste of the dead and save many living lives". Epistemically, "may" is argued to be "situated in the speaker's subjective realm and correspond to 'I think it is likely'"(Traugott, 1997: 190), expressing a greater degree of uncertainty. Even though it semantically situates propositions with possible and low authority at the remote end of the epistemic and authority scales (Werth, 1999: 276), on pragmatical dimension it indicates a conventional implicature of probability. It is this modal marker ambiguity that paradoxically heightens a sense of reliability, whereby coercion can be achieved—readers' supposedly contempt of the wolf's cruelty is manipulatively subverted into the appreciation of its resolution and mercy. In addition, the image of the wolf as sentient beings is justifiably constructed in an implicit way: Zilan's "misconduct" is not out of biological need but for a reasonable intention.

Apart from epistemic modal auxiliaries, modal adverbs are also valuable resources to legitimize the anthropomorphic representation of animals. Here is an example to illustrate:

(15)也许，这正是命运对自己野心的一种惩罚。它在同命运的抗争中又输了一个回合，输得够惨的。不，它紫岚是不会服输的，优秀的狼是永远不会在厄运面前屈服的！(Shen, 2009: 58)

Perhaps this may be a punishment from fate—because of its ambition. It lost another round in the struggle against fate, a complete loss this time. No, it will not admit defeat: a brilliant wolf will not give in to bad luck.

The use of the epistemic expression "perhaps" in the context can be viewed as a case of strategic mitigation—"perhaps" can be used strategically to "mitigate unfavorable or compromising information" (Carretero, 1996: 258). By "mitigation", it means that the epistemic possibility modal "perhaps" attempts to cast doubt and uncertainty on the proposition "this is a punishment from fate". The discourse producer's commitment to the propositional information is further reduced when "perhaps" works collaboratively with "may" as harmonic combination (Halliday, 1970). Together they act to "open up the dialogic space to alternatives" (Simon-Vandenbergen & Aijmer, 2007: 43). The "dialogically expansive" (White, 2003: 261) expression implicates an intersubjective stance, invoking "an implicit conceptualizer, which may be construed as virtual or generalized" (Marín-Arrese, 2011: 194). Thereby discourse producers presuppose the message that "those who dare to defy fate will get punished" as tacitly shared by discourse recipients, from which the expectation that "the wolf will resign itself to its fate particularly when 'it lost another round in the struggle against fate'" arises. It is evidenced by the combined use of epistemic possibility modals and the negation. "Negation always presupposes its counterpart in the discourse" (Simon-Vandenbergen & Aijmer, 2007: 190). When used in combination with negation, "perhaps" and "may" function as a concessive, i.e. in the sense of "although", and can be explained "not in terms of Speculative, but of Presupposed" (Palmer, 2001: 31), paradoxically acting to increase the emphasizing force of the counter-expectation.

The commitment of the discourse producer to the propositional information which counters the presupposed expectation is implied in the negative form of another modal marker "will". Compared to "may" and "perhaps", the modal verb "will" "expresses much stronger epistemic commitment" (Hart, 2010: 175). The epistemic use of "will" is largely manifested as making an inference, signaling language user's confidence in what to be drawn as a conclusion. As is postulated, "will" "communicates with complete conviction the definiteness of the future event" (Hart, 2010: 176). Thus, in this example, by deploying it, the sense of certainty inherent in "will" operates over the claim "No, it will not admit defeat: a brilliant wolf will not give in to bad luck", showing the discourse producer's high commitment to the proposition. In this case, the image of a wolf as being remarkably relentless and resilient is constructed. Furthermore, given that "will" is inclined to draw an inference from generally known facts (Palmer, 2001: 53), the intended representation of the wolf is implicitly endowed with legitimized authority, yielding an actuality entailment and taken as common sense.

5.4.3 Epistemic necessity modals in legitimizing anthropomorphic animal representation

As can be seen from Example 15, not merely epistemic possibility contributes to the legitimization of animal representation, but also epistemic necessity plays a role. Epistemic necessity expresses "universal quantification over possible worlds" (Mucha & Zimmermann, 2016: 31). It pertains to strong inferences or deductions made by the speaker about the truth of the proposition expressed, and can be paraphrased as "the only possible conclusion is that…".

Epistemic necessity modals share the common semantic element of strong necessity, typically exemplified by modal verbs such as "should" and "must" as well as modal adverbs like "undoubtedly", "certainly" and "definitely". In animal narratives, to endorse the anthropomorphic representation of animals, the writer attempts to substantiate the claims by resorting to different epistemic necessity modal operators. The following is an example:

(16)不能再这样和老狼拼消耗了，该想个办法。你是智慧出众的鹿王，你应当运用你的智慧来克敌制胜的，你想。(Shen, 2017: 78)

Stop fighting with the old wolf through the process of attrition. It is time to come up with a better solution. You are the deer king with brilliant wisdom, and you <u>should</u> use your wisdom to defeat your opponent, you think.

The example is extracted from *The Old Hark*. Suffering from the grave threat posed by the wolf, Hark, as the king of the deer, is determined to sacrifice its life to save the deer herb. Considering the inborn discrepancy in strength between the wolf and the deer, he is at a disadvantage in the battle against the wolf. Confronted with the adverse situation, Hark is pondering about how to turn things around. The example depicts Hark's mental activity, semantically indexed by the predicate "think". It is through the portrayal of Hark's mental world that the animal's subjective agency springs onto the paper. To legitimize the representation of the deer's subjectivity in an epistemic sense, the modal "should" is employed. "Should", "notionally one of the modal-past forms of MUST" (Palmer, 2001: 222), expresses deductive epistemic inference, which is based on a hypothesis rather than on evidence (Chafe, 1986). Chafe describes this mode of knowing as involving "an intuitive leap to a hypothesis from which conclusions about evidence can be deduced" (1986: 269). This is evident in the case of the factual use of "should". Factual uses of "should" are concerned with what calls "putative should", referring to the "putative situations that are recognized as possibly existing or coming into existence" (Quirk et al., 1985: 1014). In the example, the context is (or seems) factual—"you are the deer king with brilliant wisdom". The writer somewhat distances himself from the reality he is commenting upon (the identity of Hark as a deer king with brilliant wisdom) and mentally positions himself before that reality. That is, he feels as if he were personally on the scene where the brilliant group leader, who is in a physically inferior position, has to make a sensible assessment of the situation and decide how to outplay the opponent in the battle. And, as at that moment no decision has yet been made, the use of "should" is possible in that the meaning of "should" is embodied with both the hypothetical and temporal value (Palmer, 2001). In this way, the logic between the fact and the deductive inference is verified.

The logic necessity expressed in "should" is further strengthened in the case of the second-person pronoun use where the discourse recipient's position is consulted. The second-person pronoun "you" is deployed pragmatically to invoke empathy and to check on shared background information, contributing to the reliability of the proposition in collaboration with the use of "should". As such, the image of Hark as a sentient being endowed with the ability of logical reasoning is implicitly justified.

Another way of indicating epistemic necessity is by using "must". Epistemic "must" is critical to the development of the epistemic reading in that it represents "widescope general objective necessity" (Narrog, 2012: 177). It is also observed as conveying "the speaker's confidence in the truth of what he is saying, based on a deduction from facts known to him (which may or may not be specified)" (Coates, 1983: 41). In a similar vein, Langacker postulates that "must" places the proposition "very close to known reality—the speaker has deduced that accepting it as real seems warranted" (1991: 246). Following the line, it can be argued that epistemic necessity indicated by "must" is not merely concerned with objective verifiability in terms of knowledge but also related to the language user's subjective inference, hence can be paraphrased as something like "based upon what I know the only conclusion I can draw is...". A prototypical example can be found as follows:

(17)我想，此时此刻，它一定又看到了二十六年前惊天地泣鬼神的一幕：威武雄壮的战象驮着抗日健儿，冒着枪林弹雨，排山倒海般地冲向侵略者……
(Shen, 2008b: 16)

I guess, at this moment, it must have recalled the memory of the world-shaking battle occurring 26 years ago: the mighty and majestic war elephant carried anti-Japanese fighters, braved the rain of guns and bullets, and rushed to the invaders with the momentum of a landslide and the power of a tidal wave.

The Last War Elephant tells the story about a dying elephant who once joined the War of Resistance Against Japanese Aggression. As an elephant, it is supposed to bury itself in the elephant mound. Out of "my" expectation, it walked to the battlefield where it fought with its comrades side by side years ago, and decided to be buried there. The intentionality of the elephant's behaviors before its death is confirmed and foregrounded in the above description of "my" thought towards it. The word "guess" is an initiate of the thought, and the modal "must" invite an epistemic interpretation of "my" representation of the elephant, which is essentially an inference from known facts.

The notion of deduction or inference from known facts is the basic feature of "must" (Palmer, 2001: 53). In other words, with "must", "there is often some indication of the facts (often observable) on which the inference is based" (Palmer, 2001: 34). In this example, the known facts that "my" inference draws upon are the details depicting the elephant's behaviors before it launched the journey to the end of its life, i.e. its perseverance in wanting back its saddle, its heading for the battlefield, and the like. It is from these behaviors that a firm conclusion can be drawn—the elephant is a conscious being. Thus, as a conscious being, it is logically reasonable for the last war elephant to recall the memory of the world-shaking battle occurring 26 years ago. As such, "must" entails both the epistemic necessity and inferential reasoning (Simon-Vandenbergen & Aijmer, 2007: 288). It is the inference and confidence expressed by "must" that the anthropomorphic representation of the elephant as a sentient being can be interpreted as epistemically true and necessary.

In addition to modal verbs, adverbs of certainty are equally important in signaling epistemic necessity. Adverbs of certainty express language users' strong commitment to the truth of the assertion. They are used to serve the purpose of "rhetorical strategizing" (Simon-Vandenbergen & Aijmer, 2007: 42), functioning as strategies of persuasion, manipulation, negotiating and confrontation. Among various modal adverbs indicating epistemic necessity, "undoubtedly" is a typical one, which has a core role in legitimizing the anthropomorphic representation of animals in Shen Shixi's novels. For example,

(18)你心里出现一架天平，价值就是重量。王位固然有其特殊价值，但种族的生存和繁荣无疑要比王位的价值大得多。(Shen, 2017: 37)

There is a balance in your heart, and value is weight. Although the throne has its special value, the survival and prosperity of the deer herd is <u>undoubtedly</u> much greater than the value of the throne.

The modal adverb "undoubtedly", bearing the meaning of "less than absolute certainty", marks the discourse producer's "strong belief in the statement, on the basis of experience or probability" (Simon-Vandenbergen & Aijmer, 2007: 135). The unavoidable nature of the information suggested by "undoubtedly" entails that it presupposes an expectation that is accepted and shared by everyone. In this example, the presupposed expectation evoked by "undoubtedly" is that "collective interest far outweighs individual gain". Then it makes sense that Hark, the deer king, decided to give up the throne and sacrifice its life for the sake of the survival of the whole herd. In this way, the image of Hark as an unselfish being who exclusively keeps the public interests in mind is constructed and readers are covertly persuaded into taking the image as true.

The persuasive power is strengthened particularly when "undoubtedly", a negative expression, is applied in a highly interactional and heteroglossic context, i.e. a context of situation where there is a second person subject. This is because the kind of combination "conveys the need felt by the speaker to convince the addressee" (Simon-Vandenbergen & Aijmer, 2007: 125) as well as the need to present a stronger argument "to foresee and so forearm oneself against foreseen denial" (Downing, 2001: 257).

Notably, in expressing epistemic necessity, what also deserves attention is "unmodalized" or zero-marked propositions. An "unmodalized" proposition is "an expression of epistemic evaluation taken as an indicator of the speaker's claim to categorical truth" (Hart, 2010: 177). That is, the zero-marked option indicates the language user "accepts the designated process as part of known reality" (Langacker, 1991: 245). The total epistemic commitment expressed in unmodalized assertions is conducive to assigning the statements with veridicality, yielding the effect of legitimization. In Shen Shixi's animal narratives, unmodalized propositions are preferred especially when the writer attempts to narrate animals in an omniscient perspective. Taking the construction of the wolf image as an example:

(19)而狼就是靠这种独立不羁的嗜血本性才得以在充满激烈竞争的环境里生存下来的，这是物竞天择适者生存的结果。(Shen, 2009: 46)

Wolves rely on this independent and unruly cruelty to survive in a highly competitive environment, which is the result of natural selection.

(20)它是母狼，摆不脱母性的担忧。(Shen, 2009: 54)

It is a mother wolf, not to be out of maternal concern.

(21)狼只遵循弱肉强食的丛林法则。强者就是法律，力量就是真理。(Shen, 2009: 64)

Wolves follow only the jungle law that the weak are the prey of the strong. The strong are the law, and the strength is the truth.

The above examples represent straightforward statements of what the wolf should be like: being independent, unruly, cruel, physically and mentally strong, and sentient. The absence of any modal expressions in the propositions "communicates a categorical truth claim in a subjectification strategy" (Hart, 2010: 178), and hence the veridicality of anthropomorphic representation of the wolf is tacitly ensured. In addition, it is noteworthy that the use of zero-marked modality can be commonly found in representing animals with special reference to human society:

(22)紫岚最偏爱黑仔。这倒不是因为黑仔是长子，<u>人类社会讲究长幼次序，狼群中不讲这套。</u> (Shen, 2009: 39-40)

Zilan loves Heizai the most. This is not because it is the eldest son. <u>Human society holds respect for seniority rule; wolves do not.</u>

(23)<u>狼毕竟是狼，既不守礼节，也不讲贞操，在异性之间的交往中，只按快乐原则行事。</u> (Shen, 2009: 73)

<u>Wolves, after all, are wolves, neither morality-abiding nor chastity-respecting.</u> In the heterosexual communication, they live up to the principle of happiness.

(24)对紫岚来说，小宝贝能否平安出世自己是无能为力的。<u>狼毕竟是狼，没有人类那套科学的完善的接生方法，它只能靠命运。</u> (Shen, 2009: 3)

For Zilan, whether the baby can be born safely is out of its control. <u>Wolf is a wolf after all. In the wolf community, there is no set of scientific and perfect method of birth giving as in the human society. It is all about destiny.</u>

In making comparisons between animal characters and humans, zero-marked modality exemplified in these statements presents the difference as self-evident or as shared-knowledge. The difference, as is shown, is striking, and can be traceable in a wide range of aspects, i.e. "respect for seniority rule" "heterosexual communication" "birth giving", and the like. The disclosure of the difference between animal characters and humans serves to achieve dual effects: on the one hand, it is explicitly intended to represent animals as courageous who dare to resist against fate; on the other hand, it draws a distinctive dividing line between humans and animals—human beings are regarded as more "advanced". In this way, human species' superiority over other species is manifestly suggested. Expressed as "unmodalized", this implied message is constructed as "taken-for-granted" rather than "currently at issue or up for discussion" (Martin & White, 2005: 101). The zero-marked propositions are dialogically contractive in essence in that they "act to close down or contract the space for the alternatives" (White, 2003: 268).

5.5   Summary

Legitimization involves strategies used to endorse representations in discourse. In animal narratives, legitimization strategies provide felicity conditions under which anthropomorphic representation of animals can be accepted as true, and hence contribute to the macro-strategy of coercion. The strategies are manifested in animal narratives, as in most other discourses, through grammatical cohesion, evidentiality and epistemic modality. The use of grammatical cohesion is helpful in legitimizing anthropomorphic representation of animals through implication, presupposition and inferencing; the use of evidentiality is crucial to legitimizing anthropomorphic representation of animals through objectification; and the use of epistemic modality plays a central role in legitimizing anthropomorphic representation of animals through subjectification. The process of legitimization imbues discursive construction of animals with evidence, authority and truth, by which discourse consumers are persuaded into accepting particular construal of real animals and particular value evaluation about animals. The effects legitimization strategies impose upon readers' attitude towards animals are paradoxical: on the one hand, animals are justifiably represented as sentient beings as humans; on the other hand, it is implicitly implied yet incontrovertibly true that animals are inferior to human beings. To better understand how legitimized anthropomorphic animal representation in Shen Shixi's animal narratives shapes readers' outlook of animals, an elaboration on metaphorical conceptualization is necessary, which, when legitimization is achieved, will provide the link between language and ideology.

Chapter 6 Metaphorical Conceptualization of Anthropomorphic Representation of Animal Images

6.1 Introduction

Metaphor is pervasive in people's life. Traditionally, it has long been recognized as an aesthetic ornament which is frequently employed discursively in rhetorical and argumentative language. Insights from recent cognitive-semantic studies on metaphor have made crystal clear its flexibility as both a cognitive and a linguistic device, stressing that metaphor is a universal means of construing phenomena in the world. The view of metaphor as a device for conceptualization, known as Conceptual Metaphor Theory (CMT), is introduced by Lakoff and Johnson (1980), who argue that metaphors play a dynamic role in shaping and influencing our perception of the world. Under the framework of CMT, metaphor is first and foremost a matter of cognition, which is applicable for structuring, restructuring and even creating reality as a conceptual tool. The conceptual key of metaphor is a "conceptual mapping" between a source (concrete) domain and a target (abstract) domain. It is the systematic set of correspondences between two domains of experience that affords possible motivations for meaning. The very experiential and embodied view of conceptual metaphors thus provides "a new framework for thinking about meaning" (Colston, 2021: 409) and hence arguably brings about a paradigm shift in studies on metaphor. Within the "conceptual metaphor paradigm", research on the ideological aspect of metaphor gains a rising focus

(Wolf & Polzenhagen, 2003). It is claimed that the interest in the ideological function of metaphor use properly matches one of the fundamental tenets of CMT that "metaphors play a central role in the construction of social and political reality" (Lakoff & Johnson, 1980: 159). More specifically, conceptualizations invoked by metaphors compress complex social practice into simple and tangible mental models, which "provide a particular ideologized world view and act as heuristics legitimating social action" (Hart, 2014b: 161).

The ideological relevance of metaphors is also recognized and emphasized by a wide array of approaches, i.e. pragmatics, functional linguistics and CDS. The pragmatic approach to investigating metaphor holds that discourse producers "use metaphor to persuade by combining the cognitive and linguistic resources at their disposal" (Charteris-Black, 2004: 11). From the functional perspective, metaphor is "intimately bound with attitude and is a primary resource for the expression of affect, judgment and appreciation" (Hart, 2014b: 143) and hence enacts part of the ideology of discourses. The view of metaphor as a means to express ideology is in particular highlighted within the realm of CDS. CDS is dedicated to revealing underlying ideologies, attitudes and beliefs—and therefore constitutes a critical way of understanding more about the intricate connection between language, thought and social context. CDS researchers regard metaphor as vital in creating a coherent presentation of reality—the "order of discourse" in Foucault's term. It is claimed that in constructing reality, "metaphor choice is motivated by ideology" (Charteris-Black, 2004: 247). Balkin also postulates that metaphor should be regarded as a cognitive mechanism of ideology, which can yield ideological effects (1998: 112-113, 243-248). Therefore, critical studies of metaphor may reveal the underlying intentions of the discourse producer and "serve to identify the nature of particular ideologies" (Charteris-Black, 2004: 28).

Critical Metaphor Analysis (CMA), a term coined by Charteris-Black (2004), thus opens up possibilities for alignment between CMT and CDS, drawing upon their common feature—both believe that "discourse/metaphor constructs or confers a reality or a folk model rather than simply describing it" (Goatly, 2007:

3). It can be said that CMA suggests an approach to metaphor analysis aiming to reveal the covert intentions of discourse producers. The value of CMA lies in that it enables people to be aware of the subliminal role of metaphorical patterns in representing and shaping ideologies and social practices. As well, increased awareness of metaphor through CMA "offers alternative ways of understanding the world we live in" (Charteris-Black, 2004: 243).

From a critical perspective, one dimension CMA scholars take most interest in is the discourse model of metaphor. Discourse metaphors are "verbal expressions containing a construction that evokes an analogy negotiated in the discourse community" (Zinken, 2007: 445). In constructing the cognitive basis of ideology, discourse metaphors interact with analogical network and co-evolve in conjunction with the socio-cultural environment where they are situated. Discourse metaphors thus bear out the socio-cultural situatedness of metaphorical reasoning. The importance of discourse metaphor as a carrier of cultural beliefs and social representations is specific to social, political and literary discourses.

In literary context, discourse metaphors can be used deliberately to modularize the readers' outlook on the referent which is the target of the metaphor, acting as "part of the common conceptual apparatus shared by members of a culture" (Lakoff & Turner, 1989: 51). This is also true with animal narratives. In animal narratives, metaphor is extensively used in the anthropomorphic representation of animals, constituting aspects of animal world and inviting readers to look at animals from an intended perspective. Metaphor is therefore considered to be an ideal cognitive resource of conceptualizing animals in animal narratives. It is through metaphor that anthropomorphic representation of animals establishes interrelationships between animal and human domains and hence enables readers to construe the constituted reality about animals in discourse. To achieve this, it involves two main metaphorical patterns or "themes", namely "humans are animals" and "animals are more or less the same as humans". Each particular metaphor theme in animal representation entails and encourages specific ideological inferences, providing cognitive framework for people's view of animals.

6.2 Metaphor as the way of conceptualizing animals in animal narratives

6.2.1 Metaphor as ideological conceptualization of animal images in narratives

Narratives always intersect with cognition for the reason that they "represent the workings of the conceptual system of writers" (Csábi, 2014: 214) and "are the products of [their] cognizing minds" (Freeman, 2000: 253). In the dimension of narrative interpretation, it is found that the human conceptual system plays a significant role. As is argued, the interpretations of narratives are "the products of other [readers'] cognizing minds in the context of the physical and socio-cultural worlds in which they have been created and are read" (Freeman, 2000: 253). Therefore, "narrative cannot happen without cognition" (Trites, 2014: 5). Along with the increasing awareness of the importance of cognition in narratives, the demand for investigation into how discursive representation in narratives is conceptualized and what conceptual tools are deployed grows as well.

Conceptualization involves "the cognitive process of forming mental representations during discourse" (Hart, 2010: 10). Instead of being a direct reflection of reality, conceptualization encodes various construals and perspectives taken towards representation, and hence is inherently ideological. Discourse producers are endowed with a degree of choice in the conceptualization they intend to invoke in the addressees. Ideological conceptualization of discursive representation is realized through a spectrum of means and strategies. Among various tools, metaphorical language functions at the level of representation, encoding ideological conceptualizations.

Literary discourse abounds in metaphors. Metaphors in literature "straddle the divide between the art of persuasive argumentation [rhetoric] and the study of artistic creativity [poetics]" (Caracciolo, 2017: 207). To the ends of both persuasion and artistic effects, literary texts feature the creative deviation from ordinary language (Miall & Kuiken, 1994). The very conceptual resource they attend to when using metaphor is people's everyday metaphorical conceptual system, viewed as "part of people's enduring knowledge structures and to be a constitutive factor of all kinds of cognitive processes, including language use, reasoning, and the exercise of the imagination in literature" (Steen, 2009: 25). This is why literature, narrative included, is "perhaps the most obvious area in which conceptual metaphors can be found" (Kövecses, 2010: 71), and "the notion of conceptual metaphor is extremely important in the study of literary texts" (Kövecses, 2010: 274). It is argued that the function of conceptual change metaphor performs is closely aligned with the potential effects of literature as "schema refreshment" (Cook, 1994). In other words, literature and metaphor bear structural resemblance in perspective changing. The conventional conceptual cross-domain mappings form the foundation upon which unconventional(ized) metaphorical expressions in literature function to give novel insights and perspectives into human experience and thereupon bring about a form of conceptual change which invites readers to view aspects of reality in a new light. In this respect, discursive representation realized through metaphors in narrative context "allows authors and readers to experiment with beliefs, values and worldviews from a 'safe' distance" (Caracciolo, 2017: 211). This is, from a critical viewpoint, a process of covert ideological manipulation. As such, anthropomorphic representation of animals in animal narratives, which concerns a fundamental conceptual mapping between human and animal domains, will probably lead to ideological reconfiguration, influencing people's beliefs about animal world and their understanding of the relationship between humans and animals.

6.2.2 Discourse metaphor networks as networked conceptual constructs of anthropomorphic animal images

Representing animals as human-like in literary discourse is, among a great variety of metaphoric labels, one of the most relevant and recognized usage of metaphors. As a special genre of literary discourse, animal narrative, which attempts to close the ontological gap between humans and animals (at least it seems to be so), is dedicated to exhibiting correspondences between animal and human attributes and behaviors. Anthropomorphic representation of animals thus plays a crucial role.

Anthropomorphism refers to the attribution of human personality or characteristics to non-human objects, implying a spiritual or an existential analogy between humans and nonhumans. Analogy is argued to "play a fundamental role in some of the most impressive capabilities of the human mind" (Zinken, 2007: 445). Cognitively, the supposed analogy underlying anthropomorphic representation of animals entails a propositionally explicated conceptual mapping between the domains of human and animal, which is evoked by discourse metaphors in animal narratives. Discourse metaphors, serving as the prompt to "construct an analogical meaning that has been negotiated in the discourse" (Zinken, 2007: 450), are involved in the formation of conceptual network composed of cognitive artefacts which pop up dynamically as discourse unfolds. Metaphorical network in discourse, or metaphorical paranarrative (Biebuyck & Martens, 2011), consists of a set of connected metaphors that "stands in a complex relation to other aspects of literary narrative, enriching and complicating its meanings" (Caracciolo, 2017: 211). The networked configuration of conceptual constructs built up by discourse metaphors, together with the cognitive constants embedded in a relatively stable reservoir of cultural beliefs and social representations, acts to shape readers' construal of what is represented in discourse.

As such, in the context of animal narratives, the uncanny conceptual changing power metaphors possess is exhibited in discourse metaphor networks thematized as "humans are animals" and "animals are more or less the same as humans" respectively. Under the rubric of "humans are animals", metaphorical expressions in anthropomorphic animal representation are categorized as "impositive" metaphors which tend to project traits of human societies onto the animal groups (Goatly, 2006). The other type of metaphorical network taking "animals are more or less identified with humans" as the topic theme is related to "approximative" metaphors—connected metaphors foregrounding the subjectivity of animals, implicating that a belief human holds is readily found in animals. "Approximative" metaphor can be explained as follows:

> Depending on one's beliefs and ideology, one might see more or less grounds of similarity between the target and source. So if one were to see many salient and important grounds the metaphor would, perhaps, approximate to a literal statement, paraphrased "X is more or less Y". (Goatly, 2006: 17)

In animal narratives, impositive and approximative metaphors help to open up the analogical space between humans and animals. The different metaphorical patterns (or conceptual metaphor themes) they fall into establish a productive tension between the human perspective and the animal perspective in anthropomorphic representation of animals, leading to a perspectivated construal of the relationship of humans with the animal realm. As is argued, metaphorical patterns "can be employed to project a characteristic and partly deviant mind style" (Semino & Swindlehurst, 1996: 164). As such, metaphors in animal narratives become bound up with the perspectival nature of literary discourse—they conceptualize reader's interpretation of the overall discourse as well as modulate reader's perspective about the animal world. That is, the conceptualizations that metaphors invoke in anthropomorphic representation of animals give rise to certain mental models which "provide a particular ideologized world view and act as heuristics legitimating social action" (Hart, 2014b: 161).

6.2.3 Conceptual blending operation in the construal of anthropomorphic animal images

As a construal operation grounded in the universal ability to compare experience, the ideological and legitimating role that metaphor plays in shaping and structuring reader's understanding of animal representation in narratives seems to be evident. What needs further consideration is how metaphorical conceptualization that takes effect on reader's cognition emerges from the online processing of linguistic stimuli and contextual factors. In regard to this, Cognitive Blending Theory (CBT) offers an account of the dynamic process of online meaning construction via metaphor-mappings. It is contended that "metaphorical thought may be a special case of 'blending'" (Chilton, 2005b: 24). Conceptual blending operation represents "a viable mechanism for unpacking and relating the multifarious components of concepts" (White & Herrera, 2003: 319), which deals with a projection of conceptual structure from two (or more) mental spaces into a third blended space bringing about an emergent structure (Fauconnier & Turner, 2002). Invoked by metaphorical expressions, the ad hoc structure emerging from the blending network can "constitute more stable structures that make up world view encoded in cognitive frames and conceptual metaphors" (Hart, 2010: 142). Therefore, conceptual blending becomes an appropriate choice for describing meaning emergence and ideology construction. As the online construal operation, it serves to offer explanations for the ideological and legitimating functions of metaphor in discourse in that "the dynamic conceptualization invoked by metaphor provides a local guide for thinking, feeling and acting" (Hart, 2010: 142). In view of that, CBT is counted as a productive interpretive framework in a wide range of research fields and has been "fruitfully applied to works of literature" (Dancygier, 2014: 301). It is, then, also applicable to explaining the process in which metaphor works to guide readers' knowledge and belief about animal group at different ideological directions through anthropomorphic representation of animals in narratives.

In a nutshell, that metaphor is a way of conceptualizing animals in animal narratives is closely related to the notions of conceptual metaphor and blending. The former pertains to relatively stable conceptual organization while the latter stresses the dynamic process of conceptualizing. The relationship between them is intricate and dialectical (Hart, 2010: 121-124). In understanding how anthropomorphic representation of animals is construed, conceptual blending is powerful in disclosing the way mental spaces evoked by metaphors are blended into one coherent interpretation on the one hand; on the other hand, conceptual metaphor as an abstracted blending pattern defines the possibilities of particular blends and contributes to the systematicity of metaphorical expressions in animal representation.

6.3   Impositive metaphor "humans are animals": Conceptualizing animal world as the projected human society in *Dream of the Wolf King*

6.3.1 Metaphor of competition and success in *Dream of the Wolf King*

Narrative, as a form of literature, is "no less than a joint endeavor" (Werth, 1999: 48) of writer and reader given that "literature is designed to be re-read, re-interpreted, representing its own revisitable textual context" (Csábi, 2013: 211). Representation constructed discursively in narrative acts as "a guide for the conceptualizations built up in the minds of the spatio-temporally displaced writer and reader" (Lahey, 2013: 288). This is obvious in the context of animal narratives. In animal narratives, anthropomorphic representation of animals suggests a controversial manner of representation which could be interpreted as literal or metaphorical (Crist, 1999). Anthropomorphic way of representation embodies an approach to knowing animals that affirms a powerful alignment between humans and animals, drawing upon their underlying analogies or similarities which are encapsulated in the statement "humans are animals". Construals of "humans are animals" vary—some regard human as literally sophisticated animals on the basis of evolutionary continuity while others view this metaphorically. Diverse as they are, it is agreed that metaphorical interpretations of "humans are animals" construct and reproduce ideologies and justify or reproduce certain behaviors (Fairclough, 1989; Gibbs, 1999). In particular, the metaphor "humans are animals" connoted in anthropomorphic representation of animals brings a reality about animals into being. And ideologically how it is exploited in animal narratives to promote one particular image of reality over another is worth exploration.

The ideological aspect of metaphor use in anthropomorphic representation is well demonstrated by the impositive "humans are animals" metaphor. "Impositives" (Mack, 1975: 248) highlight the ideological orientation of metaphors; impositive metaphors are "expressions of desirability and idealism rather than statements of a perceived reality" (Goatly, 2006: 17). Within the impositive metaphor "humans are animals", "traits of human societies are projected onto the animal groups under consideration, to create a hyponymic relationship, if not a synonymous one, maximizing the comparison into something more literal" (Goatly, 2006: 19). The metaphorical projection of values and structure of current human society onto animal group encourages an apprehension of the social world as a natural world, "dissolving the ontological boundaries between the different species so that the non-human animal can be viewed and measured in terms of the human" (Danta, 2018: 2). Instead of naively conflating human and animal qualities, this kind of cross-space mapping between biological and social knowledge counts upon an extended metaphorical network thematized as "humans are animals". The concatenation of semantically related metaphorical expressions connected to a wide range of aspects of contemporary life work together in describing a coherent scenario, contributing to the metaphorical theme "humans are animals".

Among an extensive array of correspondence established between animal and human, grounds of competitiveness and aggression "often seem to project features of human society on to animal" (Goatly, 2006: 17). Stressing competitiveness and aggression as the intrinsic features shared by human and animals is closely related to the notions of "evolutionary continuity" and "natural selection" proposed by Darwin. It is held by Darwinism that life is a struggle in which only the fittest survive. In order to survive, animals are bound to be competitive and aggressive. It follows that given the presupposition that humans are sophisticated animals, the ways in which animals behave are natural to humans. As such, competitiveness and aggression are viewed as a natural, biological phenomenon that is an outcome of the human evolutionary heritage. The evolutionary continuity between animals and humans has received resounding affirmation in anthropomorphic representation of animals which puts significant emphasis upon constructing metaphor of competitiveness and aggression through a prolific set of related metaphors such as "life is struggle", "the strong is the winner", "activity is fighting", "fate is enemy", and the like. Telling evidence can be found in the following examples:

(1)假如狼不是自幼便割弃那种强烈的恋母情结，便会削弱它们的独立精神，软化它们桀骜不驯的野性；而狼就是靠这种独立不羁的嗜血本性才得以在充满激烈竞争的环境里生存下来的，这是<u>物竞天择适者生存</u>的结果……对幼狼来说，吃奶实际上是一种<u>生存预习</u>。(Shen, 2009: 46)

If wolves are not free to abandon that strong maternal complex, it will weaken their independent spirit, soften their unruly wildness; while wolves rely on this independent and unruly bloodthirsty nature to survive in a highly competitive environment, which is the result of <u>the natural selection of the fittest</u>... For young wolves, <u>feeding is actually a survival preview</u>.

(2)狼生来就是用强者的姿态去征服弱者的。<u>在严酷的丛林法则的支配下，</u>狼身上每一个细胞，血管里的每一滴血浆，都<u>带着攻击食草类弱小动物的烙印</u>……(Shen, 2009: 159)

Wolves are born to use the posture of the strong to conquer the weak. Under the domination of <u>the harsh laws of the jungle</u>, every cell in the wolf and every drop of plasma in its blood vessels <u>are imprinted with the brand of attacking weak herbivorous animals</u>...

(3)它忘了这是一场你死我活的搏斗，它用一种弱者的生活逻辑来判断，还以为只要投降称臣就能得到宽宥从而苟全生命。它忘了狼的生存信念：用死亡的恐怖来统治这个世界；它忘了<u>弱肉强食的丛林法则</u>……(Shen, 2009: 135)

It forgot that this was a life-and-death fight. It used the life logic of the weak to judge, rendering that as long as it bent the knee, it would be forgiven and barely managed to survive. It forgot the wolf's belief in survival: to rule the world with the horrors of death; it forgot <u>the law of the jungle—the weak are the prey of the strong</u>...

Dream of the Wolf King tells a story that the animal protagonist, a female wolf named Zilan, is determined to cultivate one of her successors to be the next wolf king, for which she tries every means and pay a heavy price. To make the wolf king's dream come true, competing with other wolves is an unavoidable choice. Therefore, competitiveness and aggression hold a keynote position in the story. Although extracted from different episodes described in the novel with Example 1 concerned with feeding, Example 2 associated with hunting and Example 3 presenting an unusual scene of fighting, the above three examples are all dedicated to shaping the image of wolf as a competitive and aggressive fighter.

To this end, the author arranges metaphors masterfully and in a conscious manner. Most notably, life is metaphorically constructed as competition under the heading "life is struggle" directly indicated by the expressions "the natural selection of the fittest", "the harsh laws of the jungle" and "the law of the jungle—the weak are the prey of the strong", indirectly complemented by some "micrometaphors" (Kövecses, 2010: 59), i.e. "the strong is the winner" (expressed in "the weak are the prey of the strong" and "activity is fighting", exemplified as "feeding is actually a survival preview" as well as "... are imprinted with the brand of attacking weak herbivorous animals"). These metaphors extend through large portions of the novel, and may not tangibly surface in the literary discourse.

However, drawing upon the evolutionary link between animal and human, readers can establish the mapping smoothly in the process of interpretation even if they are not explicitly instructed about the specific correspondence between elements of different images. The metaphorical jungle law of natural selection, which acts through the competition of the inhabitants and consequently leads to success in the battle for life as described in the novel, invokes cognitive associations and produces projected analogy between animal world and human society. As is pointed out, "metaphor creates similarity by projection" (Vandaele, 2021: 454). The projected conceptual mappings arising from "natural selection" bring out a reliable inference that "competition is a positive force for development" and "human behavior and social structure should be valued in terms of their contribution to fitness". In this way, metaphors construct a covert evaluation about "competition". Moreover, implicated evaluation about the fighters—those who join the war of competition for survival is also inscribed in metaphorical expressions:

(4)虽然狼的生活不可避免地充满暗礁险滩，隐伏着无数杀机，但它愿意再和命运拼搏一番。(Shen, 2009: 140)

The wolf's life will inevitably be full of dangerous beaches and hidden risks, but it is willing to fight with fate again.

(5)也许，这正是命运对自己野心的一种惩罚。它在同命运的抗争中又输了一个回合，输得够惨的。不，它紫岚是不会服输的，优秀的狼是永远不会在厄运面前屈服的。(Shen, 2009: 58)

Perhaps this is a punishment from fate for its own ambitions. It lost another round in the struggle against fate, and it lost badly enough. No, it will not lose, the good wolf will never give in to unfortunate fate again.

In these two examples, the author metaphorically constructs fate as the enemy of the wolf. The "fate is enemy" metaphor structures the theme of competitiveness and aggression in an elaborate way by creating the oppositional tension between fate and wolf. In the meanwhile, it conceptualizes the image of wolf as a warlike fighter, implicitly conveying a positive evaluation—"fundamental structural traits are determined by success in the war of competition for survival, and that the best win the war, the logical conclusion is that the best are the most warlike" (Goatly, 2006: 343). Metaphors like this, therefore, articulate imperceptibly the author's points of view and turn into effective persuasive tools. Competitiveness and aggression bolstered by metaphors as the feature shared by humans and animals fashion the minds of people, implicating that men as sophisticated animals should always be in competition for honor and dignity—"fighting and war are the natural expression of human instinctive aggression" (Laland & Brown, 2002: 60).

6.3.2 Metaphor of economy in *Dream of the Wolf King*

The metaphoric sketch of a hard image of animal life conjures up the nonnegotiable requirement to compete well so as to survive in a competitive environment where resource is scarce. In a way, it can be said that competition for survival is parallel to competition for resource. Striving for the dream of being the wolf king could be understood as the pursuit of power among the same species, which is also regarded as a form of resource. Considering resource competition, economic concern comes naturally. Thus, in constructing anthropomorphic representation of animals, the metaphor of economy, together with metaphor of competitiveness, comprises dominant ideological strands of the impositive metaphor "humans are animals" running through the whole story. In the story *Dream of the Wolf King*, as the name suggests, the dream to be the wolf king becomes a recurring theme for the literary discourse and thus acts as an organizing principle which gives the story a discursive cohesion. Narrating how to achieve the dream provides a critical link.

Whether the dream of the wolf king can come true is subject to various factors, which are mediated by one constant parameter "competition"—the bottom line for the success is efficiency in fighting. Efficiency requires a delicately designed plan to improve the physical and mental strength of the successor who is endowed with high expectation. Working out a delicate plan to go for the wolf king's dream involves a process of calculating thought, which falls exactly into the scope of economy in that "economic terms semantically include a calculating attitude" (Crist, 1999: 120). Therefore, it can be found that in providing a detailed portrayal of how the animal character Zilan manages to materialize the wolf king's dream metaphor of economy expressed in economic and social-category concepts performs as metaphorical chains gathering up the thread of the story. Consider the following examples:

(6)但从培育未来狼王的角度看，对黑仔所表现出来的超级胆量不但不应该制止，还应放纵和鼓励，<u>超前教育才能塑造出杰出的"超狼"</u>。(Shen, 2009: 53)

From the point of view of cultivating the future wolf king, the super courage shown by Heizai should not only not be stopped, but also be indulged and encouraged, and only <u>advanced education can shape an outstanding "super wolf"</u>.

(7)蓝魂儿已经完全<u>按照它的设计</u>成长起来了……蓝魂儿已用自己超众的胆魄为将来争夺狼王宝座<u>铺垫了坚实的基础</u>……(Shen, 2009: 87)

Lanhuner has grown up exactly <u>as it was designed</u>... It has used its superior courage to <u>build a solid foundation</u> for the future competition for the throne of the wolf...

(8)你是我最得意的<u>杰作</u>，你身上寄托着我的全部理想和希望。(Shen, 2009: 96)

You are my proudest <u>masterpiece</u>, and you have all my ideals and hopes in you.

(9)它开始着手<u>重新塑造双毛的形象</u>，从肉体到精神。(Shen, 2009: 102)

It began to <u>reshape</u> the image of Shuangmao, physically and spiritually.

(10)紫岚露出了欣慰的微笑，瘸腿的痛苦和扮演被奴役者角色所付出的<u>代价</u>在这一刻都得到<u>补偿</u>。它心爱的狼儿终于按它设计的<u>蓝图</u>成长起来了。(Shen, 2009: 122)

Zilan smiled with relief, the pain of lameness and <u>the price paid for</u> playing the enslaved character <u>were compensated</u> at this moment. Its beloved wolf pup finally grew up according to <u>the blueprint it had designed</u>.

As can be seen from the above examples, economic and social category terms are pervasively deployed in anthropomorphic representation of the female wolf Zilan. With a determined mind to raise one of its wolf pups to be the wolf king, Zilan has devoted its entire energy and tried every possible means. Though frustrated by unexpected failures, it never gives up the dream—all of its three male wolf pups, Heizai, Lanhuner and Shuangmao respectively, are arranged to be the ideal candidates to go after the throne of the wolf king on succession. So, as the story progresses, readers can witness one episode after another which exhibit a comprehensive picture of how Zilan raises its young. Different episodes could be bound together by metaphorical markers implying economic and social connotations, i.e. "cultivation", "advanced education can shape the outstanding super wolf", "designed", "build a solid foundation", "masterpiece", "reshape... physically and spiritually" and "the price paid for playing the enslaved character were compensated" in these examples.

Economic expressions "can surface into the landscape of animal experience through the embodiment of economic ideas" (Crist, 1999: 122). Economic ideas in anthropomorphic representation of the wolf are loaded with a broad spectrum of economy-relevant submetaphors of the conduit metaphor complex. For example, in the statements exemplified above, there are conceptual metaphors such as "life is object" (e.g. "reshape... physically and spiritually", "masterpiece"), "affection/ relationship is money/wealth" (e.g. "the price paid for playing the enslaved character were compensated"), "raising offsprings is constructing buildings" (e.g. "designed" "build a solid foundation") and fundamentally, "humans are animals".

6.3.3 Conceptual blending operation of the metaphor "humans are animals" in *Dream of the Wolf King*

To well account for the online construal operation underlying these conceptual metaphors as well as the way they contribute to influencing readers' outlook of animals, the theory of conceptual blending is in demand. As a productive interpretive framework to describe meaning emergence, blending "has also been fruitfully applied to works of literature" (Dancygier, 2014: 301). In literary discourse, writers "use the device of creating fantastic blends with great skill and can thus convey subtle messages that can only be fully understood" (Kövecses, 2010: 274). Figure 6.1 summarizes the blending operation of architect metaphor and the metaphor of "humans are animals" in the previous examples.

As the figure suggests, the two conceptual metaphors are set up through two independent blending operations, while in the meantime they emerge from the same pattern of generic space. Both of the two conceptual blendings are targeted at disclosing the construal operation of the wolf's (Zilan in the case) way of parenting in the story. In Blending 1, Situation Space 1 is framed by the schema image of wolf's parenting, and contains the elements of Zilan, raise and wolf pups; Situation Space 2 is structured by the architect frame, and the counterpart elements of Zilan, raise and wolf pups are architect, construct and building respectively. These counterpart elements are compressed into a blended space, namely, Blended Situation Space 1, giving rise to structure that wolf, like human, is granted with a calculating shrewdness, or "Machiavellian intelligence". And the invocation of a Machiavellian ethos "stems from the resonance between economic concepts and the calculating, gainful orientation of an investing or merchant mentality" (Crist, 1999: 124).

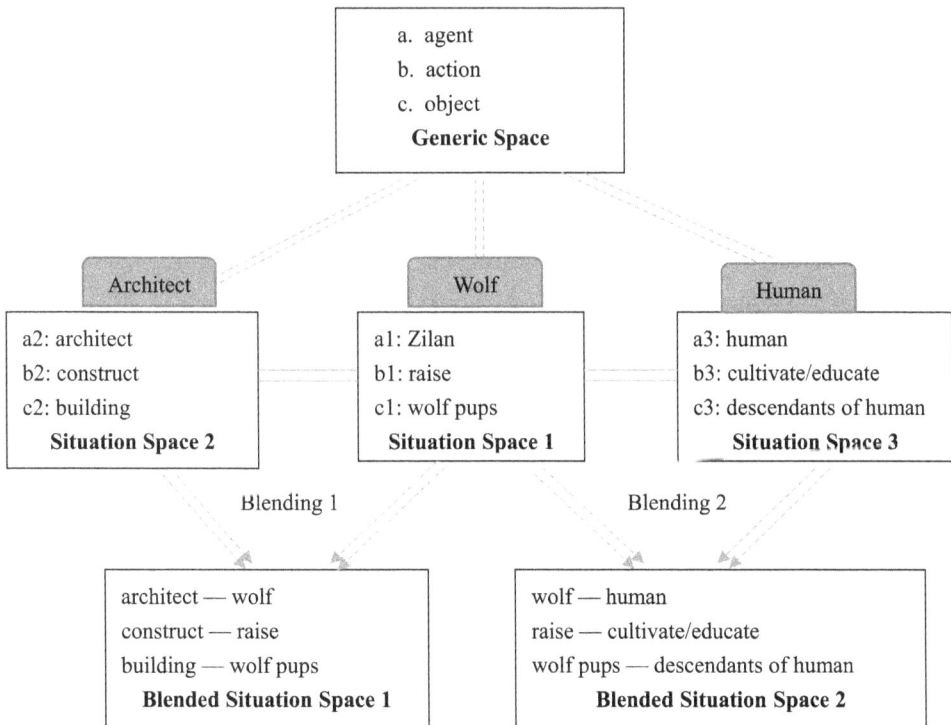

Figure 6.1   Blending of architect metaphor and the metaphor of "humans are animals"

In the other blending operation, the wolf's way of parenting is compared to that of humans. In a similar vein, two different input spaces are fused into an emergent structure—Blended Situation Space 2 where correspondence between wolf and human is established. Such being the case, the propositional tier works together with a dispersed metaphorical network to yield a powerful inferencing potential, tacitly legitimizing the impositive metaphor "humans are animals". Animals are viewed through the lens of human society—a calculating attitude affiliated with economic action is passed on to the animals. As Gould once said, "natural selection was essentially Adam Smith's economics read into nature" (cf. Goatly, 2007: 132).

6.3.4 Biological continuity: A sociobiological interpretation

In *Dream of the Wolf King*, the theme of craving for success and power mediated by competition creates a nexus of interconnected metaphors encapsulated in economic terms, which "becomes the dominant representational means of animal action and life and develops into a conceptual medium that strengthens a success-oriented, competitive neo-Darwinian vision of evolution" (Crist, 1999: 118). Neo-Darwinian approach to animal behavior is a manifestation of the sociobiological view of animal life which is "erected on the cornerstone ideas of success, competition, and selfishness" (Crist, 1999: 113). Predicated on Darwinism, sociobiologists tend to accept the notion that life is a struggle in which only the fittest survive and depict animal behavior in complete conceptual continuity with human action. Following the guideline, value judgments sanctioned by human society, albeit to a greater or lesser degree, are tagged on the representation of animals in narratives, which excludes the recognition of animal life as a lifeworld. In addition, clinging to the naturalistic fallacy that "what happens in nature is good" (Goatly, 2007: 129) and it is natural and right to behave like animals makes possible the breeding of the idea that "societies competing against each other for supremacy was a realization of the evolutionary struggle for survival" (Goatly, 2007: 380) and hence provides "an apologia for imperialism" (Goatly, 2007: 380).

6.4   Approximative metaphor "animals are more or less the same as humans": Conceptualizing animals as being more or less identified with humans in *Gorge Leaping Gorals*

6.4.1 Symbiosis and interdependence: A dissenting view

Impositive metaphor "humans are animals", directed at projecting human society to animal world, highlights the competitive struggle for survival: animals are viewed as fiercely competitive and aggressive and evolution is seen as based upon the struggle for existence. Resonating with the themes of competition and success, anthropomorphic representation of animals is permeated with an atmosphere of unrelenting coldness which is run by selfish genes and crafty minds expressed in economic and social category language. Impositive metaphorical network pervading through animal representation produces a vision of essential isolation—"to be an animal is essentially to live alone, to fight hard, and to die, often prematurely" (Crist, 1999: 128). Given the genealogical kinship between humans and animals, a valid metaphorical entailment is inferred that humans, the natural cognate, are basically selfish and competitive, which is reflected and reinforced by the metaphorical themes.

Nevertheless, such a sociobiologically oriented interpretation of conceptual mappings between humans and animals has been confronted with challenges which emphasize more on the symbiotic nature of evolution. Ryan (2002) advocates that the symbiotic principle behind evolution should be equally stressed in establishing the analogical connection between humans and animals, which revamps our worldview towards the relationship between them. His *Darwin's Blind Spot: Evolution beyond Natural Selection* (2002), popped up as a query to the Darwinian account of evolution, "puts a new cooperative and symbiotic slant on (animal) nature, and therefore, perhaps human nature, but ties in interestingly with Gaia theory" (Goatly, 2007: 140). Gaia theory, popularized by James Lovelock, stresses wholeness and interrelatedness—earth is seen as one integrated and self-regulating organism made up of physical, chemical and biological components. With a special emphasis on the interdependence of organisms, symbiotic principle holds that "formative symbiotic unions can merge together thousands of genes into a new hybrid organism" (Goatly, 2007: 142), generating interrelated biological and genetic complexity—a dissenting view from natural selection which "acts on gene mutations to modify existing genes over a long period" (Goatly, 2007: 142) . Recognition of symbiotic associations in a sense promotes the idea that the boundaries between classes of organisms become blurred. Admittedly, symbiosis "brings a wonderful new perspective on life in general and human society in particular" (Ryan, 2002: 6). When it comes to the relationship between humans and animals, drawing upon the symbiotic basis, not only human nature shares a lot with animal nature and they two maintain an intimate interconnectedness (referred to as *exosymbiosis*), but also cooperative qualities and principles can be perceived in animals themselves (referred to as *endosymbiosis*). This symbiotic tendency has metaphorical correspondences between human domain and animal domain as its plain manifestation. Rather than treating humans as animals, as is indicated in the impositive metaphor "humans are animals", it is postulated that possibilities exist that this metaphorical equation can be reversed and animals can be valued through the lens of human society on account that metaphor involves a two-way transfer between source and target (Black, 1962; Goatly, 2007). Thus, the impositive metaphor "humans are animals" which centers on projecting human society to animal world also makes animals become more like human. Accordingly, approximative metaphor "animals are more or less the same as humans" is allowed to view animals from the lens of humans.

6.4.2 Metaphor of cooperation and altruism in Gorge Leaping Gorals

Contrary to the impositive metaphor "humans are animals" that foregrounds the traits of competitiveness and aggression, the metaphorical theme of "animal is human" prioritizes instinctive cooperation and even self-sacrifice, born out of symbiosis, and thereby animals are conceived to be more or less like humans in that "cooperativeness is the very hallmark of humanity" (Goatly, 2007: 144). It follows naturally the view that animals are worth our sympathy and have equal rights to exist as humans. The use of metaphors thematized as cooperation and symbiosis in anthropomorphic representation of animals thus becomes a formidable vehicle for uniting the animal and human realms. This is manifest in representing the image of gorals in the novel *Gorge Leaping Gorals*:

(11)也许，它确实因为神经高度紧张而误以为<u>那道虚幻的彩虹是一座实实在在的桥，可以通向生的彼岸</u>；也许，它清楚那道色泽鲜艳远看像桥的东西其实是水汽被阳光折射出来的幻影，但既然走投无路了，<u>那就怀着梦想和幻觉走向毁灭，起码可以减轻死亡的恐惧</u>。(Shen, 2008a: 68)

Perhaps, it was so nervous that it mistakenly thought that <u>the illusory rainbow was a real bridge leading to the other shore of life</u>; perhaps, it was clearly aware that the bright colored stuff which looked like the bridge from faraway was actually the shadow of water vapor reflected by the sunshine. But since there is no choice, <u>it is better to walk to destruction with dreams and illusions, which at least could alleviate the fear caused by death</u>.

(12)试跳成功，紧接着，一对对斑羚凌空跃起，<u>山涧上空画出一道道令人眼花缭乱的弧线</u>，每一只年轻斑羚的成功飞渡，都意味着又一只老年斑羚摔得粉身碎骨。

<u>山涧上空，和那道彩虹平行，架起了一座桥，那是一座用死亡做桥墩架设起来的桥</u>。没有拥挤，没有争夺，次序井然，快速飞渡……<u>它们心甘情愿用生命为下一代开通一条生存的道路</u>。(Shen, 2008a: 73)

The test jump was a success. And then pairs of gorals leaped in the air in succession. <u>There appeared dazzling arcs over the mountain creek</u>. Every time a young goral jumped successfully, an old one fell to pieces.

<u>Over the mountain brook, parallel to the rainbow, a bridge was erected—a bridge built upon death</u>. No crowding, no competition, gorals flied orderly and fast… <u>They are</u>

willing to sacrifice their lives to pave the way for the survival of the next generation.

(13)我没想到，在面临种族灭绝的关键时刻，斑羚群竟然能想出牺牲一半挽救一半的办法来赢得种群的生存机会。我没想到，老斑羚们会那么从容地走向死亡。(Shen, 2008a: 73)

I didn't expect that, at a critical moment of facing the risk of extinction, the goral herd would come up with the way to sacrifice one half to save the other half for the sake of the survival of the population. <u>I didn't expect the old gorals would walk toward death so calmly.</u>

(14)砰，砰砰，猎枪打响了，我看见，镰刀头羊旷阔的胸部冒出好几朵血花，它摇晃了一下，但没倒下去，迈着坚定的步伐，走向那道绚丽的彩虹。弯弯的彩虹一头连着伤心崖，一头连着对岸的山峰，像一座美丽的桥。
它走了上去，消失在一片灿烂中。(Shen, 2008a: 74)

The shotgun rang, I saw several blood flowers flocking out of the sickle-head goral's broad chest. It wobbled a bit, but did not fall down. <u>It marched a firm pace towards that gorgeous rainbow.</u> One end of the curved rainbow is connected to Heartbroken Cliff, and the other is attached to the mountains on the oppositional side, <u>which looked like a beautiful bridge.</u>
<u>It went up and disappeared into a splendid brightness.</u>

The novel *Gorge Leaping Gorals* fictionally depicts a group of desperate gorals who, for the sake of the survival of the whole goral population, sacrifice half of them to save the lives of the other half. Self-sacrifice for the wellbeing of offspring is referred to as altruism. It is commonly acknowledged that "when a person (or animal) increases the fitness of another at the expense of his own fitness, he can be said to have performed an act of altruism" (Crist, 1999: 142). The theme of sacrifice and altruism thereby functions as the thread running through the storyline. Descriptions of the episodes of altruism and sacrifice in the animal novel *Gorge Leaping Gorals*, together with delicate affection that suffuses the writing, create a bond between humans and animals, for the reason that self-sacrifice is "the potential humans carry in extreme circumstances given their instinctive properties such as love, friendship, and togetherness" (Ryan, 2002: 248). Similarly, animals perform cooperative behaviors—actions of sacrifice under extreme circumstances. The extreme situation where the group of gorals are faced with is that they are forced to a cliff—a deadend cliff in the hunter's pursuit. For them, the only choice to escape the hunt is to leap across the mountain to the other side, which seems impossible due to the long distance. When confronted with the "to die or not to die" dilemma, for the survival of the goral population, the elder gorals volunteer to sacrifice their lives and are willing to be the stepping stone. As the story proceeds, the symbolic theme of altruism and sacrifice floats, depending on the processing of a network of metaphors predominantly concerned with life and death. For instance, in "I didn't expect the old gorals would walk toward death so calmly", conceptual metaphors "life is journey" and "death is the termination" are invoked. Modified by the adverb "calmly", metaphorical expressions in this statement convey the old gorals' determination and willingness to give their lives as sacrifice for the survival of their descendants, calling up readers to conjure up a scenario with gorals fearless of death. In this way, metaphor is deployed to evoke an emotional response, i.e. respect and admire, based on which a positive evaluation towards gorals is elicited.

6.4.3 Conceptual blending operation of the metaphor "animals are more or less identified with humans" in Gorge Leaping Gorals

The global metaphoricity of "life" and "death" is given more weight by the repetition of the bridge metaphor. Bridge metaphors in *Gorge Leaping Gorals* are applied to establish correspondences between the target bridge and multivalent sources. Multivalency can "help create or prepare the way for metaphoric parallels between two or more topics... It can also bring about or suggest certain thematic equivalences" (Goatly, 2005: 266). In this context, there are rainbow bridge (as in Examples 11, 12, 14) and goral bridge (as in Example 13). And, more thematically related and more abstract, there is a symbolic bridge of life, one end of which connects the hope of survival, the other linked to death. The processing of "bridge" metaphor replete with multivalent parallels "depends upon both local and global metaphoricity and they interact with each other" (Steen, 1994: 119). The online construal operation can be illustrated in Figure 6.2.

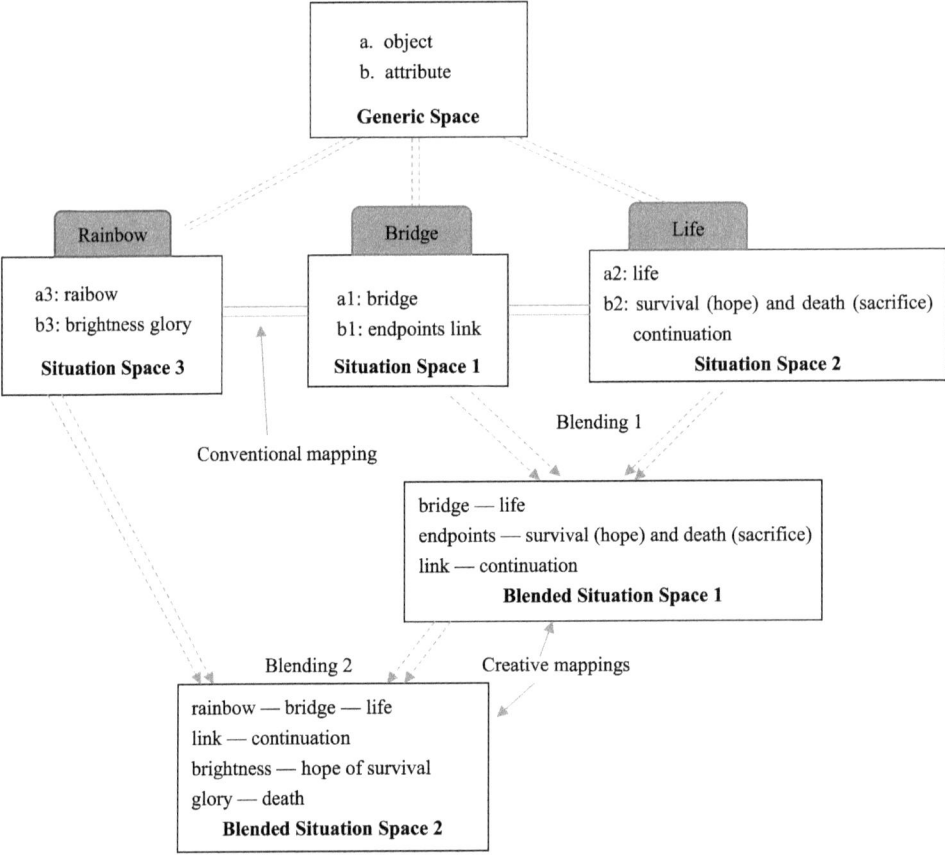

Figure 6.2   Blending of bridge metaphors

As the figure suggests, under the framework of the bridge metaphor, there exist sub-metaphorical analogies between bridge and its multivalent sources, i.e. rainbow and life. Sub-metaphors of the bridge network interplay with each other, contributing to anthropomorphic representation of gorals in the story. The metaphorical correspondence between rainbow and bridge is verified by conventional agreement because it matches an external reality. It is postulated that a conventional metaphor like this reflects underlying conventional mappings between distinct conceptual domains, which "are held to be part of people's enduring knowledge structures and to be a constitutive factor of all kinds of cognitive processes, including language use, reasoning, and the exercise of the imagination in literature, the arts, and other domains of human performance" (Steen, 2009: 25). Nevertheless, conceptual mappings between bridge and life are constructed creatively. Creative (active) metaphor is frequently used in literary texts "to capture the qualitative and often almost inexpressible properties of various experiences" (Caracciolo, 2016: 214). It requires readers to search for, instead of easily recall, encyclopedic knowledge to construct the analogical schema. Compared to conceptual metaphors, they are more effective in attracting attention—psychological foregrounding is an automatic effect of active metaphors (van Peer, 1986), hence evoking more cognitive associations as intended. Creative metaphor is used to create life as the bridge blend in which survival implying hope and death is conceptualized as two endpoints of the bridge. At the same time, bridge is metaphorically framed as the link between survival and death, which implicates the continuation of life. This corresponds to the theme of the story that the goral population is free from extinction owing to the older gorals' altruistic behaviors.

Another process of blending is operated when the emergent structure blended from conceptual parallels between life and bridge is compared to rainbow. The symbolic articulation of bridge acts as the mediating force that connects the domains of rainbow and life. The resulting blended space foregrounds particular traits of rainbow (i.e. glory, brightness) which are fused with their counterpart elements of life frame (i.e. hope of survival, sacrifice), giving rise to the metaphorical entailment that "hope is light" and "virtue (altruism) is light". A blending process as such involves metaphorical highlighting (Lakoff & Johnson, 1980), or a form of "partial metaphorical utilization" (Kövecses, 2010: 93), which aims at achieving specific ideological effects by intensifying selected perceptions and ignores others. On this point, the statement "it went up and disappeared into a splendid brightness" at the end of the story provides valid evidence. The statement describes the last scene of the story and portrays the goral, who makes its mind to sacrifice itself, as being undaunted in the face of death. The metaphorical expression "a splendid brightness" in this sentence equates its heroic and altruistic behavior with the glory of rainbow, which deeply penetrates the readers' minds with its rich emotional and evaluative connotations.

Metaphors in discourse, as Charteris-Black elucidates, use language "to activate unconscious emotional associations" (2004: 53), and blended spaces are "cognitive loci for reasoning, drawing inferences and developing emotions" (Fauconnier & Turner, 1996: 115). Using metaphors in this way is "particularly effective at rendering the integratedness of experience itself" (Caracciolo, 2017: 214), potentially invoking a sense of closeness and intimacy between readers and animal characters. The emotional force connoted in metaphors makes them value-laden and ideologically attitudinal, directing readers to conceptualize the animal characters as desired, as Goatly puts forward, "since we share these passions with animals, we are less different from them than the traditionalists assert, who regard reason as what distinguishes us from animals" (2007: 350). The "emotional similarity" underlying the theme of sacrifice and altruism in anthropomorphic representation of animals exerts significant influence on people's construal of animals in reality in that "people will be more likely to map elements that have the same positive or negative valence" (Thagard & Shelly, 2006: 36). As such, animals are viewed as being more or less the same as humans.

6.5 Summary

In this chapter, the importance of metaphor as a way of conceptualizing animals in animal narratives is highlighted. The ideological and legitimizing effects that metaphors impose upon people's construal of animals are disclosed. It is revealed that metaphors used in anthropomorphic representation of animals help to construct interrelationships between animal and human domains and hence enable readers to construe the constituted reality about animals in discourse. The two main metaphorical patterns, "humans are animals" and "animals are more or less the same as humans", are under scrutiny. The impositive metaphor "humans are animals", foregrounding the traits of competitiveness and aggression, tends to tag value judgments sanctioned by human society on anthropomorphic representation of animals in narratives, which excludes the recognition of animal life as a lifeworld. The approximative metaphor "animals are more or less the same as humans", highlighting the features of symbiosis and cooperation, attempts to manifest the "emotional similarity" between animals and humans, and animals are appraised from the lens of humans. By so doing, animals as subjective beings are stressed and the distance between animals and humans is potentially bridged—animals are considered as being more or less the same as humans.

Chapter 7   Ecological Attribute of Anthropomorphic Representation of Animal Images in Shen Shixi's Animal Narratives

7.1   Introduction

Previous chapters have provided detailed analysis of discursive strategies in anthropomorphic representation of animal images in Shen Shixi's animal narratives. Meanwhile, the legitimizing process and the metaphorical conceptualizing mechanism of anthropomorphic animal representation are explored. This chapter continues the investigation into the ecological attribute of anthropomorphic representation of animal images in Shen Shixi's animal narratives. It will firstly discuss the negotiation between human perspective and animal perspective in anthropomorphic animal representation; and then be dedicated to an introduction of Chinese ecosophy constitutive of traditional Chinese ecological wisdom, based on which ecological attribute of discursive animal representation in the Chinese context can be identified.

7.2   Anthropomorphic representation of animals in Shen Shixi's animal narratives: Negotiation between the human perspective and the animal perspective

The way animals are represented in discourse is a leading exponent of the change in relationships between humans and animals, which "deserves to be a key area in ecolinguistics" (Cook & Sealey, 2018: 551). Discursive representation of animals "entails consequences in terms of how animal life is understood and how it is pictured in the reader's imagination" (Crist, 1999: 140). Among various ways of representing animals in discourses, anthropomorphic mode carves out a niche. Anthropomorphic representation of animals in animal narratives in particular, performatively shapes people's construal of animals, and hence contributes significantly to establishing a bond between humans and animals. For quite some time, anthropomorphism, a tendency to attribute human personality or characteristics to non-human entities, has breasted considerable controversy. Voice of doubt primarily concerns whether anthropomorphism is a metaphorical extension of language from the human realm to the animal realm. In contrast, advocators take it more positively as a means to bridge the gap between humans and animals. As Doniger contends, "anthropomorphism and zoomorphism are two different attempts to reduce the otherness between humans and animals, to see the sameness beneath the difference" (2005: 34). Controversial as it is, the value of the anthropomorphic language in literary discourse, animal narratives included, cannot be overlooked. Anthropomorphic language "can often be found in literature" (Heuberger, 2018: 611), and is increasingly recognized as "ineradicable in the description of animal behavior" (Crist, 1999: 140). One possible reason is that "to give an accounting of the practices of human-animal relations... inevitably includes anthropomorphic tendencies and explanations of animal subjectivity" (Taylor, 2011: 274). Therefore, instead of regarding it as a fault to be avoided, a modest assumption about anthropomorphism is proposed that it "has no specific substantive content" (Crist, 1999: 139) and it performs to signify linguistic usage that lifts a mirror between humans and animals.

By "mirror", two levels of connotations are implied. Both rest upon the tacit conviction that humans and animals bear great resemblance to each other on account of evolutionary continuity. Discrepancy lies in that one sees the similarity as the potential to identify real correspondences between human and animal behaviors from the animal perspective, and thus to crumble the human-animal border; the other views the analogy as the medium to stand in for humans by projecting the wealth of human experience onto the animal world from the human perspective, and thus to serve for boundary maintenance between human and animal species. It thus can be said anthropomorphic representation of animals in animal narratives helps to create "a productive tension between the human perspective and the animal perspective" (Danta, 2018: 39).

This is proved to be a justified conclusion on the basis of an exploration into anthropomorphic representation of animal images in Shen Shixi's animal narratives. Animal narrative, a medium of realist description and explanation of the facts of animal life in Shen Shixi's view, allows for the co-existence of the wonder of the fictional world and of the realities known to the readers. Attentive readers of animal narratives are able to "explore animal issues and reach their own conclusions on the texts and their possible parallels to reality" (Manty, 2014: 259). For the sake of presenting a realistic portrayal, animals in Shen Shixi's narratives are not transformed into sapient creatures that talk and reason like humans, which is a distinctive feature of animal fables. However, animals in Shen Shixi's animal narratives are not deprived of means of communication, i.e. they use the visual or acoustic mode for the perception and transmission of information in a shared physical environment with animal companions and humans. The analogical connection between humans and animals, in his writings, is encapsulated in the descriptions of animal behaviors. Anthropomorphism emanates from his endeavors to depict animal behaviors in ordinary language of actions, which functions to render animal behaviors meaningful and authored. Considering that "action is associated with intentionality" (Taylor, 2011: 274), mental life of animals springs up as a result, in the ascription of particular mental predicates. The use of a vocabulary of mental activity which characterizes animals as sentient beings, together with the use of action verbs replete with meaningfulness and authorship, allows the transparency of animal subjectivity—animals emerge as subjects. In addition to these predication strategies, subjectivity of animals in Shen Shixi's animal narratives can also be recognized in the ways animals are referred to. Referential strategies in anthropomorphic representation of animals, the individualization strategy realized by names and naming and the assimilation strategy realized by the pronoun use of "you", function to individualize animals as subjective beings and blur the boundaries between humans and animals. As such, representation strategies in anthropomorphic representation of animals help to disclose genuine analogies between humans and animals and submit a commanding form of witnessing animal life from an animist worldview which closes the ontological gap between humans and animals.

This way of representing animals is endorsed by legitimization strategies—through grammatical cohesion, evidentiality and epistemic modality. What deserves consideration is that when animals are justifiably represented as sentient beings as humans by way of legitimization, quite paradoxically, a covertly implied message comes forward that humans and animals are different, which implicates a prioritized human perspective. Examples can be seen as:

(1)人类<u>毕竟是</u>人类，<u>实在</u>精明……(Shen, 2009: 11)
Human beings are human beings; they are <u>really</u> smart…

(2)鹿<u>就是</u>鹿，<u>永远无法</u>和高级动物人类相媲美的。(Shen, 2017: 44)
Deer <u>are</u> deer, and <u>can never</u> be compared with advanced animals—humans.

(3)狼<u>毕竟是</u>狼，没有人类那套科学的完善的接生方法，<u>只能靠命运</u>。(Shen, 2009: 3)
Wolves <u>are</u> wolves. They have no scientific and sophisticated methods of

delivering their baby wolves. They <u>can only</u> rely on destiny.

Adopting factual epistemological stance, the above statements imply an anthropocentric tendency, which seems to affirm human being's precedence over animals. This is accredited by the impositive metaphor "humans are animals" at the level of conceptualization, which involves the projection of human reality onto animal life via anthropomorphic representation of animals. In this strand, animals are portrayed as "either stand-ins for humans, representing a number of characteristics that humans have or that the author wants to teach to the reader" (DeMello, 2012: 307). Nevertheless, for the reason that "the human element cannot be avoided in any human interpretation of others" (Taylor, 2011: 265), in animal narratives, the functioning of a human perspective in anthropomorphic representation of animals, which displays an understanding of animal life comparable to that of human experience, appears to be indispensable, and that does "not necessarily lead to, or stem from, an assumption of human superiority" (Taylor, 2011: 265). As Sun postulates, "animal novels have shown that humans are nothing more than advanced animals in animal world, whereas other animals are endowed with some valuable qualities that human being do not have" (2010: 13). In animal narratives, animals display their magic power and talent in their own ways. Animals increasingly gain their unique identity that is no longer subsumed under the recognition of humans. Look at the following examples:

(4)你明白，这将是一场力量悬殊的搏斗。首先你要克服自私与怯懦的天性，但动物要改变天性谈何容易，简直比登天还难，<u>人类也不例外</u>。(Shen, 2017: 16)

You understand that it's going to be a David and Goliath struggle. First of all, you have to overcome the selfish and cowardly nature of deer, but it's never easy for animals to change natural instincts, which seems to be more difficult than ascending to heaven. <u>In this regard, human beings are no exception.</u>

(5)我对嘎羧肃然起敬，<u>它虽然只是一头象，被人类称之为兽类，却具有很</u>
<u>多称之为人的人所没有的高尚情怀</u>。在它行将辞世的时候，它忘不了这片它曾
经洒过热血的土地，特意跑到这儿来缅怀往事，凭吊战场。(Shen, 2008b: 16)

I respect the elephant Gasuo. <u>Although it is only an elephant, referred to as</u>
<u>a beast by human beings, it has a lot of noble qualities that human beings do not</u>
<u>possess</u>. Upon death, it cannot forget the land where it used to shed its blood. For this
particular reason, it comes to the battlefield to muse over the memories of the past.

In these exemplified representations of animals, animals are granted with
ontological standing which is equal to human beings. By stating that "human
beings are no exception" in Example 4 and "it [the elephant] has a lot of noble
qualities that human beings do not possess" in Example 5, human's position of
authority and superiority within the ecological hierarchy is decentered. More to
the point, humanity in Shen Shixi's animal narratives is sometimes degraded:

(6)聪明的大象好像知道人类<u>觊觎</u>它们发达的门牙，生怕遭到<u>贪婪</u>的人类的
<u>洗劫</u>，通常都把象冢选择在路途艰险人迹罕至的密林深处，再有经验的猎人也
休想找得到。但如果采取<u>卑鄙</u>的跟踪手段，悄悄尾随在死期将临的老象后面，
就有可能找到那遥远而又神秘的象冢。(Shen, 2008b: 14-15)

Smart elephants seem to know that humans <u>covet</u> their well-developed teeth.
To save their teeth from being <u>ransacked</u> by <u>greedy</u> humans, they usually locate the
elephant mounds in the depths of dense forests so that even experienced hunters
are not able to find them. But if you take <u>mean</u> tracking, quietly trailing behind an
old elephant that is dying, it is possible to find the distant and mysterious elephant
mounds.

As is shown, lexical items such as "covet", "ransacked", "greedy" and "mean"
evoke negative evaluation of human beings, which is further strengthened in
comparison with "smart" elephants who have sacrificed their lives to help humans.
This way of animal representation is conducive to challenging the commonly

accepted hierarchical relation between humans and animals. As the boundaries become less and less clear, animals are more likely to be viewed as relatively similar to humans. Within the dimension of conceptualization, parallel to the strand of viewing animals as "stand-ins for humans" from the human perspective, there stands another way of metaphorical conceptualization—conceptualizing animals as being more or less the same as humans under the framework of approximative metaphor "animals are more or less the same as humans". It is argued that "humans are perceived to share the capacity for sensation with animals" (Bastian et al., 2012: 422). Seeing animals as human-like may "raise concerns about moral inclusivity" (Bastian et al., 2012: 422) and fundamentally "reorient human perspective toward the earth and the non-human animal" (Danta, 2018: 30). Accordingly, an animal perspective encoded in anthropomorphic representation of animals in Shen Shixi's narratives, with an emphasis on the behavioral, mental and emotional correspondences between animal and human, makes it possible for animals to "have agency and play a part in human-animal interactions in ways that traditional thought negates" (Danta, 2018: 275).

In his animal narratives, Shen Shixi deploys anthropomorphism as the rhetorical device, conceptualizing tool and compromised conduit to evoke a potentially more complicated continuity between humans and animals. To some extent, human perspective and animal perspective negotiate with one another in anthropomorphic representation of animals which touches upon far more than a mere transposition of human attributes to animals. The juxtaposition of human perspective and animal perspective in anthropomorphic representation of animals in some way pictures a continuum between the human and the animal domains. Both humans and animals are seen as interrelated actants going through a fluid process of interaction and reconciling with each other in a shared text world. In this way, anthropomorphism in Shen Shixi's narratives acts as the conduit of complex negotiations between human and animal actants. It is the negotiation that gives rise to the definition of their identities considering that "beings do not preexist their relating" (Haraway, 2003: 6). Therefore, it could be said that "practices of anthropomorphism lead to hybridity... such practices and their outcomes essentially disrupt the enlightenment logic that proclaims essential differences between human and animal" (Taylor, 2011: 270). Anthropomorphic representation of animals in Shen Shixi's narratives, in this manner, offers prospects for eradicating dualist conceptuality with regard to humans and animals and moving toward a holistic and organic worldview which connotes that "the poles of transcendence and immanence integrate within each other to construct a more dynamic and developmental cosmic whole" (Palmquist & Chan, 2016: 222). This seems to resonate with Chinese philosophical thinking, "Chinese ecosophy" in the ecological sense, which highlights integratedness and wholeness.

7.3 Rethinking human-animal relationship: On Chinese ecosophy

Relationship between humans and animals is an important proposition for sustainable human development. Traditional cosmopolitan ideal of "human dignity as self-raising of the human animal above the animal being" (Adorno, 2004: 82) reifies human difference from and superiority over animals. This fundamentally anthropocentric orientation is further strengthened by social practice which reduces animals to objects for exploitation, and reinforced by the Western philosophical thought of human and nature dichotomy, which prevails in enlightenment cosmopolitanism and our contemporary ideal of civil society. The relationship between humans and animals thus "looks set to become even more distant and more mediated" (Jacobs & Stibbe, 2006: 2). In the postmodern era when the process of industrialization brings about tremendous changes to the earth and the society, people are urged to embark on rethinking and redefining the relationship between humans and animals.

The great urgency to "repair" human relations with animals calls forth a need to foster ecological consciousness in deconstructing hegemony with regard to animals and eliminating the dichotomy between humans and animals, which counts significantly upon discursive and spiritual recourses. In response, "ecosophy" as an interdisciplinary notion emerges. The term "ecosophy" is coined as "an obvious point of contact between ecology and philosophy" (Schonfeld, 2016: 178). It refers to a philosophical worldview or system with regard to the conditions of life in the ecosphere (Naess, 1995). It is concerned with ecological wisdom in which "harmony, above all other ideas, is dominant" (Fill & Penz, 2018: 759). In the case of human-animal entanglement, ecosophy highlights a stance of harmonious coexistence with animals, which fits well in with the spirit of traditional Chinese philosophy, namely, Confucianism and Taoism. The Confucian-Taoist thought of "the union of nature and man" (*tian ren he yi,* 天人合一) implies a harmonious relationship between nature and man. The background assumption is that "persons and all things are interconnected through complex networks of dynamic, causally efficacious relationships" (Brasovan, 2016: 206). It foregrounds that "relationships are internal and essential to the constitution of any phenomenon" (Brasovan, 2016: 205). It spontaneously propagates undifferentiated wholeness that all the individual entities in the universe, same or different, are ontologically co-dependent constituents within a holistic totality. Accordingly, humans and animals are interrelated to each other as a complex whole. There is no absolute qualitative difference between them, and both of them deserve to enjoy their own intrinsic value. The equality between humans and animal natures forms the very basis of the respect that humans owe to animals (Palmquist & Chan, 2016). As such, Chinese ecological vision is inherent in holistic cosmology which emphasizes interconnected inclusiveness, contributing to establishing a harmonious relationship between humans and animals. Taking Confucian-Taoist harmony as its central philosophical orientation and hence termed as "harmosophy" (Zhou & Huang, 2017), Chinese ecosophy can "provide rich spiritual and philosophical recourses and conceptual tools for rethinking current ecological problems" (Zhou & Huang, 2017: 266). At home, the Chinese ecosophy of interconnectional inclusivism and harmonious benevolence has concrete manifestation in the process of promoting the mission of building a harmonious society and constructing ecological civilization in contemporary China. Moreover, it has been epitomized in the principles guiding Chinese ecological discursive practice. The way animals are represented in the discourse of animal narratives is a case in point. The unity of nature and man suggests an anthropocosmic worldview, which provides an epistemological alternative to Western philosophical thought on human-animal relationship and seems much in tune with today's theme of sustainability. Thus, Chinese ecosophy is envisioned as "a positive response to the 'ecological turn' in new Confucian humanism", as a way of "coping with anthropocentricism" (Zhou & Huang, 2017: 266). Chinese ecological discourse adhering to Chinese ecosophy "can be perceived as one Eastern eco-discursive paradigm" (Zhou & Huang, 2017: 265), which is helpful in a joint endeavor with other ecological strands to fulfill the substantial role of ecological harmonious discourse.

7.4   Toward an ecologically harmonious discursive representation

Chinese ecological holism, the view of a cosmic whole, as the specific Chinese cultural connotation, is deeply engraved in Chinese animal narratives, which are intersected together into a three-dimensional cultural pattern of human-nature symbiosis (Chen, 2018: 3). Anthropomorphic representation of animals in Shen Shixi's narratives also carries with it the profound cultural orientation, imprinted with traditional Chinese ecological thoughts. By writing out different perspectives, anthropomorphic animal representation in Shen Shixi's animal novels brings about a stereoscopic display of plural symbiosis between humans and animals—a life pattern of interdependency between different species is unfolded in the perception of integration. The interconnection of animal world and human society in anthropomorphic representation of animal images in Shen Shixi's writing is not simply a mechanical analogy; instead, it represents a pleasant blending of human and animal horizons. By means of anthropomorphism, human's emotional appeal and animal nature are effectively fused together in the discursive representation of animals. Anthropomorphic animal representation in Shen Shixi's narratives is therefore permeated with the emotional interactions between humans and animals, acting as "a response to the emotional ground of animal-worship in the animal totem myth [in ancient China]" (Chen, 2018: 283).

"Animal worship" and "animism" are a pair of primitive natural concepts that have left indelible cultural imprint on the Chinese nation (Chen, 2018). The use of anthropomorphism in representing animals in Shen Shixi's novels is exactly an index of commitment to "animism", the doctrine involving the attribution of conscious life to all the creatures in the universe. The intrinsic value of anthropomorphized animals is not merely constrained to their biological qualities; moreover, they are endowed with humanized mentality which allows for thinking, voicing, and thereupon expressing their subjectivity on the one hand, as well as speaking for humans on the other hand. Anthropomorphic representation as such helps to achieve a harmonious convergence between humans and animals.

Highlighting harmonious coexistence with other creatures in the universe is always the core of Confucian ecological vision. Confucian scholars view the way of Heaven as an ongoing organismic process, asserting that the most fundamental value of being human is to facilitate the spontaneous transformation of the cosmos, and build up moral, affective interconnection with other creatures (Fox, 2005). Thus harmony in the Confucian sense has nothing to do with molding a humanized nature; it stresses more about "human projecting their emotions into objective existence in nature" (cf. Sun, 2010: 143). This kind of emotional harmony grows out of mutual recognition and respect between human and nature (animal), which is illustrated as follows:

> "Human project their emotions into objective existence in nature" means that
> people endow a high degree of trust and dependence on natural creatures, emphasizing
> their role as emotional entrustment. This helps to eliminate the possible contradictions
> between man and nature, smoothly unblock the connection between man and the

universe, and greatly promote the harmony between man and the natural world. (cf. Sun, 2010: 143)

Harmony like this is a map of Chinese cosmic view of the unity of nature and man. Approaching the world as a whole in which all creatures are placed in a network of relationship allows the inclusion of animals into human spaces, making possible "ontological hybridity" (Taylor, 2011: 271). This is entirely different from the dualist post on which Western thoughts are based. Cartesian tradition in the Western society posits an enduring distinction between objective and subjective worlds, between humans and animals. The "divided natures" of Cartesian legacy have exerted profound influence upon Western ecolinguistics. A case in point is the binarism of categorizing ecological discourse into either "beneficial" or "destructive" discourse (Stibbe, 2012, 2015). Even though a mediating link under the rubric of "ambivalent discourse" is proposed, the imprint of dualism cannot be wiped out clean. It is argued that the Cartesian views which "European ecological discourse turns to has put itself onto an increasing disadvantage of philosophical disharmony" (Zhou & Huang, 2017: 266). In counterpoint to Western ideas on the purification of hybrid categories, Chinese holistic approach to looking at the relationship between human and nature provides spiritual resources with great authority and legitimacy for harmonious discursive representation of animals in animal narratives. In resonance with Chinese harmosophy, Chinese animal narratives represent an artistic practice which seeks to restore harmonious human animal relationship (Sun, 2010). For example, anthropomorphism in Shen Shixi's animal narratives is used to describe and denote both animals and humans, whereby creating the emotional harmony among the species. In this way, the presumed political hierarchy between humans and animals can be translated into the acknowledged biological diversity, bringing about an amelioration of the status of animals and fostering equality among humans and animals. Anthropomorphic representation in Shen Shixi's novels therefore offers an appealing and insightful way of seeing animals, which enriches the notion of "universality"—what secures cosmopolitan harmony—with concrete examples through discursive practice. From this perspective, anthropomorphic representation of animal images in Shen Shixi's animal narratives is deemed as ecologically harmonious.

7.5 Summary

Based on investigations into representation strategies, legitimization and metaphorical conceptualization of anthropomorphic animal representation in previous chapters, this chapter is an attempt to identify the ecological attribute of anthropomorphic representation of animal images in Shen Shixi's animal narratives. It is suggested that the human perspective and the animal perspective negotiate with each other in anthropomorphic animal representation, which in some way pictures a continuum between the human and the animal domains and offers prospects for eradicating dualist conceptuality with regard to humans and animals. It is postulated that holistic cosmology which emphasizes interconnected inclusiveness is inherent to Chinese ecosophy, contributing to establishing a harmonious relationship between humans and animals. It is argued that anthropomorphic representation of animal images in Shen Shixi's animal narratives resonates with Chinese harmosophy, and hence is ecologically harmonious.

Chapter 8   Conclusion

This chapter is intended as a summary of the previous chapters which have investigated into anthropomorphic representation of animal images in Shen Shixi's animal narratives from the perspective of ecological critical discourse studies. As the conclusion of the present study, this chapter will review the main aspects the present study has covered, sum up the major findings, discuss the significance and point out the limitations, based upon which some feasible and interesting research projects relevant to the present study will be suggested.

8.1   Overview of the present study

Animal narratives in contemporary society appear to be the perfect medium for "reminding" people of animals that are increasingly erased from the human world. Animal narratives are committed to making visible the ontological value of individual animal lives and reconstructing the intimate interlacing between animal world and human life by means of realistic portrayal and ecological interpretation of animal world. They are defined as both the distillation of animal world and the artistic reflection of human life. The very dualism of animal narratives is realized through the anthropomorphic representation of animal images. Anthropomorphism in animal narratives serves the dual purposes of rendering back the visibility of animals as the subject of a lifeworld and evoking a reflection on human selves and society. Anthropomorphic representation in animal narratives creates a method of interpretation, involving meaning construction and construal.

The results of a literature review on researches from three interdependent fields, namely, studies on animal representation in literature, studies on the linguistic dimension of animal representation, and studies on Shen Shixi's animal narratives, call for an interdisciplinary approach to exploring how anthropomorphic representations of animal images in Shen Shixi's animal narratives are realized by linguistic means and how they will affect the addressees' cognition. For this purpose, several research questions are put forward:

What discursive strategies are applied to achieve anthropomorphic representation of animal images in Shen Shixi's animal narratives?

How is anthropomorphic representation of animal images in Shen Shixi's animal narratives legitimized?

What is the cognitive mechanism of anthropomorphic depictions? More precisely, how can anthropomorphic representation of animal images be metaphorically conceptualized?

What is the ecological attribute of anthropomorphic representation of animal images in Shen Shixi's animal narratives in terms of Chinese ecosophy?

In an attempt to answer the above questions, a three-level framework of ecological critical discourse studies is constructed to examine animal representation in animal narratives. Taking the cognitive perspective as the entry point, the study proceeds to provide a detailed analysis on how discourse strategies contribute to anthropomorphic representation of animals under the framework, and how anthropomorphic animal representation is conceptualized. The project centers on the qualitative analysis and interpretation of the materials. The study then attempts to place anthropomorphic representation of animals in Shen Shixi's narratives in a broad social, cultural and historical context to inquire into the underlying ideological orientations. The ecological attribute of anthropomorphic representation of animals in Shen Shixi's animal narratives is identified in terms of Chinese ecosophy.

8.2   Major findings of the present study

The major findings of the present study will be elaborated with regard to the research questions.

The study identifies different representation strategies in constructing anthropomorphic representation of animal images in Shen Shixi's animal narratives. It is found that referential strategies involve individualization and assimilation. It is suggested that the referential strategy of naming in anthropomorphic animal representation in Shen Shixi's animal narratives acts to foreground the individuality animals referred to, thus to highlight their intrinsic value as subjective beings; the pronoun use of "you" plays its role in eliciting direct or perceptually mediated effects on transcending the boundaries between human readers and animal characters. It is also found that the predication strategy of using verbs is effective in constructing animal behaviors as meaningful and authored; the predication strategy of using mental predication functions to shape animals as sentient beings in Shen Shixi's narratives. It is demonstrated that referential and predication strategies work together to construct the constituted reality about animals in discourse.

The study explores legitimization strategies in endorsing anthropomorphic representation of animal images in Shen Shixi's animal narratives. It is observed that legitimization of anthropomorphic animal representation in Shen Shixi's narratives is realized through grammatical cohesion, evidentiality and epistemic modality: grammatical cohesion is used to legitimize anthropomorphic representation of animal images by means of implication, presupposition and inferencing; evidentiality is deployed to legitimize anthropomorphic representation of animals through objectification; epistemic modality is exploited to legitimize anthropomorphic representation of animals through subjectification. It is suggested that the effects legitimization strategies impose upon readers' attitude towards animals are paradoxical: on the one hand, animals are justifiably represented as sentient beings as humans from the animal perspective; on the other hand, animals are constructed implicitly yet incontrovertibly as subordinated objects from the human perspective.

The study investigates metaphorical conceptualization of anthropomorphic animal representation in Shen Shixi's animal narratives. It is revealed that metaphor as an important way of conceptualizing animals in animal narratives is inherently ideological, imposing ideological and legitimizing effects upon people's construal of animals. It is found that two metaphorical networks, thematized as "humans are animals" and "animals are more or less the same as humans", are manipulatively operated in anthropomorphic animal representation. It is suggested that the impositive metaphor "humans are animals", foregrounding the traits of competitiveness and aggression, tends to tag value judgment sanctioned by human society on anthropomorphic representation of animals in narratives, which excludes the recognition of animal life as a lifeworld. It is also found that the approximative metaphor "animals are more or less the same as humans", highlighting the features of symbiosis and cooperation, attempts to appraise animals from the lens of humans on the basis of emotional similarity, manifest the "emotional similarity" between humans and animals, whereby the distance between humans and animals is possibly bridged.

It is unveiled that the human perspective and the animal perspective negotiate with each other in anthropomorphic representation of animal images in Shen Shixi's animal narratives, which offers prospects for eradicating dualistic conceptuality on the relationship between humans and animals. It is argued that anthropomorphic representation of animal images in Shen Shixi's animal narratives carries with it the profound cultural orientation which takes root in Chinese philosophical thinking, i.e. the Confucian-Taoist thought of the unity of nature and man. It is postulated that Chinese ecosophy, with holistic cosmology at its core, provides an epistemological alternative to the Western dualist thought on human-animal relationship and seems much in tune with today's theme of sustainability. It is suggested by writing out a pleasant blending of human and animal horizons, anthropomorphism in Shen Shixi's animal narratives entails a notion of "universality" and is in resonance with Chinese harmosophy, and therefore can be envisioned as ecologically harmonious.

8.3   Significance of the present study

In exploring the anthropomorphic representation of animal images in Shen Shixi's animal narratives, the present study has made achievements in the following aspects.

Firstly, the present study provides a relatively comprehensive survey of anthropomorphic representation of animal images in Shen Shixi's animal narratives. It investigates discursive strategies in representing animals anthropomorphically. It answers how anthropomorphic representation of animals is legitimized ideologically by linguistic means. And it reveals the underlying mechanism of metaphorically conceptualizing the anthropomorphic representation of animals. It is hoped that this detailed account of the way animals are represented in the discourse of animal narratives will contribute an insightful observation of the topic. It is also expected that animal representation study in China will bring fresh vigor to the realm of ecolinguistic research.

Secondly, the present study is a modest attempt to take up the challenge of constructing a three-level (macro-, meso- and micro-) framework to examining animal representation in animal narratives. This framework makes it possible to analyze discursive representation of animals in a systematic and comprehensive way. Of particular note is that it tends to see the anthropomorphic representation of animals as a dynamic process which involves both meaning production and construal, and endeavors to approach the topic from a cognitive perspective. It serves to inspire the introduction of a cognitive dimension to ecolinguistic study which is still underexplored.

Thirdly, the present study, taking animal narratives as a form of discursive practice, probes into uncovering the dialectical relationship between human, discourse and animal by means of detailed and systemic linguistic analysis. It is an interdisciplinary endeavor drawing upon a wide range of theoretical and methodological inspirations from various fields such as discourse study, literature, ecology and sociology. The study thus offers a complementary contribution to the current prevailing cross-interdisciplinary studies. Taking the field of literature as an example, a linguistic approach to studying animal representation opens up a new way into studying animal narratives. It is hoped that the survey will to some extent broaden the scope of animal narrative research and add a valuable extension to the literature.

Fourthly, the investigation of anthropomorphic representation of animal images in Shen Shixi's animal narratives and the forces that influence that representation, in some way, can provide discursive recourses for raising people's ecological consciousness in addressing the global ecological crisis and encouraging a more harmonious human-animal relationship. It is also expected that the study will be of certain instructive significance to ecological discursive practice at home.

Fifthly, the present study discusses the role of traditional Chinese philosophy, the core idea of which is inclusiveness and wholeness, in anthropomorphic representation of animals in Shen Shixi's animal narratives. It is argued that Chinese ecosophy, adhering to Confucianism-Taoism thoughts of harmonious coexistence between human and nature, is holistic cosmology, which provides an epistemological alternative to traditional Western dualistic conceptuality. It is hoped that the study will not only help to establish culturally normative harmony-oriented attitudes toward animals, but also facilitate an intercultural dialogue between the Eastern and Western eco-discursive paradigms, thereby making a joint effort in improving ecological consciousness worldwide.

8.4　Limitations and future direction

Despite the above-mentioned significant findings, it has to be acknowledged that it is far from safe to say that the present study is immune to limitations. The following will concentrate on the limitations in this study and suggest some areas for future research.

Firstly, there is the problem of the confusing terms. In academic circles, defining and understanding the terms "anthropomorphism" and "animal narrative" has always been a point of controversy. The situation gets more complicated when they are applied and examined in the interdisciplinary background. It requires the researcher to conduct an extensive, if not exhaustive, literature review, and handle the work rigorously. Even so, there is still room to improve.

Secondly, although the present study has made endeavors to offer a rich and detailed perspective on the examples (selected as typical as possible), the main disadvantage of the qualitative approach is that the findings cannot be extended to wider populations with the same degree of certainty. It is hard to decide whether the results are statistically significant or more likely to be due to chance. Therefore, the findings are anticipated to be seen as less than statements.

Thirdly, the study does not tackle other linguistic devices that contribute to representing animals in the discourse of animal narrative. It should be mentioned that discursive strategies disclosed in the study are by no means the only possible ones that human language has evolved to serve for constructing animal representation in discourse. It could be quite plausibly argued that evaluation strategy, for example, plays an important role in discursive representation of animals and deserves further investigation.

Accordingly, it is predictable that remaining issues for future research lie in the following several aspects.

Firstly, comparative inquiries into discursive animal representation can be conducted. Discursive strategies in animal representation may vary in the aspects of different genres. As far as the genre of animal narrative is concerned, comparisons between animal representation in and out of China, as well as between animal representation in Shen Shixi's and other contemporary writer's writings are worth exploring, the investigation into which will prove fruitful. In addition, a diachronic approach to studying discursive strategies of animal representation in animal narratives will also be insightful.

Secondly, the investigation of discursive representation of animals in animal narratives may be expanded by studying how these resources co-occur with other linguistic devices, i.e. evaluation strategy and other conceptualizing tools, in animal narratives.

Thirdly, a qualitative approach to exploring discursive representation of animals in animal narratives is merely the primary step to investigating the topic. The findings will shed light on the studies of discursive representation of animals in a wider range of corpora. Further exploration into the general discursive representation of animals with the help of expanded corpora is suggested, which is sure to be of academic value.

References

Chen, J. J., 2018. *On Typologies of Animal Narratives in Contemporary China*. Beijing: China Social Sciences Press. [陈佳冀，2018. 中国当代动物叙事的类型学研究. 北京：中国社会科学出版社.]

Chen, Q., 2007. Non-realism tendency of Shen Shixi's animal fiction. Hangzhou: Zhejiang Normal University. [陈琦，2007. 论沈石溪动物小说创作的非写实性倾向. 杭州：浙江师范大学.]

Dong, G. Y., 2011. Study on Shen Shixi's humanoid animal novels. Qingdao: Ocean University of China. [董广云，2011. 沈石溪类人动物小说研究. 青岛：中国海洋大学.]

Feng, G. Y., 2013. *Language Ecology*. Beijing: People's Publishing House. [冯广艺，2013. 语言生态学. 北京：人民出版社.]

He, W. & Zhang, R. J., 2017. An ecological analytical framework for discourse. *Foreign Languages in China* (5): 56-64. [何伟，张瑞杰，2017. 生态话语分析模式构建. 中国外语（5）：56-64.]

Huang, G. W. & Xiao, J. Y., 2017. The concept of "anthropocene" and ecolinguistic studies. *Foreign Languages Research* (5): 14-30, 112. [黄国文，肖家燕，2017. "人类世"概念与生态语言学研究. 外语研究（5）：14-30，112.]

Qu, X. L., 2011. Mirroring human society: Study on the sociality in Shen Shixi's animal novels. *Journal of Chongqing University of Science and Technology (Social Sciences Edition)* (16): 129-130, 138. [曲秀丽，2011. 观照人类社会的一面镜子——浅谈沈石溪动物小说中的社会性. 重庆科技学院学报（社会科学版）（16）：129-130，138.]

Shen, S. X., 1999. *The Seventh Hound*. Cheng, Q. (trans.). Taiyuan: Hope Publishing House. [沈石溪，1999. 第七条猎狗. 太原：希望出版社.]

Shen, S. X., 2008a. *Gorge Leaping Gorals*. Hangzhou: Zhejiang Children's Publishing House. [沈石溪，2008a. 斑羚飞渡. 杭州：浙江少年儿童出版社.]

Shen, S. X., 2008b. *The Last War Elephant*. Hangzhou: Zhejiang Children's Publishing House. [沈石溪，2008b. 最后一头战象. 杭州：浙江少年儿童出版社.]

Shen, S. X., 2009. *Dream of the Wolf King*. Hangzhou: Zhejiang Children's Publishing House. [沈石溪，2009. 狼王梦. 杭州：浙江少年儿童出版社.]

Shen, S. X., 2017. *The Old Hark*. Hangzhou: Zhejiang Children's Publishing House. [沈石溪，2017. 老鹿王哈克. 杭州：浙江少年儿童出版社.]

Shi, R. H., 1995. The stylistic consciousness on Shen Shixi's animal fictions. *Journal of Yunnan Normal University (Philosophy and Social Sciences Edition)* (6): 76-81. [施荣华，1995.沈石溪动物小说的文体自觉.云南师范大学哲学社会科学学报（6）：76-81.]

Sun, Y., 2010. *Animal Novels: The Ecological Thinking of Human Beings*. Shenyang: Liaoning University Press. [孙悦，2010. 动物小说——人类的绿色凝思. 沈阳：辽宁大学出版社.]

Tang, K. L., 2010. *Literary Study of Animal Narratives in Contemporary China*. Tianjin: Nankai University Press. [唐克龙，2010. 中国现当代文学动物叙事研究. 天津：南开大学出版社.]

Xin, Z. Y. & Huang, G. W., 2013. Systemic functional linguistics and ecolinguistic analysis. *Foreign Language Education* (3): 7-10, 31. [辛志英，黄国文，2013. 系统功能语言学与生态话语分析. 外语教学（3）：7-10，31.]

Yang, W., 2013. The discussion of authenticity issues of Shen Shixi's animal novels. Qingdao: Ocean University of China. [杨伟，2013. 论沈石溪动物小说的真实性问题.青岛：中国海洋大学.]

You, Z. S., 2010. *Foreign-oriented Political Discourse in Contemporary China: Construction Model and Social Changes*. Beijing: Science Press. [尤泽顺，2010. 中国当代对外政治话语：建构模式与社会变迁. 北京：科学出版社.]

You, Z. S. & Chen, J. P., 2009. Orders of discourse and the discursive construction of foreign policy: A diachronic analysis of lexical variations in the AWR. *Journal of Guangdong University of Foreign Studies* (2): 44-49. [尤泽顺，陈建平，2009. 话语秩序与对外政策构建：对政府工作报告的词汇变化分析. 广东外语外贸大学学报（2）：44-49.]

Zhou, W. J., 2017. Theory and practice of ecolinguistic studies in China: Review of Huang Guowen's ecolinguistic studies. *Journal of Xi'an International Studies University* (3): 24-28. [周文娟，2017. 中国语境下生态语言学研究的理念与实践——黄国文生态语言学研究述评. 西安外国语大学学报（3）：24-28.]

Zhu, Z. Q., 2005. About animal or human: On the artistic model and thought of Shen Shixi's animal novels. In Zhu, Z. Q. (ed.). *On Children's Literature*. Qingdao: China Ocean University Press: 358-370. [朱自强，2005. 从动物问题到人生问题——论沈石溪动物小说的艺术模式与思想//朱自强. 儿童文学. 青岛：中国海洋大学出版社：358-370.]

Abram, D., 1996. *The Spell of the Sensuous*. New York: Vintage.

Abram, D., 2010. *Becoming Animal: An Earthly Cosmology*. New York: Pantheon Books.

Adorno, T. W., 2004. *Aesthetic Theory*. Hullot-Kentor, R. (trans.). London: Continuum.

Aikhenvald, A. Y., 2004. *Evidentiality*. Oxford: Oxford University Press.

Aikhenvald, A. Y., 2018. Evidentiality: The framework. In Aikhenvald, A. Y. (ed.). *The Oxford Handbook of Evidentiality*. Oxford: Oxford University Press: 1-55.

Aldrin, E., 2016. Names and identity. In Hough, C. (ed.). *The Oxford Handbook of Names and Naming*. Oxford: Oxford University Press: 424-436.

Alexander, R. J., 2009. *Framing Discourse on the Environment: A Critical Discourse Approach*. New York: Routledge.

Alexander, R. J., 2018. Investigating texts about environmental degradation using critical discourse analysis and corpus linguistic techniques. In Fill, A. F. & Penz, H. (eds.). *The Routledge Handbook of Ecolinguistics*. London: Routledge: 357-383.

Alexandra, Y. A. (ed.)., 2018. *The Oxford Handbook of Evidentiality.* Oxford: Oxford University Press.

Anderson, L. B., 1986. Evidentials, paths of change, and mental maps: Typologically regular asymmetries. In Chafe, W. L. & Nichols, J. (eds.). *Evidentiality: The Linguistic Coding of Epistemology*. Norwood: Ablex: 273-312.

Auer, P., 1992. Introduction: John Gumperz' approach to contextualization. In Auer, P. & Diluzio, A. (eds.). *The Contextualization of Language*. Amsterdam: John Benjamins Publishing Company: 1-37.

Austin, J. L., 1962. *How to Do Things with Words*. Oxford: Oxford University Press.

Balkin, J. M., 1998. *Cultural Software: A Theory of Ideology*. New Haven: Yale University Press.

Baron, R. A. & Byrne, D., 1997. *Social Psychology*. Boston: Allyn & Bacon.

Barthes, R., 1975. *An Essay*. Miller, P. (trans.). New York: Macmillan.

Bastian, B. et al., 2012. When closing the human-animal divide expands moral concern: The importance of framing. *Social Psychological and Personality Science* (4): 421-429.

Baudrillard, J., 1994. *Simulacra and Simulation*. Ann Arbor: University of Michigan Press.

Beardsworth, A . & Bryman, A., 2001. The wild animal in late modernity. The case of the Disneyization of zoos. *Tourist Studies* (1): 83-104.

Bednarek, M., 2006. Epistemological positioning and evidentiality in English news discourse: A text-driven approach. *Text & Talk*, 26(6): 635-660.

Bergen, B. & Chang, N., 2005. Embodied construction grammar in simulation-based language understanding. In Ostman, J.-O. & Fried, M. (eds.). *Construction Grammars: Cognitive Grounding and Theoretical Extensions*. Amsterdam: John Benjamins Publishing Company: 147-190.

Berger, J., 1980. *About Looking*. New York: Vintage.

Berman, T., 2005. The rape of mother nature? Women in the language of environmental discourse. In Fill, A. F. & Mühlhäusler, P. (eds.). *The Ecolinguistics Reader: Language, Ecology and Environment*. London: Continuum: 258-269.

Biber, D. et al., 1999. *Longman Grammar of Spoken and Written English*. London: Longman.

Biebuyck, B. & Martens, G., 2011. *Beyond Cognitive Metaphor Theory: Perspectives on Literary Metaphor*. New York: Routledge.

Billig, M., 2003. Critical discourse analysis and the rhetoric of critique. In Weiss, G. & Wodak, R. (eds.). *Critical Discourse Analysis: Theory and Interdisciplinarity.* Basingstoke: Palgrave Macmillan: 35-46.

Black, M., 1962. *Models and Metaphors.* Ithaca: Cornell University Press.

Blommaert, J., 2005. *Discourse: A Critical Introduction.* Cambridge: Cambridge University Press.

Bowers, C., 2014. *The False Promises of the Digital Revolution: How Computers Transform Education, Work, and International Development in Ways that Undermine an Ecologically Sustainable Future.* New York: Peter Lang.

Boye, K., 2012. Epistemic Meaning: *A Crosslinguistic and Functional-Cognitive Study.* Berlin: Mouton de Gruyter.

Brasovan, N. S., 2016. An exploration into neo-Confucian ecology. *Journal of Chinese Philosophy*, 43(3-4): 203-220.

Brown, C. H., 1984. *Language and Living Things: Uniformities in Folk Classification and Naming.* New Brunswick: Rutgers University Press.

Brunyé, T. T. et al., 2009. When you and I share perspectives: Pronouns modulate perspective taking during narrative comprehension. *Psychological Science*, 20(1): 27-32.

Brunyé, T. T. et al., 2011. Better you than I: Perspectives and emotion simulation during narrative comprehension. *Journal of Cognitive Psychology*, 23(5): 659-666.

Cap, P., 2006. *Legitimisation in Political Discourse: A Cross-Disciplinary Perspective on the Modern US War Rhetoric.* Newcastle: Cambridge Scholars Publishing.

Cap, P., 2013. *The Pragmatics of Symbolic Distance Crossing.* Amsterdam: John Benjamins Publishing Company.

Caracciolo, M., 2017. Creative metaphor in literature. In Semino, E. & Demjén, Z. (eds.). *The Routledge Handbook of Metaphor and Language.* London: Routledge: 206-218.

Carretero, M., 1996. A new angle on an old theme: Epistemic modality reconsidered. *Estudios Ingleses de la Universidad Complutense* (4): 253-263.

Chafe, W., 1986. Evidentiality in English conversation and academic writing. In Chafe, W. & Nichols, J. (eds.). *Evidentiality: The Linguistic Coding of Epistemology.*

Norwood: Ablex: 261-272.

Charteris-Black, J., 2004. *Corpus Approaches to Critical Metaphor Analysis*. Basingstoke: Palgrave Macmillan.

Chilton, P., 1988. *Orwellian Language and the Media*. London: Pluto.

Chilton, P., 1996. *Security Metaphors: Cold War Discourse from Containment to Common House*. New York: Peter Lang.

Chilton, P., 2004. *Analysing Political Discourse: Theory and Practice*. London: Routledge.

Chilton, P., 2005a. Missing links in mainstream CDA: Modules, blends and the critical instinct. In Wodak, R. & Chilton, P. (eds.). *A New Research Agenda in Critical Discourse Analysis: Theory and Interdisciplinarity*. Amsterdam: John Benjamins Publishing Company: 19-52.

Chilton, P., 2005b. Manipulation, memes and metaphors: The case of *Mein Kampf*. In Saussure, L. de & Schulz, P. (eds.). *Manipulation and Ideologies in the Twentieth Century Discourse, Language, Mind*. Amsterdam: John Benjamins Publishing Company: 15-44.

Chilton, P. & Lakoff, G., 1995. Foreign policy by metaphor. In Schäffner, C. & Wenden, A. (eds.). *Language and Peace*. Aldershot: Ashgate: 37-60.

Chilton, P. & Schäffner, C., 1997. Discourse and politics. In van Dijk, T. A. (ed.). *Discourse as Social Interaction*. London: Sage: 206-230.

Chilton, P. & Schäffner, C., 2002. Introduction: Themes and principles in the analysis of political discourse. In Chilton, P. & Schäffner, C. (eds.). *Politics as Text and Talk: Analytic Approaches to Political Discourse*. Amsterdam: John Benjamins Publishing Company: 1-44.

Clark. T., 2011. *The Cambridge Introduction to Literature and the Environment*. Cambridge: Cambridge University Press.

Coates, J., 1983. *The Semantics of the Modal Auxiliaries*. London: Croom Helm.

Colston, H. L., 2021. Cognitive linguistics and figurative language. In Xu, W. & Taylor, J. R. (eds.). *The Routledge Handbook of Cognitive Linguistics*. London: Routledge: 408-420.

Condor, S. & Antaki, C., 1997. Social cognition and discourse. In van Dijk, T. A. (ed.).

Discourse Studies: A Multidisciplinary Introduction (Vol. 1). London: Sage: 320-347.

Cook, G., 1994. *The Discourse of Literature: The Interplay of Form and Mind*. Oxford: Oxford University Press.

Cook, G., 2015. "A pig is a person" or "You can love a fox and hunt it": Innovation and tradition in the discursive representation of animals. *Discourse and Society*, 26(5): 587-607.

Cook, G. & Sealey, A., 2018. The Discursive representation of animals. In Fill, A. F. & Penz, H. (eds.). *The Routledge Handbook of Ecolinguistics*. London: Routledge: 551-574.

Cosmides, L. & Tooby, J., 2000. Consider the source: The evolution of adaptations for decoupling and metarepresentations. In Sperber, D. (ed.). *Metarepresentations: A Multidisciplinary Perspective*. Oxford: Oxford University Press: 53-116.

Cramer, J., 2010. Do we really want to be like them? Indexing Europeanness through pronominal use. *Discourse & Society*, 21(6): 619-637.

Crist, E., 1999. *Images of Animals: Anthropomorphism and Animal Mind*. Philadelphia: Temple University Press.

Csábi, S., 2014. Metaphor and stylistics. In Burke, M. (ed.). *The Routledge Handbook of Stylistics*. New York: Routledge: 206-220.

Damasio, A. R., 1994. *Descartes Error: Emotion, Reason, and the Human Brain*. New York: Putnam.

Dancygier, B., 2014. Stylistics and blending. In Burke, M. (ed.). *The Routledge Handbook of Stylistics*. New York: Routledge: 297-312.

Danler, P., 2005. Morpho-syntactic and textual realizations as deliberate pragmatic argumentative linguistic tools? In Saussure, L. de & Schulz, P. (eds.). *Manipulation and Ideologies in the Twentieth Century Discourse*. Amsterdam: John Benjamins Publishing Company: 45-60.

Danta, C., 2018. *Animal Fables after Darwin Literature, Speciesism, and Metaphor*. Cambridge: Cambridge University Press.

Daston, L. & Mitman, G., 2005. *Think with Animals: New Perspectives on*

Anthropomorphism. New York: Columbia University Press.

Deleuze, G. & Guattari, F., 1987. *A Thousand Plateaus: Capitalism and Schizophrenia.* Minneapolis: University of Minnesota Press.

DeMello, M., 2008. Online animal (auto-)biographies: What does it mean when we "give animals a voice?". In Krebber, A. & Roscher, M. (eds.). *Animal Biography: Reframing Animal Lives.* London: Palgrave Macmillan: 227-242.

DeMello, M., 2012. *Animals and Society: An Introduction to Human-Animal Studies.* New York: Columbia University Press.

Devall, B. & Sessions, G., 1985. *Deep Ecology: Living as if Nature Mattered.* Salt Lake City: Gibbs Smith.

Ding, J. X., 2018. *Linguistic Prefabrication: A Discourse Analysis Approach.* Singapore: Springer.

Dirven, R., Frank, R. & Putz, M. (eds.)., 2003. *Cognitive Models in Language and Thought Ideology, Metaphors and Meanings.* Berlin: Mouton de Gruyter.

Doniger, W., 2005. Zoomorphism in ancient India: Humans more bestial than the beasts. In Daston, L. & Mitman, G. (eds.). *Thinking with Animals: New Perspectives on Anthropomorphism.* New York: Columbia University Press: 17-36.

Downing, A., 2001. "Surely you knew!" Surely as a marker of evidentiality and stance. *Functions of Language,* 8(2): 253-285.

Dunayer, J., 2001. *Animal Equality: Language and Liberation.* Derwood: Ryce.

Durkheim, E., 1995. *The Elementary Forms of Religious Life.* Fields, K. E. (trans.). New York: The Free Press.

Erwin, P., 1995. A review of the effects of personal name stereotypes. *Representative Research in Social Psychology,* 20(7): 41-52.

Evans, V. & Green, M., 2006. *Cognitive Linguistics: An Introduction.* Edinburgh: Edinburgh University Press.

Fairclough, N., 1989. *Language and Power.* London: Routledge.

Fairclough, N., 1992. *Discourse and Social Change.* Cambridge: Polity Press.

Fairclough, N., 1993. Critical discourse analysis and the marketization of public discourse: The universities. *Discourse and Society,* 4(2): 133-168.

Fairclough, N., 1995. *Critical Discourse Analysis: The Critical Study of Language*. London: Longman.

Fairclough, N., 1999. Global capitalism and critical awareness of language. *Language Awareness*, 8(2): 71-83.

Fairclough, N., 2003. *Analysing Discourse: Textual Analysis for Social Research*. New York: Routledge.

Fairclough, N., 2010. *Critical Discourse Analysis*. 2nd ed. London: Longman.

Fairclough, N., 2012. Critical discourse analysis. In Gee, J. & Handford, M. (eds.). *The Routledge Handbook of Discourse Analysis*. New York: Routledge: 9-20.

Fairclough, N., 2018. CDA as dialectical reasoning. In Flowerdew, J. & Richardson, J. E. (eds.). *The Routledge Handbook of Critical Discourse Studies*. New York: Routledge: 13-25.

Fairclough, N. & Wodak, R., 1997. Critical discourse analysis. In van Dijk, T. A. (ed.). *Discourse as Social Interaction. Discourse Studies: A Multidisciplinary Introduction (Vol. 2)*. London: Sage: 258-284.

Fan, Q. & Chen, M., 2018. Review of *Ecolinguistics: Language, Ecology and the Stories We Live By*. *Australian Journal of Linguistics* (2): 1-3.

Fauconnier, G., 1997. *Mappings in Thought and Language*. Cambridge: Cambridge University Press.

Fauconnier, G. & Turner, M., 1996. Blending as a central process of grammar. In Goldberg, A. E. (ed.). *Conceptual Structure, Discourse and Language*. Stanford: CSLI Publications: 113-130.

Fauconnier, G. & Turner, M., 2002. *The Way We Think: Conceptual Blending and the Mind's Hidden Complexities*. New York: Basic Books.

Fill, A. F. & Mühlhäusler, P. (eds.), 2001. *The Ecolinguistics Reader: Language, Ecology and Environment*. London: Continuum.

Fill, A. F. & Penz, H. (eds.), 2018. *The Routledge Handbook of Ecolinguistics*. New York: Routledge.

Fischer, M. H. & Zwaan, R. A., 2008. Embodied language: A review of the role of the motor system in language comprehension. *Quarterly Journal of Experimental*

Psychology, 61: 825-850.

Flowerdew, J. & Richardson, J. E. (eds.), 2018. *The Routledge Handbook of Critical Discourse Studies*. London: Routledge.

Fowler, R., 1991. *Language in the News: Discourse and Ideology in the Press*. London: Routledge.

Fowler, R. & Kress, G., 1979. Interviews. In Fowler, R. et al. (eds.). *Language and Control*. London: Routledge and Kegan Paul: 89-110.

Fowler, R. et al., 1979. *Language and Control*. London: Routledge and Kegan Paul.

Fox, A., 2005. Process ecology and the "ideal" Dao. *Journal of Chinese Philosophy*, 32(1): 47-57.

Freeman, C., 2009. This little piggy went to press: The American news media's construction of animals in agriculture. *Communication Review* (12): 78-103.

Freeman, M. H., 2000. Poetry and the scope of metaphor: Toward a cognitive theory of literature. In Barcelona, A. (ed.). *Metaphor and Metonymy at the Crossroads: A Cognitive Perspective*. Berlin: Mouton de Gruyter: 253-281.

Garrard, G., 2012. *Teaching Ecocriticism and Green Cultural Studies*. London: Palgrave Macmillan.

Gibbons, A. & Macrae, A. (eds.), 2018. *Pronouns in Literature: Positions and Perspectives in Language.* London: Palgrave Macmillan.

Gibbs, R., 1999. Researching metaphor. In Cameron, L. & Low, G. (eds.). *Researching and Applying Metaphor*. Cambridge: Cambridge University Press: 122-145.

Giddens, A., 1991. *The Consequences of Modernity*. Cambridge: Policy Press.

Givón, T., 2001. *Syntax.* Amsterdam: John Benjamins Publishing Company.

Glenberg, A. M., 2007. Language and action: Creating sensible combinations of ideas. In Gaskell, G. (ed.). *The Oxford Handbook of Psycholinguistics*. Oxford: Oxford University Press: 361-370.

Glenn, C., 2004. Constructing consumables and consent: A critical analysis of factory farm industry discourse. *Journal of Communication Inquiry*, 28(1): 63-81.

Goatly, A., 2001. Green grammar and grammatical metaphor, or language and myth of power, or metaphors we die by. In Fill, A. F. & Mühlhäusler, P. (eds.). *The*

Ecolinguistics Reader: Language, Ecology and Environment. London: Continuum: 203-225.

Goatly, A., 2005. *The Language of Metaphors*. London: Routledge.

Goatly, A., 2006. Humans, animals, and metaphors. *Society and Animals*, 14(1): 15-37.

Goatly, A., 2007. *Washing the Brain—Metaphor and Hidden Ideology*. Amsterdam: John Benjamins Publishing Company.

Gough, V. & Talbot, M., 1996. "Guilt over games boys play": Coherence as a focus for examining the constitution of heterosexual subjectivity on a problem page. In Caldas-Coulthard, C. R. & Coulthard, M. (eds.). *Texts and Practices: Readings in Critical Discourse Analysis*. London: Routledge: 214-230.

Grishakova, M., 2018. Multi-teller and multi-voiced stories: The poetics and politics of pronouns. In Gibbons, A. & Macrae, A. (eds.). *Pronouns in Literature: Positions and Perspectives in Language*. New York: Palgrave Macmillan: 193-216.

Gross, A. & Vallely, A., 2012. *Animals and the Human Imagination: A Companion to Animal Studies*. New York: Columbia University Press.

Guthrie, S. E., 1993. *Faces in the Clouds: A New Theory of Religion*. New York: Oxford University Press.

Guthrie, S. E., 1997. Anthropomorphism: A definition and a theory. In Mitchell, R. W., Thompson, N. S. & Miles, H. L. (eds.). *Anthropomorphism, Anecdotes, and Animals*. Albany: State University of New York Press: 52-58.

Halliday, M. A. K., 1970. Functional diversity in language as seen from a consideration of mood and modality in English. *Foundations of Language* (4): 225-254.

Halliday, M. A. K., 1991. New ways of meaning: The challenge to applied linguistics. *Journal of Applied Linguistics* (6): 7-36.

Halliday, M. A. K., 2000. *An Introduction to Functional Grammar*. London: Arnold.

Halliday, M. A. K. & Hasan, R., 1976. *Cohesion in English*. London: Longman.

Halliday, M. A. K. & Matthiessen, C. M. I. M., 1999. *Construing Experience Through Meaning: A Language-based Approach to Cognition*. London: Continuum.

Hanks, W. F., 2014. Forward: Evidentiality in social interaction. In Nuckolls, J. & Michael, L. (eds.). *Evidentiality in Interaction*. Amsterdam: John Benjamins Publishing

Company: 1-12.

Hansen, A., 2018. Using visual images to show environmental problems. In Fill, A. F. & Penz, H. (eds.). *The Routledge Handbook of Ecolinguistics*. London: Routledge: 329-356.

Haraway, D., 2003. *The Companion Species Manifesto: Dogs, People and Significant Otherness*. Chicago: Prickly Paradigm Press.

Hart, C., 2008. Critical discourse analysis and metaphor: Toward a theoretical framework. *Critical Discourse Studies*, 5(2): 91-106.

Hart, C., 2010. *Critical Discourse Analysis and Cognitive Science*. London: Palgrave Macmillan.

Hart, C., 2011. Moving beyond metaphor in the cognitive linguistic approach to CDA. In Hart, C. (ed.). *Critical Discourse Studies in Context and Cognition*. Amsterdam: John Benjamins Publishing Company: 171-192.

Hart, C., 2014a. Construal operations in online press reports of political protests. In Hart, C. & Cap, P. (eds.). *Contemporary Critical Discourse Studies*. London: Bloomsbury: 167-188.

Hart, C., 2014b. *Discourse, Grammar and Ideology: Functional and Cognitive Perspectives*. London: Bloomsbury.

Hart, C., 2018. Cognitive linguistic critical discourse studies. In Flowerdew, J. & Richardson, J. E. (eds.). *The Routledge Handbook of Critical Discourse Studies*. London: Routledge: 77-91.

Hart, C. & Cap, P. (eds.), 2014. *Contemporary Discourse Studies*. London: Bloomsbury.

Hartung, F. et al., 2016. Taking perspective: Personal pronouns affect experiential aspects of literary reading. *PLoS One*, 2016, 11(5): 1-18.

Haugen, E., 1972. *The Ecology of Language*. Palo Alto: Stanford University Press.

Haynes, J., 1989. *Introducing Stylistics*. London: Hyman.

Herman, D., 2002. *Story Logic: Problems and Possibilities of Narrative*. Lincoln: University of Nebraska Press.

Herman, L. & Vervaeck, B., 2005. *Handbook of Narrative Analysis*. Lincoln: University of Nebraska Press.

Heuberger, R., 2018. Overcoming anthropocentrism with anthropomorphic and physiocentric uses of language?. In Fill, A. F. & Penz, H. (eds.). *The Routledge Handbook of Ecolinguistics*. London: Routledge: 602-622.

Hidalgo-Downing, L., 2017. Evidential and epistemic stance strategies in scientific communication: A corpus study of semi-formal and expert publications. In Marín-Arrese, J. I. et al. (eds.). *Evidentiality Revisited: Cognitive Grammar, Functional and Discourse-Pragmatic Perspectives*. Amsterdam: John Benjamins Publishing Company: 225-248.

Hobgood-Oster, L., 2008. *Holy Dogs and Asses: Animals in the Christian Tradition*. Chicago: University of Illinois Press.

Hodge, R. & Kress, G., 1993. *Language as Ideology*. 2nd ed. London: Routledge.

Hodges, A., 2018. Discursive underpinnings of war and terrorism. In Wodak, R. & Forchtner, B. (eds.). *The Routledge Handbook of Language and Politics*. London: Routledge: 673-686.

Hough, C. (ed.), 2016. *The Oxford Handbook of Names and Naming*. Oxford: Oxford University Press.

Howlett, M. & Raglon, R., 1992. Constructing the environmental spectacle: Green advertisements and the greening of the corporate image. *Environmental History Review*, 16(4): 53-68.

Hunston, S., 1993. Professional conflict: Disagreement in academic discourse. In Baker, M., Francis, G. & Tognini-Bonelli, E. (eds.). *Text and Technology: In Honour of John Sinclair*. Amsterdam: John Benjamins Publishing Company: 115-134.

Jacobs, G. & Stibbe, A., 2006. Guest editors introduction: Animals and language. *Society & Animals*, 14(1): 1-7.

Jones, P. E., 2000. Cognitive linguistics and the Marxist approach to ideology. In Dirven, R., Hawkins, B. & Sandicioglu, E. (eds.). *Language and Ideology (Vol. 1)*. Amsterdam: John Benjamins Publishing Company: 227-252.

Kean, H., 2018. Finding a man and his horse in the archive?. In Krebber, A. & Roscher, M. (eds.). *Animal Biography: Re-framing Animal Lives*. London: Palgrave Macmillan: 41-56.

Kennedy, J. S., 1992. *The New Anthropomorphism.* New York: Cambridge University Press.

Knoll, E., 1997. Dogs, Darwinism, and English sensibilities. In Mitchell, R. W. et al. (eds.). *Anthropomorphism, Anecdotes, and Animals.* Albany: State University of New York Press: 12-21.

Koller, V., 2005. Critical discourse analysis and social cognition: Evidence from business media discourse. *Discourse & Society*, 16(2): 199-224.

Kövecses, Z., 2010. *Metaphor: A Practical Introduction.* 2nd ed. Oxford: Oxford University Press.

Kragh, K. J. & Lindschouw, J. (eds.), 2013. *Deixis and Pronouns in Romance Languages.* Amsterdam: John Benjamins Publishing Company.

Krebber, A. & Roscher, M., 2018. Introduction: Biographies, animals and individuality. In Krebber, A. & Roscher, M. (eds.). *Animal Biography: Re-framing Animal Lives.* London: Palgrave Macmillan: 1-16.

Kress, G., 1989. *Linguistic Processes in Sociocultural Practice.* Oxford: Oxford University Press..

Kripke, S., 1980. *Naming and Necessity.* Cambridge, MA: Harvard University Press.

Lahey, E., 2013. Stylistics and text world theory. In Burke, M. (ed.). *The Routledge Handbook of Stylistics.* London: Routledge: 284-294.

Lakoff, G. & Johnson, M., 1980. *Metaphors We Live By.* Chicago: University of Chicago Press.

Lakoff, G. & Turner, M., 1989. *More than Cool Reason: A Field Guide to Poetic Metaphor.* Chicago: University of Chicago Press.

Laland, K. N. & Brown, G. R., 2002. *Sense and Nonsense: Evolutionary Perspectives on Human Behavior.* Oxford: Oxford University Press.

Lampert, G. & Lampert, M., 2010. Where does evidentiality reside? Notes on (alleged) limiting cases: *seem* and *be like. Language Typology and Universals*, 63(4): 308-321.

Langacker, R. W., 1991. *Foundations of Cognitive Grammar (Vol. II): Descriptive Application.* Palo Alto: Stanford University Press.

Langacker, R. W., 2017. Evidentiality in cognitive grammar. In Marín-Arrese, J. I., Haßler,

G. & Carretero, M. (eds.). *Evidentiality Revisited: Cognitive Grammar, Functional and Discourse-Pragmatic Perspectives*. Amsterdam: John Benjamins Publishing Company: 13-56.

Langdon, A., 2017. *Animal Languages in the Middle Ages Representations of Interspecies Communication*. London: Palgrave Macmillan.

Lawson, E. D., 1996. Personal name stereotypes. In Eichler, E. et al. (eds.). *International Handbook of Onomastics (Vol. 2)*. Berlin: de Gruyter: 1744-1747.

Leibring, K., 2016. Animal names. In Hough, C. (ed.). *The Oxford Handbook of Names and Naming*. Oxford: Oxford University Press: 662-675.

Linhares-Dias, R., 2006. *How to Show Things with Words*: *A Study on Language*. Berlin: Mouton de Gruyter.

Livingstone, S., 1998. *Making Sense of Television: The Psychology of Audience Interpretation*. Oxford: Butterworth-Heinemann.

Latour, B., 2004. *Politics of Nature: How to Bring the Sciences into Democracy*. Porter, C. (trans.). Cambridge, MA: Harvard University Press.

Mack, D. 1975. Metaphoring as speech act: Some happiness conditions for implicit similes and simple metaphors. *Poetics* (4): 221-256.

Maitland, K. & Wilson, J., 1987. Pronominal selection and ideological conflict. *Journal of Pragmatics* (11): 495-512.

Manty, S., 2014. Animal representation in the *Harry Potter* series. In Tüür, K. & Tønnessen, M. (eds.). *The Semiotics of Animal Representations*. Amsterdam: Rodopi B.V.: 239-262.

Marín-Arrese, J. I., 2011. Effective vs. epistemic stance and subjectivity in political discourse: Legitimising strategies and mystification of responsibility. In Hart, C. (ed.). *Critical Discourse Studies in Context and Cognition*. Amsterdam: John Benjamins Publishing Company: 193-223.

Marín-Arrese, J. I. et al., 2017. *Evidentiality Revisited: Cognitive Grammar, Functional and Discourse-Pragmatic Perspectives*. Amsterdam: John Benjamins Publishing Company.

Martin, J. R., 1999. Grace: The logogenesis of freedom. *Discourse Studies*, 1(1): 29-56.

Martin, J. R., 2004. Positive discourse analysis: Solidarity and change. *Revista Canaria de Estudios Ingleses*, 49: 179-200.

Martin, J. R. & White, P. R. R., 2005. *The Language of Evaluation: Appraisal in English*. London: Palgrave Macmillan.

McHugh, S., 2018. Taxidermy's literary biographies. In Krebber, A. & Roscher, M. (eds.). *Animal Biography: Re-framing Animal Lives*. London: Palgrave Macmillan: 141-160.

Miall, D. S. & Kuiken, D., 1994. Foregrounding, defamiliarization, and affect: Response to literary stories. *Poetics*, 22(5): 389-407.

Middelhoff, F., 2018. Recovering and reconstructing animal selves in literary autozoographies. In Krebber, A. & Roscher, M. (eds.). *Animal Biography: Re-framing Animal Lives*. London: Palgrave Macmillan: 57-80.

Mildorf, J., 2016. Reconsidering second-person narration and involvement. *Language and Literature*, 25(2): 145-158.

Mills, S., 2003. Caught between sexism, anti-sexism and "political correctness": Feminist women's negations with naming practices. *Discourse & Society*, 14(1): 87-110.

Mitchell, R. W., 1997a. Anthropomorphic anecdotalism as method. In Mitchell, R. W. et al. (eds.). *Anthropomorphism, Anecdotes and Animals*. Albany: State University of New York Press: 151-169.

Mitchell, R. W., 1997b. Anthropomorphism and anecdotes: A Guide for the perplexed. In Mitchell, R. W. et al. (eds.). *Anthropomorphism, Anecdotes and Animals*. Albany: State University of New York Press: 407-427.

Mitchell, S. D., 2005. Anthropomorphism and cross-species modeling. In Daston, L. & Mitman, G. (eds.). *Thinking with Animals: New Perspectives on Anthropomorphism*. New York: Columbia University Press: 100-118.

Moscovici, S., 1981. On social representations. In Forgas, J. P. (ed.). *Social Cognition: Perspectives in Everyday Understanding*. London: Academic Press: 181-209.

Moscovici, S., 1984. The phenomenon of social representations. In Farr, R. M. & Moscovici, S. (eds.). *Social Representations*. Cambridge: Cambridge University Press: 3-69.

Moscovici, S., 1988. Notes towards a description of social representations. *European*

Journal of Social Psychology (18): 211-250.

Moscovici, S. & Duveen, G., 2000. *Social Representations: Explorations in Social Psychology*. Cambridge: Polity Press.

Moscovici, S. & Hewstone, M., 1983. Social representations and social explanations: From the "naïve" to the "amateur" scientist. In Hewstone, M. (ed.). *Attribution Theory, Social and Functional Extensions*. Oxford: Blackwell: 98-125.

Mucha, A. & Zimmermann, M., 2016. TAM coding and temporal interpretation in West African languages. In Blaszczak, J. et al. (eds.). *Modality Revisited*. Chicago: The University of Chicago Press: 6-44.

Mushin, I., 2001. *Evidentiality and Epistemological Stance in Narrative Retelling*. Amsterdam: John Benjamins Publishing Company.

Musolff, A., 2004. *Metaphor and Political Discourse: Analogical Reasoning in Debates about Europe*. Basingstoke: Palgrave Macmillan.

Musolff, A., 2012. The study of metaphor as part of critical discourse analysis. *Journal of Critical Discourse Studies*, 9(3): 301-310.

Musolff, A. & Zinken, J. (eds.), 2009. *Three Kinds of Metaphor in Discourse: A Linguistic Taxonomy Gerard Steen Metaphor and Discourse*. London: Macmillan.

Naess, A., 1973. The shallow and the deep, long-range ecological movement: A summary. *Inquiry* (4): 95-100.

Naess, A., 1995. The shallow and the long range, deep ecology movement. In Drengson, A. & Inoue, Y. (eds.). *The Deep Ecology Movement: An Introductory Anthology*. Berkeley: North Atlantic Books: 3-10.

Narrog, H., 2012. *Modality, Subjectivity, and Semantic Change: A Cross-Linguistic Perspective*. Oxford: Oxford University Press.

Nielsen, H. S., 2018. Pronouns in literary fiction as inventive discourse. In Gibbons, A. & Macrae, A. (eds.). *Pronouns in Literature: Positions and Perspectives in Language*. London: Palgrave Macmillan: 217-234.

Nuckolls, J. & Michael, L. (eds.), 2014. *Evidentiality in Interaction*. Amsterdam: John Benjamins Publishing Company.

Nuyts, J., 2001. *Epistemic Modality, Language, and Conceptualizatio*n. Amsterdam: John

Benjamins Publishing Company.

Nuyts, J., 2017. Evidentiality reconsidered. In Marín-Arrese, J. I. et al. *Evidentiality Revisited: Cognitive Grammar, Functional and Discourse-Pragmatic Perspectives*. Amsterdam: John Benjamins Publishing Company: 57-86.

Nyström, S., 2016. Names and meaning. In Hough, C. (ed.). *The Oxford Handbook of Names and Naming*. Oxford: Oxford University Press: 57-60.

O'Halloran, K., 2003. *Critical Discourse Analysis and Language Cognition*. Edinburgh: Edinburgh University Press.

O'Halloran, K., 2007. Casualness vs commitment: The use in critical discourse analysis of Lakoff and Johnson's approach to metaphor. In Hart, C. & Lukeš, D. (eds.). *Cognitive Linguistics in Critical Discourse Analysis: Application and Theory*. Newcastle: Cambridge Scholars Publishing: 159-179.

Pacherie, E., 2014. How does it feel to act together?. *Phenomenology and the Cognitive Science*, 13(1): 25-46.

Palmer, F. R., 2001. *Mood and Modality*. Cambridge: Cambridge University Press.

Palmquist, S. R. & Chan, K. K. A., 2016. Confucian-Kantian response to environmental eco-centrism on animal equality. *Journal of Chinese Philosophy*, 43(3-4): 221-238.

Parker, J., 2018. Placements and functions of brief second-person passages. In Gibbons, A. & Macrae, A. (eds.). *Pronouns in Literature: Positions and Perspectives in Language*. London: Palgrave Macmillan: 97-112.

Parry, C., 2017. *Other Animals in Twenty-First Century Fiction*. London: Palgrave Macmillan.

Peirce, C. S., 1955. Logic as semiotic: The theory of signs. In Buchler, J. (ed.). *The Philosophical Writings of Peirce*. New York: Dover Books: 98-119.

Phillips, M., 1985. *Aspects of Text Structure: An Investigation of the Lexical Organization of Text*. Amsterdam: North-Holland.

Pinker, S., 1997. *How the Mind Works*. London: Penguin.

Poole, R., 2017. Review of *Ecolinguistics: Language, Ecology and the Stories We Live By. Journal of Critical Discourse Studies* (2): 1-3.

Quirk, R. et al., 1985. *A Comprehensive Grammar of the English Language*. London:

Longman.

Reisigl, M. & Wodak, R., 2001. *Discourse and Discrimination: Rhetorics of Racism and Anti-Semitism*. London: Routledge.

Rembowska-Płuciennik, M., 2018. Second-person narration as a joint action. *Language and Literature*, 27(3): 159-175.

Rocci, A., 2005. Are manipulative texts "coherent"? Manipulation, presuppositions and (in-)congruity. In Saussure, L. de & Schulz, P. (eds.). *Manipulation and Ideologies in the Twentieth Century Discourse, Language, Mind*. Amsterdam: John Benjamins Publishing Company: 85-113.

Russell, N., 2010. Navigating the human-animal boundary. *Reviews in Anthropology* (39): 3-24.

Ryan, F., 2002. *Darwin's Blind Spot: Evolution Beyond Natural Selection*. New York: Houghton Mifflin.

Sanders, J. & Spooren, W., 1996. Subjectivity and certainty in epistemic modality: A study of Dutch epistemic modifiers. *Cognitive Linguistics*, 7(3): 241-264.

Sanford, A. J. & Emmott, C., 2012. *Mind, Brain and Narrative*. Cambridge: Cambridge University Press.

Sato, M. & Bergen, B. K., 2013. The case of missing pronouns: Does mentally simulated perspective play a functional role in the comprehension of person? *Cognition*, 12(7): 361-374.

Saussure, L. de, 2005. Manipulation and cognitive pragmatics preliminary hypotheses. In Saussure, L. de & Schulz, P. (eds.). *Manipulation and Ideologies in the Twentieth Century Discourse*. Amsterdam: John Benjamins Publishing Company: 113-146.

Schonfeld, M., 2016. Introduction: Ecology and Chinese philosophy. *Journal of Chinese Philosophy*, 43(3-4): 178-184.

Sealey, A. & Charles, N., 2013. "What do animals mean to you?" Naming and relating to nonhuman animals. *Anthrozoös*, 26(4): 485-503.

Sealey, A. & Oakley, L., 2013. Anthropomorphic grammar? Some linguistic patterns in the wildlife documentary series *Life*. *Text and Talk*, 33(3): 399-420.

Sealey, A. & Oakley, L., 2014. Why did the Canada goose cross the sea? Accounting for the behaviour of wildlife in the documentary series *Life. International Journal of Applied Linguistics*, 24(1): 19-37.

Searle, J., 1969. *Speech Acts: An Essay in the Philosophy of Language*. Cambridge: Cambridge University Press.

Semino, E. & Swindlehurst, K., 1996. Metaphor and mind style in Ken Kesey's *One Flew over the Cuckoo's Nest. Style*, 30(1): 143-166.

Shah, M., 2018. Animal life stories; or, the making of animal subjects in primatological narratives of fieldwork. In Krebber, A. & Roscher, M. (eds.). *Animal Biography: Re-framing Animal Lives*. London: Palgrave Macmillan: 119-138.

Silva-Corvalán, C., 1995. Contextual conditions for the interpretation of *poder* and *deber* in Spanish. In Bybee, J. & Fleischman, S. (eds.). *Modality in Grammar and Discourse*. Amsterdam: John Benjamins Publishing Company: 67-107.

Simon-Vandenbergen, A.-M. & Aijmer, K., 2007. *The Semantic Field of Modal Certainty: A Corpus-based Study of English Adverbs*. Berlin: Mouton de Gruyter.

Skabelund, A., 2018. A dog's life: The challenges and possibilities of animal biography. In Krebbe, A. & Roscher, M. (eds.). *Animal Biography: Re-framing Animal Lives*. London: Palgrave Macmillan: 83-102.

Smith, B., 2012. Language and the frontiers of the human: Aymara animal-oriented interjections and the mediation of mind. *American Ethnologist* (39): 313-324.

Smith, G. W., 2016. Theoretical foundations of literary onomastics. In Hough, C. (ed.). *The Oxford Handbook of Names and Naming*. Oxford: Oxford University Press: 338-353.

Smith-Harris, T., 2004. There's not enough and there's no sense: Language usage and human perceptions of other animals. *Revision*, 27(2): 12-15.

Sperber, D., 2000. Metarepresentations in an evolutionary perspective. In Sperber, D. (ed.). *Metarepresentation: A Multidisciplinary Perspective*. New York: Oxford University Press: 117-138.

Stallwood, K., 2018. Topsy: The elephant we must never forget. In Krebber, A. & Roscher, M. (eds.). *Animal Biography: Re-framing Animal Lives*. London: Palgrave Macmillan: 227-242.

Steen, G., 1994. *Understanding Metaphor in Literature*. Harlow: Longman.

Steen, G., 2009. Three kinds of metaphor in discourse: A linguistic taxonomy. In Musolff, A. & Zinken, J. (eds.). *Metaphor and Discourse*. New York: Palgrave Macmillan: 23-39.

Stella, B., 2014. *Evaluation in Advertising Reception: A Socio-Cognitive and Linguistic Perspective*. London: Palgrave Macmillan.

Stibbe, A., 2001. Language, power and the social construction of animals. *Society & Animals*, 9(2): 145-161.

Stibbe, A., 2012. *Animals Erased: Discourse, Ecology, and Reconnection with the Natural World*. Middletown: Wesleyan University Press.

Stibbe, A., 2014. An ecolinguistic approach to critical discourse studies. *Critical Discourse Studies*, 11(1): 117-128.

Stibbe, A., 2015. *Ecolinguistics: Language, Ecology and the Stories We Live By*. New York: Routledge.

Stibbe, A., 2018. Positive discourse analysis. In Fill, A. F. & Penz, H. (eds.). *The Routledge Handbook of Ecolinguistics*. London: Routledge: 301-328.

Storch, A., 2018. Evidentiality and the expression of knowledge: An African perspective. In Aikhenval, A. Y. (ed.). *The Oxford Handbook of Evidentiality*. Oxford: Oxford University Press.

Stubbs, M., 1997. Whorf's children: Critical comments on critical discourse analysis (CDA). In Ryan, A. & Wray, A. (eds.). *Evolving Models of Language*. Clevedon: British Association for Applied Linguistics: 100-116.

Subramaniam, R., 2018. The elephant's I: Looking for Abu'l Abbas. In Krebber, A. & Roscher, M. (eds.). *Animal Biography: Re-framing Animal Lives*. London: Palgrave Macmillan: 207-226.

Sun, J. T.-S., 2018. Evidentials and person. In Aikhenvald, A. Y. (ed.). *The Oxford Handbook of Evidentiality*. Oxford: Oxford University Press: 100-122.

Swan, T. & Westvik, J. (eds.), 1997. *Subjectification and the Development of Epistemic*. Berlin: Mouton de Gruyter.

Taylor, N., 2011. Anthropomorphism and the animal subject. In Boddice, R. (ed.). *Anthropocentrism: Humans, Animals, Environments*. Leiden: Brill NV: 265-280.

Taylor, N., 2013. *Humans, Animals, and Society: An Introduction to Human-Animal Studies*. New York: Lantern Books.

Thagard, P. & Shelley, C., 2006. Emotional analogies and analogical inference. In Thagard, P. (ed.). *Hot Thought: Mechanisms and Applications of Emotional Cognition*. Cambridge, MA: The MIT Press: 27-50.

Tønnessen, M., 2013. Discourses gone astray: Restoring animality, humanity, and language. *Journal of Multicultural Discourse* (3): 254-259.

Trampe, W., 2005. Language and ecological crisis: Extracts from a dictionary of industrial agriculture. In Fill, A. F. & Mühlhäusler, P. (eds.). *The Ecolinguistics Reader: Language, Ecology and Environment*. London: Continuum: 232-240.

Traugott, E. C., 1989. On the rise of epistemic meanings in English: An example of subjectification in semantic change. *Language* (65): 31-55.

Traugott, E. C., 1997. Subjectification and the development of epistemic meaning: The case of promise and threaten. In Swan, T. & Westvik, O. J. (eds.). *Modality in Germanic Languages*. Berlin: Mouton de Gruyter.

Trites, R., 2014. *Literary Conceptualizations of Growth Metaphors and Cognition in Adolescent Literature*. Amsterdam: John Benjamins Publishing Company.

Usonienė, A. & Šinkūnienė, J., 2013. A cross-linguistic look at the multifunctionality of the English verb *seem*. In Marín-Arrese, C. et al. (eds.). *English Modality: Core, Periphery and Evidentiality*. Berlin: Walter de Gruyter: 281-316.

van Dijk, T. A., 1987. *Communicating Racism: Ethnic Prejudice in Thought and Talk*. London: Sage.

van Dijk, T. A., 1990. Social cognition and discourse. In Giles, H. & Robinson, W. P. (eds.). *Handbook of Language and Social Psychology*. New York: John Wiley: 163-183.

van Dijk. T. A., 1993. Principle of critical discourse analysis. *Discourse & Society*, 4(2): 249-283.

van Dijk, T. A., 1995. Discourse analysis as ideology analysis. In Schäffner, C. & Wenden, A. I. (eds.). *Language and Peace*. Amsterdam: Harwood Academic Publishers: 17-36.

van Dijk, T. A., 1997. The study of discourse. In van Dijk, T. A. (ed.). *Discourse Studies:*

A Multidisciplinary Introduction (Vol. 1). London: Sage: 1-34.

van Dijk, T. A., 1998. *Ideology: A Multidisciplinary Approach*. London: Sage.

van Dijk, T. A., 2001. Critical discourse analysis. In Schiffrin, D., Tannen, D. & Hamilton, H. E. (eds.). *The Handbook of Discourse Analysis*. Oxford: Blackwell: 352-371.

van Dijk, T. A., 2002. Ideology: Political discourse and cognition. In Chilton, P. & Schäffner, C. (eds.). *Politics as Text and Talk: Analytic Approaches to Political Discourse*. Amsterdam: John Benjamins Publishing Company: 203-238.

van Dijk, T. A., 2006. Discourse and manipulation. *Discourse and Society* (17): 359-383.

van Dijk, T. A., 2008. *Discourse and Context: A Sociocognitive Approach*. Cambridge: Cambridge University Press.

van Dijk, T. A., 2009. *Society and Discourse: How Social Contexts Influence Text and Talk*. Cambridge: Cambridge University Press.

van Dijk, T. A., 2014. *Discourse and Knowledge: A Sociocognitive Approach*. Cambridge: Cambridge University.

van Dijk, T. A., 2018. Socio-cognitive discourse studies. In Flowerdew, J. & Richardson, J. E. (eds.). *The Routledge Handbook of Critical Discourse Studies*. New York: Routledge: 26-43.

van Eemeren, F. H., 2005. Foreword: Preview by review. In Saussure, L. de & Schulz, P. (eds.). *Manipulation and Ideologies in the Twentieth Century Discourse*. Amsterdam: John Benjamins Publishing Company: x-xvi.

van Eemeren, F. H., Grootendorst, R. & Henkemans, F. S. (eds.), 2002. *Argumentation: Analysis, Evaluation, Presentation*. London: Routledge.

van Langendonck, W., 2007. *Trends in Linguistics*. Berlin: Mouton de Gruyter.

van Langendonck, W. & van de Velde, M., 2016. Names and grammar. In Hough, C. (ed.). *The Oxford Handbook of Names and Naming*. Oxford: Oxford University Press: 35-56.

van Leeuwen, T., 2007. Legitimation in discourse and communication. *Discourse & Communication*, 1(1): 91-112.

van Leeuwen, T. & Wodak, R., 1999. Legitimizing immigration control: A discourse-historical analysis. *Discourse Studies*, 10(1): 83-118.

van Peer, W., 1986. *Stylistics and Psychology: Investigations of Foregrounding*. London: Croom Helm.

Vandaele, J., 2021. Cognitive poetics and the problem of metaphor. In Xu, W. & Taylor, J. R. (eds.). *The Routledge Handbook of Cognitive Linguistics*. London: Routledge: 450-483.

Werth, P., 1999. *Text Worlds: Representing Conceptual Space in Discourse*. Harlow: Longman.

Wesling, D., 2019. *Animal Perception and Literary Language*. London: Palgrave Macmillan.

White, M. & Herrera, H., 2003. Metaphor and ideology in the press coverage of telecom corporate consolidations. In Dirven, R., Langacker, R. W. & Taylor, J. R. R. (eds.). *Cognitive Models in Language and Thought Ideology*. Berlin: Mouton de Gruyter: 277-326.

White, P., 2003. Beyond modality and hedging: A dialogic view of the language of intersubjective stance. *Text*, 23(2): 259-284.

Widdowson, H. G., 2004. *Text, Context, Pretext: Critical Issues in Discourse Analysis*. Oxford: Blackwell.

Willett, T., 1988. A crosslinguistic survey of grammaticalisation of evidentiality. *Studies in Language* (12): 51-97.

Wodak, R., 2001. What is CDA about: A summary of its history, important concepts and its developments. In Wodak, R. & Meyer, M. (eds.). *Methods of Critical Discourse Analysis*. London: Sage: 1-13.

Wodak, R. & Meyer, M. (eds.), 2001. *Methods of Critical Discourse Analysis*. London: Sage.

Wolf, D. C., 2018. The rise and dawn of a humanimalistic identity. In Krebber, A. & Roscher, M. (eds.). *Animal Biography: Re-framing Animal Lives*. London: Palgrave Macmillan: 161-184.

Wolf, H-G. & Polzenhagen, F., 2003. Conceptual metaphor as ideological stylistic means: An exemplary analysis. In Dirven R. et al. (eds.). *Cognitive Models in Language and Thought: Ideology, Metaphors and Meanings*. New York: Mouton de Gruyter:

247-276.

Wolfe, C., 2003. *Animal Rites: American Culture, the Discourse of Species, and Posthumanist Theory*. Chicago: University of Chicago Press.

Wood, L. A. & Kroger, R. O., 2000. *Doing Discourse Analysis: Methods for Studying Action in Talk and Text*. Thousand Oaks: Sage.

Zhou, W. J. & Huang, G. W., 2017. Chinese ecological discourse: A Confucian-Daoist inquiry. *Journal of Multicultural Discourses*, 12(3): 264-281.

Zinken, J., 2007. Discourse metaphors: The link between figurative language and habitual analogies. *Cognitive Linguistics*, 18(3): 445-466.

Postscript

This book grew out of my doctoral dissertation at Fujian Normal University where I acquired sufficient academic training. I would like to express my appreciation to my doctoral advisor, Professor You Zeshun, whose intellectual support provides the basis of the book; my indebtedness to his instruction is more than obvious to the readers of the book. I should also like to thank Professor Li Rongbao of Fujian Normal University for comments and suggestions on various aspects of the book at its different stages. I also owe a lot to Professor Yang Xinzhang of Xiamen University: my experience of visiting Xiamen University as a visiting scholar several years ago was helpful in expanding new intellectual horizons for me. In particular, I would like to thank Professor Xin Zhiying of Xiamen University, whose earlier research on ecolinguistics was the inspiration for my dissertation topic. I also wish to thank Professor Chen Wenge for his suggestions on how to conduct doctoral research.

I would like to thank all my friends and colleagues in Fujian Agriculture and Forestry University for providing a wonderful environment for work. I would like to thank Chen Yan for encouraging me to pursue a doctoral degree.

I'm grateful to Zhejiang University Press for offering me the opportunity to publish the book.

Above all, I would like to thank my family—my parents, my husband and my son. Your love, understanding, indulgence and support are always the driving force of my work.

Lin Jing

November 2022